Modernism Since Postmodernism

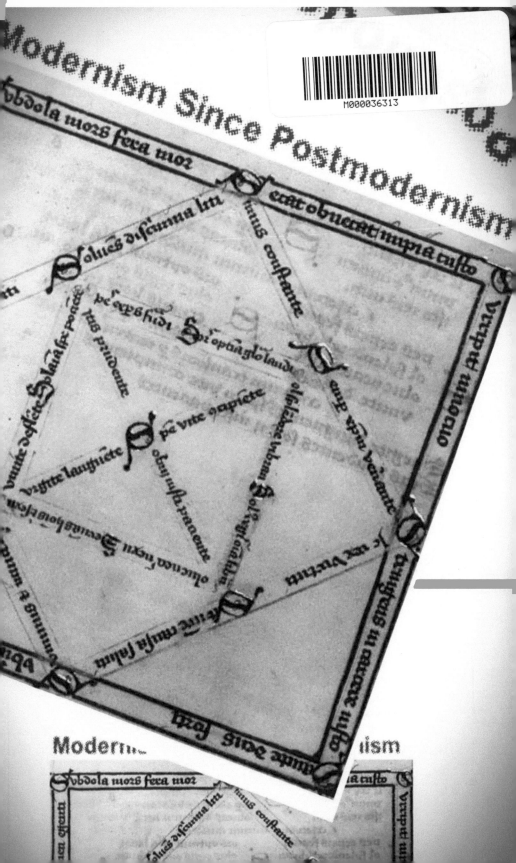

Intermedia Chart

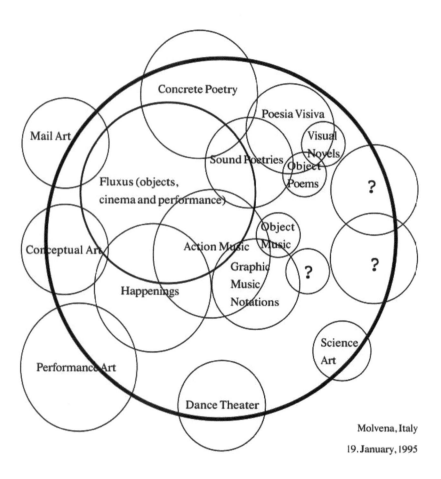

Concrete Poetry

Poesia Visiva

Mail Art

Visual Novels

Sound Poetries

Object Poems

Fluxus (objects, cinema and performance)

?

Object Music

Conceptual Art

Action Music

Graphic Music Notations

?

?

Happenings

Performance Art

Science Art

Dance Theater

Molvena, Italy
19. January, 1995

Some intermedia. Here we see only *some* of the overlaps among the forms and the extent to which some of these are purely intermedia. Parts of many fall outside those areas; that is, they include individual works that are not intermedial. The circles with question marks may be named by the reader.

Modernism Since Postmodernism

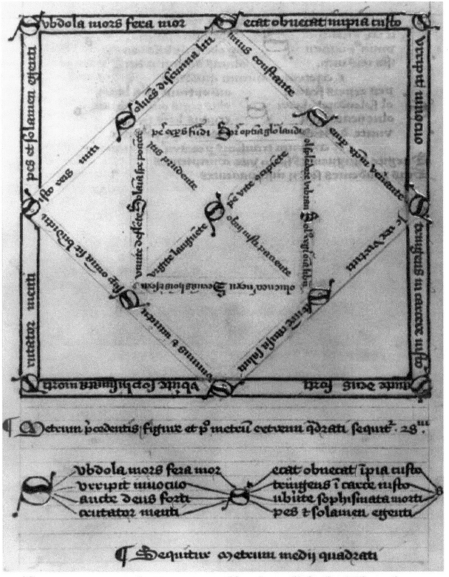

Essays on Intermedia by Dick Higgins

SAN DIEGO STATE UNIVERSITY PRESS | 2019 | THIRD PRINTING

SAN DIEGO STATE UNIVERSITY PRESS

Modernism Since Postmodernism: Essays on Intermedia, by Dick Higgins,
is published by San Diego State University Press, San Diego, CA 92182-6020.

Credits and Acknowledgments

"A Book" first appeared in *New Wilderness Letter* 11 (1983); "Early Sound Poetry" in *Literature in Performance* 5 #2 (Apr. 1985); "Five Myths of Postmodernism" in *Art Papers* 13 #1 (Jan.-Feb. 1989); "Fluxessay for a Few of my Fluxfriends" in *Freibord* 26 (Feb. 1992); "The Golem in the Text" in Vincent Barras and Nicholas Zurbrugg, eds., *Poésies Sonores* (Geneva: Contrechamps Éditions, 1993); "John Cage: Perception and Reception" in *Art Papers* 15 #6 (Nov.-Dec. 1991); "Mediocracy" in *Something Else Newsletter* 3 #2 (Oct. 1983); "Music from Outside" in René Block, ed., *The Readymade Boomerang: Certain Relations in 20th Century Art* (Sydney: Biennale of Sydney and Museum of Contemporary Art, 1990 [catalog of The Eighth Biennale of Sydney, curator René Block]); "The Naive and Its Function in Meaning" in *The Smith* 19 (1977); "The Origin of 'Happening,'" in *American Speech* 51 #3-4 (Fall-Winter 1976); "Two Sides of a Coin: Fluxus and the Something Else Press" in *Visible Language* 26 #1-2 (Winter/Spring, 1992) [Special issue, Estera Milman, ed., *Fluxus: A Conceptual Country*]; and "A [very short] Autobiography of Originality" in *Something Else Newsletter* #3 (Nov. 1983). Dick Higgins, *Fluxus: Theory and Reception* was originally a pamphlet (Barrytown, NY: privately published, 1987). "The Importance of Caravaggio" and "Modernism Since Postmodernism" appear here for the first time. Thanks are also due to Jeff Katz, Head Librarian at the Bard College Library, Annandale, New York, for helping me locate some of the rarer items referred to in this book.

A note on the front cover detail: Iacobus Nicholai de Dacia (=Jakob Nielsen, fl. 1363-79) from "Ms. Cotton Claudius A X IV," piece "XXVIII." The notations of sound poetry are often quite striking visually, both in contemporary pieces and old ones. This is the notation for a section not described in our text from a metrics by Dacia cited in the text. The manuscript (in the British Library in London) is on vellum, the text is written in black, the letters have gold embellishments, and the squares are gold or blue. "Dacia" was the bishopric that included Copenhagen, and the author was a Danish cleric who worked in England. The work was commissioned by Margaret, widow of the Earl of Pembroke, a great patron of the arts. The full work was published as Iacobus Nicholai de Dacia, *Liber de Distinccione Metrorum,* ed. Aage Kabell (1967). Reproduced by permission.

Front and Back Cover Design by Guillermo Nericcio García, ©1997/2014 memogr@phics designcasa; Book Design by Harry Polkinhorn and William Nericcio. All rights reserved. Printed in the United States of America. No part of this book may be used or reproduced in any manner whatsoever without written permission except in the case of the brief quotations embodied in critical articles and reviews. All reasonable effort has been made to notify copyright holders.

ISBN-13: 978-1-879691-43-8
ISBN-10: 1-879691-43-4

FIRST EDITION | PRINTED IN THE UNITED STATES OF AMERICA

Copyright © 1997 by San Diego State University Press | sdsupress.sdsu.edu

Third Printing, June 2019

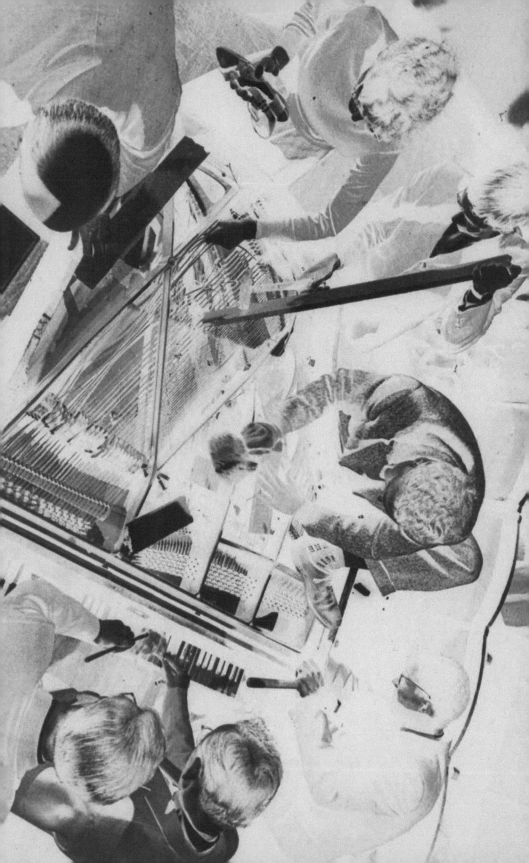

Contents

List of Figures

Foreword

This book is intended to complete the history and speculations that were begun in *A Dialectic of Centuries: Notes Towards a Theory of the New Arts* (1978) and continued with *Horizons: The Poetics and Theory of the Intermedia* (1984). On the positive level, I wanted to present a historical critique of the arts in which the intermedia would be placed squarely at stage center, coequal with the pure media (though no "better" than they). This view implied the presentation of a theoretical position to justify one's experience of intermedial works as worthy of such a central position, and this I found in hermeneutics, initially in Heidegger and Gadamer, and more recently in Jauss. Needing historical exhibits to back up these conceptual tools, I made an aside into the world of pattern poetry in *Pattern Poetry: Guide to an Unknown Literature* (1987), which shows visual poetry through the centuries. Besides its intrinsic interest, pattern poetry shows how the intermedia are as old as the rest of the arts, that, as I like to say, it is a human instinct to wish to combine the various aspects of one's cultural experience into a whole, to fuse them conceptually. As a second historical exhibit I needed an early example of the theory of intermedia (and semiotics), and this I found in Giordano Bruno's *On the Composition of Images, Signs and Ideas* (1591), which my friend Charles Doria translated from the Latin and which I annotated and edited. It was published in 1991.

But I still had not completed my discussion of an appropriate theory for intermedial arts and for what seems to me the most exciting part of the ongoing arts today. Thus, I needed to take a look at "the state of things now," the history of the intermedia and the history of the art tendency with which I have been most closely associated in my art life as distinct from my historical or critical one, namely Fluxus. No matter that Fluxus has been over for a long time now, some would say since 1965, others since 1978 or perhaps 1982; most of the Fluxus artists are still alive, and, though most do not feel they are still doing Fluxus work, much of their recent work represents an outgrowth of their earlier concerns. Furthermore, the hermeneutic approach I suggest in this book is, I continue to feel, the most useful entry into the more recent works as well. This explains my tri-fold division of this book into a theoretical analysis that is an attack and clearing away, negative in tone, but with the purpose of showing how the forms of theory that were enormously popular in the 1960s, 1970s, and 1980s (especially in academia) are inappropriate for the new arts and thus irrelevant except, at best, as intrinsically interesting exercises. I also suggest some of the positive ideas and tools which seem to fit the needs of this "pre-millenarian" time. To this I have added some historical materials—a presentation of "outside music" and "sound poetry," a discussion of John Cage, and so on—and an application of hermeneutics to Fluxus. The last two sections pretty much speak for themselves, but the first requires a bit more framing, in my opinion.

Paul Mann (1991) suggests that art, like history, is condemned to repeat itself—the first time as modernity, the second time as kitsch. As Mann says, "There is no post: everything that claims to be so blindly repeats what it thinks it has left behind" (141). In dealing, therefore, with the issue of so-called "postmodernism," one must not only deal with the various theories that have been current and show their inapplicability to the stronger forms of new art, but one must also start the process of dumping the work that the theoreticians identified as postmodern or, if it seems worth the trouble, reclassifying it more appropriately.

Of course kitsch can be fun. Already 125 years ago, Rimbaud recognized this when, in the second section of *A Season in Hell*, he speaks of liking dumb paintings, door panels, stage sets, backdrops for acrobats, street signs, old-time literature and such-like. Who doesn't? But usually, as Matei Calinescu points out (1987:248), "The fun of kitsch is just the other side of terrible and inconsequential boredom." "Kitschspeak" is the term I use (though more in conversation, not in this book) for the fashionable kitsch language about the arts, sometimes delightful for a while, as with Jacques Derrida, for instance, but ultimately locked so closely into fashion and the world of second-rate and derivative art that it is all but impossible to use with major work and thus destined to pass into academia or oblivion once its novelty has passed.

There are, of course, many schools of postmodernism—and they are just that, schools—but for a preliminary discussion there is no need to identify all of them. However, it can be argued that most of them are of two sorts: pop-academic, in which the professors cite each other to build up a lattice of assumptions into a polemic that may or may not have any correspondence with the realities of the arts that lie outside what is known in their trade as "the discussion." The academic trades are known collectively among participants in such discussions as "the profession," much as prostitutes refer to "the life," and one will find this kind of jargon in writers such as Gerald Graff or Frank Lentricchia, often associated with canon formation, whom I do not intend to discuss further. As for "the profession," it seems to exclude lay-participants, thus intensifying the academic exclusivity associated with the postmodern project. (Incidentally, even Ihab Hassan, whom I consider the best of the postmodernist critics and theoreticians, uses this tendentious "the profession" term on occasion, for instance, in Hassan (1987:138).)

"Canon formation" should mean the formation of a canon of significant works for this or that purpose, but, usually in the name of relevance or presumable fairness to someone or other, in practice it has meant a rejection of value judgments in works ("Whose values will we accept?" is the valid question of the best of these people), leading to an assumption that all art works (except fascistic or difficult ones) are of equal value. Socially and linguistically this may be true. But it sometimes seems to beg the question of whether gays, women, or members of racial minorities have anything to say or learn from works by members of other groups. At best these assumptions can be valuable in saying that, when two works might be taught the identity of the author, artist, or composer can be a consideration in determining which to pick, assuming that diversity is of interest. At worst it can lead to a severe underestimation of the capabilities of the very people whom one wishes to reach or include. Can only women understand writings by women? Is Dante's *Inferno* beyond the comprehension of blacks or Native Americans? Is *every* gay novel as valuable as Baldwin's *Giovanni's Room*? Questions such as these are being begged by the current theoreticians involved in canon formation.

Alas, the prevalence of all the postmodernist faddism has led to a profound distaste for all theory, at least in the United States. Increasingly one hears that it is inherently an academic matter. One Ben Yagoda, writing in the *New York Times* (Sunday, September 4, 1994, Editorial Section, p. 6), notes a Modern Language Association panel on "Posttheory," and discusses the interest in theory during the period I have mentioned as something over and done with.

But if so, then we would be stuck with no access to ongoing possible artistic and cultural innovations; we would have only what we already know, and one gets tired of this. Artists *have* to be able to imagine what still needs doing in order to do it, and critics and audiences *must* have a self-consciousness of what they have known in order to match it against the new possibilities that come their way (including newly experienced works from the past). Thus, there is always a need for theory in order to have a way of providing a framework for understanding what one is doing, performing, and experiencing. It would be a pity if the discussion of this were confined to academia.

So when I speak of works with evident fondness, I am suggesting that the works of which I am obviously approving be added to the canon, but to the canon of work generally available to everyone who wants it, on a sex-blind, color-blind, class-blind nature, and so on. There is nothing wrong with having an avant-garde; it is where one starts. The avant-garde simply constitutes a temporary elite, one which *all* may enter should they choose to do so but that remains an elite in the sense that it requires certain involvement with knowledge of what is going on in order to discover that, in fact, one has become a part of this elite. In time, hopefully, this elite will grow and become communality; it will not be an arcane suggestion that so-and-so has done good work but will be received opinion that he or she has done so. Meanwhile, the next avant-garde will be passing along to its elite the works that have been ignored by their time. So it goes; when things are working right, the avant-garde informs the elite, and the elite grows into a general public. It is to point out and, hopefully, to help enable this progression, that I have dedicated this book, for I believe the avant-garde is eternal.

Barrytown, New York
18 November 1994

Section One
The State of Things Now

I. Modernism Since Postmodernism

> Orpheus is no fable; you have only to sing, and the
> rocks will crystallize; sing and the plant will orga-
> nize; sing, and the animal will be born.
>   —Ralph Waldo Emerson[1]

> Making sense is fatidic.
>   —Ihab Hassan[2]

1. The Postmodern Project

THE POSTMODERN PROJECT has become tiresome, owing to its
persistent citation of the same, often mediocre texts, paintings, and musical works by academics who often exclude a
lay public. The temptation is to reject the concept altogether
in favor of some other view, which would be throwing out the
baby with the bath water. However, certain insights can still
be drawn from it. We shall get to these after a review of what
it includes. When postmodernism is said to have begun is still
under discussion among those who accept the term as useful.
The term's first use appears to have been in 1884, Toynbee
used it in the 1940s, and there are other early usages.[3] But its
first use in precisely its present form was as applied to
architecture, where it refers to recent eclectic building styles
as opposed to the austerities of Mies van der Rohe and other
"modern" architects. Van der Rohe's famous dictum that
"less is more" led to "postmodern architect" Robert Venturi's
response that "less is a bore"[4] Passing for the moment over
visual art and music, in literature the term was used by
Randall Jarrell as early as 1946. Samuel Beckett's works of the
1940s are often cited as early postmodern ones, and there is
said to be a major flow of postmodern works in the 1950s. The

term became more prevalent in the 1960s in France among structuralists and semioticians[5] such as Roland Barthes, and with the spread of this kind of thinking to the USA in the 1960s a new focus on theory more or less for its own sake began in the 1970s and crested in the 1980s, leading to poststructuralism and deconstructionism. These approaches have in common a certain heuristic value, since theory had been, in the main, underestimated (and under-taught) in the 1940s and 1950s. It was healthy for academics and critics to apply philosophical and other methods, brought in from outside the critical traditions of music, visual art, and litera-ture to these areas, applying linguistic methods to nine-teenth-century texts to decode aspects of them that had been inaccessible. But what of now, now that we are in the 1990s? How do we deal with—or do we need at all—the avalanche of theory with which we have been inundated since the early 1960s? As for the structuralists, it strikes me that their argu-ments assume a super-reader of themselves and the works they discuss, a reader or receiver who has already fused his or her horizons with innumerable works of the nineteenth century. The result is that Barthes' approach becomes subjec-tive and impressionistic, not at all the scientific and objective one that led to their method in the first place. Further, in order to write "scientifically" about works, Barthes must minimalize the role of style. But style is one of the ways in which works produce meaning for a receiver, not only when the style is itself a self-conscious focal point, as in Joyce's *Finnegans Wake*, but when it evokes and manipulates further styles, as in Stravinsky's neoclassical musical works such as *Pulcinella*. To choose a more recent example, in Górecki's *Three Pieces in The Old Style* (1963) the style of the piece is an integral part of its message. Naturally a semiotics of music or the other arts could be worked out that takes this kind of thing into account, but we know of no systematic work that does this.

In my essay "Five Myths of Postmodernism," printed elsewhere in this book, I have called into question five typical assumptions of pop-academic postmodernism: the charges that modernism is unfair to women, that theory is the art wave of the future, that after "the revolution" there can be no avant-garde (this is borrowed from the Marxian tradition), that innovative ideas in art works have reached a closure and that stressing them makes one "neo-modern" and therefore passé, and that modernism is essentially utopian and therefore has very limited relevance to our world which is seen as uniquely entropic and on the way downhill.

But there are also more thoughtful postmodernist critics who seem to ask themselves questions at every stage that go beyond the purely heuristic or fashionable ("in the discussion") approaches. These would include the late Paul de Man and Ihab Hassan. De Man's approach changed so dramatically over the years that it is hard to say what he stood for as a whole: one must break down his writings into stages or periods. Hassan, for all his annoying pontifications (such as "Schizophrenia heralds and hastens the end of capitalism"[6]) has made the most sincere and effective attempt to date to work out a theoretical basis for his discussions empirically rather than simply by relation to other theoreticians. He has even given us a list of eleven criteria of postmodernism:[7] 1) indeterminacy, 2) fragmentation, 3) decanonization, 4) self-lessness/depth-lessness, 5) the unpresentable/unrepresentable, 6) irony, 7) hybridization, 8) carnivalization, 9) performance/participation, 10) constructionism, and 11) immanence. Missing from his list is an emphasis on myth as an allusive device but also as a creative strategy, which seems central to Hassan's earlier writings.[8] These terms are mostly self-explanatory, except that for Hassan "decanonization" means questioning authority and rejecting many of the given assumptions of what constitutes a masterpiece; "hybridization" means formal or genre hybridization; "carnivalization" (which Hassan gets from Bakhtin) means a sort of polyphony or contrapuntal approach and not just a ludic element; "constructions" means that a work constructs a reality of some kind; and "immanence" is a secular concept here referring to the ability of the mind to construct itself by means of symbols, or icons. Hassan expresses doubt that these eleven "definiens" (he prefers the term to criteria) add up to any explicit definition of postmodernism and also that they fully distinguish what he calls "postmodern" from "modern." He is surely right about this; what he has defined or at least suggested is much of what characterizes the best art works of our time, but no case has been made here for a radical rupture with the various forms of modernism that came before so-called "postmodernism." Thus, it seems to me that, though Hassan would surely disagree with me, he has given here the case for a change of what we mean by "modernism" rather than a rejection of the term in favor of one that, for its very validity, must refer to a consensus about the term modernism that is questionable.[9]

Modernism has always changed, not only in the view of its practitioners but also of subsequent observers. Claudio Monteverdi, I should think, was an avant-gardist in his music in the seventeenth century. The Schlegel brothers, Beethoven, and Blake were all modernists in theirs (and Blake seems to prefigure in a curious way Hassan's list). Matthew Arnold, writing in the late nineteenth century, called the linchpin of modernism its "adequacy," that is, its ability to engage on all levels. But few would deny that the term "modern," if you simply say it to a layman, means the innovative works of the early twentieth century. The problem arises when one assumes that this is the only modern work. That may suffice for an English department in which the subject is too large for just one course, so Professor X teaches "Modern Literature," that is, twentieth-century literature up to the end of World War II, while Professor Y teaches "Postmodern Literature," meaning art from that watershed until the present moment. But it has no real correspondence with anything that *happened* in literature. Beckett's prose style is traditional, has few of the characteristics of "modern style" as we find it in Stein, Joyce, or even Faulkner. But the same is true of Yeats or Frost,

Sherwood Anderson or Theodore Dreiser, all of whom are usually classed as "modern." Every decade has its characteristics, and, confronted by any given work of music, visual art, or literature, a reasonably sophisticated listener, viewer, or reader can identify fairly accurately the date that the work reflects. "Modern" is a term that is progressively less useful as the work recedes into its chronological past. Viewed in this light the concept of "postmodern" becomes heuristic, basically a teaching device. However, a list such as Hassan's is more than this: it relates to the *Zeitgeist*, to which we shall return shortly. Hassan's list is invaluable for an approach to many works of the 1950s and 1960s, but it applies to the modernism of those decades, not to those of before or perhaps afterward.

But first: another sign of the continuation of modernist approaches into what the academics called the postmodern period is the work of artists such as Robert Rauschenberg. Resolutely innovative and iconoclastic, he matured in the 1950s, became famous in the 1960s, and his work continues strong today. In no way does his work fit into the past-obsessed and professionalistic, eclectic myopia of so many visual artists associated with postmodernism in visual art. He is the very epitome of what a postmodernist critic such as Peter Bürger would dismiss as "neo-modern." Yet his work seems to point towards other possibilities besides what he himself has realized, thus suggesting that it is not at the end of a stream of work but somewhere at its beginning or middle. Had modernism been replaced by postmodernism as a source of lively thought, would this be likely?

Art critics have traditionally been tempted to use their field as a Procrustean bed, undervaluing artists of various sorts in order to fit them into their criteria. As new artists come along who don't fit into their paradigms, either new critics become necessary or else the criteria can and should be adjusted. Trying to fit Rauschenberg into postmodernism is a rather thankless task, and the same holds true of discussions of John Cage's music and poetry, Diter Rot's art, Fluxus (all arts)[10] and Language poetry, especially its major practitioners—Charles Bernstein and Steve McCaffery, though others, such as Lyn Hejinian, Ray di Palma, Bruce Andrews, and Ron Silliman, have made important contributions as well. All these have usually been classified as "postmodern," whereas they cannot be understood except in the spectrum of modernism. As Paul Mann put it, "There is no post: everything that claims to be so blindly repeats what it thinks it has left behind."[11]

ii. The Zeitgeist

In the 1920s and 1930s it was a commonplace observation that if an art work did not reflect the spirit of its time, its *Zeitgeist*, it would probably not reflect anything significant about the world and would be doomed to irrelevance.[12] This was in contradistinction to the earlier assumption that art was eternal, forever outside its moment. But both these distinctions usually imply a should—art *should* reflect its time, or art *should not* reflect its time. Whether or not it should do so, we might observe that it *usually does* reflect its time, so that, in order to gain insight into a particular work, along with the inductive use of biography, we can relate it to its moment before we then bring it into ours. One can often go so far as to guess accurately the date of an unfamiliar work by spotting its general spirit, its reflection of the *Zeitgeist*. One matches what one experiences in a work with what one knows of the characteristics of the various decades to which it might belong.

Let us, for example, skate quickly over the decades of the past century in one country, the United States. The 1880s saw the climax of the long depression that started around 1873, and it alleviated itself during the 1890s, "the gay nineties," a very up decade in comparison to the 1880s, which was staid and a bit on the gloomy side in general. The start of the twentieth century was a come-down after the 1890s in the United States (as in France, for instance) since the adventuresome magazines were collapsing, the panic of 1907 deprived many artists of their livelihoods, and the arts (Albert Ryder, for example) show a corresponding introversion and gloom, but also a good deal of rejection of conventions much as the artists in their own way, like the radicals in the social movements of the time (World War I, for example) do in theirs. The 1910s started with a heroic upturn as the experimentation of the 1900s reached an apogee (as witnessed in the famous Armory Show of 1913, which introduced the European avant-gardes in America). Suddenly there was a sort of strained idealism as Americans entered World War I to "make the world safe for democracy." The 1920s begin at the end of the war with a time of economic problems and a "return to normalcy" (President Harding's campaign slogan in 1922), with the Palmer raids in which scores of radicals were railroaded into jails and many American artists and writers went off to Europe (the "lost generation" in Gertrude Stein's phrase) to escape the stultifying Philistinism of the United States. The decade became more mellow as it passed, however, and the works of the late 1920s, when they are not characterized by the frenetic energy of the "roaring twenties," often have a striking lyrical quality as in Gertrude Stein's *Lucy Church Amiably* (1927), the "Anna Livia Plurabelle" section of James Joyce's *Work in Progress* (*Finnegans Wake*, 1927), both written in France of course, or the Stravinsky-Ballanchine ballets, such as *Pulcinella*, which began at this time and suggest the possibility of neoclassicism, a term with which Stravinsky and have both been associated. In the 1930s confidence was lost for a time, as the world economy collapsed, and in the resulting rage a new social focus was probably inevitable, given the need to struggle against fascism (Bertolt Brecht), capitalism (the earlier John Dos Passos of *USA*). This rage continued into the 1940s, which are all but seamless with the 1930s, against Stalinism (Arthur Koestler).

By the late 1940s this area seemed played out, and a new cycle began, not only with Abstract Expressionism and new forms of modern dance, but the beginning of aleatoric art (John Cage and others). The 1960s are a crest of innovation and experimentation in the arts, not only with establishment "movements" (Pop Art, which celebrates the world, the Urban American world at least, as seen in the mass media, to the delight of corporate executives) but officially rejected ones as well (romantically called "underground," but in fact meaning simply underfunded and thus cruel to their participants) such as Fluxus, Concrete and Sound Poetry, and so on. The 1970s represent a kind of Thermidor, solidifying the gains and taking stock of whatever had been achieved that was positive, more introspective than the 1960s but still at heart looking for progress. Often it is dismissed as the "me generation," which is unfair, but it does seem to have an unusually high degree of introspection. The 1980s is a curious phenomenon, a retrogressive time, rejecting equally progress and introspection in favor of a past which never existed. This is the decade, par excellence, of the art that is favored by most postmodernist art critics (literary critics tend to focus on a slightly earlier period). This brings us to the 1990s, which will probably be seen as a decade in which the retrogressive current died out but in which any progressive forces, in art or politics or even economics, have been inchoate, seeming to be desperately searching for an identity and a voice. Many people appear to agree that changes are needed, but there is no consensus as to how to bring these about, and the establishment of this time seems all too glad to prevent any change by coopting all popular wishes and needs through commercialism and using our mass media to repress them. It is a time of what I have called "mediocracy"—a polysemic word suggesting rule at once by the media and by the mediocre.[13]

Not every work, of course, focuses literally on its time. However, usually an artist evolves from becoming tired of what has been done, of feeling that it is irrelevant to him or her, and begins looking for a new vision in his or her moment. It is here that the *Zeitgeist* enters in. In the terminology of Jaussian hermeneutics, a horizon of expectations (*Erwartungshorizont*) is felt which does not match the horizon of what has been offered.[14] So far this is the horizon of expectation that is shared with the viewer or receiver, listener or reader (the "horizon of expectation of æsthesis"). But the artist also tries to select what is missing from what he or she has experienced and to achieve it, whether by means of a new form, a new subject, whatever seems appropriate. This is the "horizon of expectation of poiesis." Put differently, let us consider this model:

    i) someone initiates a model, call it the "commissioner," whether public, organization , private sponsor.

    ii) The artist (or curator?) now matches his or her horizon of expectations with that of the commissioner. Does he or she reject or accept it?

        a) It may be accepted, resulting in a work which is not radically broken or separated from its matrix.

        b) It may be rejected (Baudelaire, dadaists, most Fluxus works, exhibitions in which a subject is re-evaluated). This would be the horizon of expectation of poiesis expressed in idfferent terms.

    iii) The receiver now experiences the work, expects x and receives y. How close is y to x?

        a) What are the possible effects when x and y are very close?

        b) Or very far apart? How many of these models are covered (and how) when, for example, the piece is a piano work being performed by a pianist for an audience? What in this last case is the role of notation? What horizons does it imply?

This is the first part of the horizon of expectations of æsthesis, and the performer, artist, or curator here becomes another receiver. The work perceived is now able to be digested by the receiver onto his or her own intellectual plane.

a) the work becomes part of the newly altered horizon of experience, when

b) it is compared to other experiences.

c) New meanings are assigned to the work, which may either remain central to the receiver, or they may be rejected or placed somewhere between acceptance and rejection ("I remember liking that song, but I no longer care about it.").

This model is implicit in the discussions in this essay and elsewhere in this book, and it is applicable to the historical discussion which was suggested earlier and to which we should now return. Given the fine tuning of the historical overview that surely any reader might wish to make of my account, decade by decade, from the 1880s to the present, and granted that I might have begun with the 1490s C.E. or B.C.E. and used more examples from this or that other art, country, or continent, it does not seem at all surprising that the arts of the 1970s and 1980s should have turned to eclectic sources, myths, images, and archetypes (the so-called "new age" concerns at worst but, at best, a much-needed correction to areas that had been ignored in the previous few decades). These are often the main concerns of the artists classified as "postmodern." The titles of the painters' shows are allusive in a way that would have been very unusual in the 1960s. The names of the books on the shelves are more often mythic than was the case before, from Derek Walcott's *Omeros* to Hassan's *Dismemberment of Orpheus*, already cited. But the citation of myth is more usually not a reference and enriching by association with the *meaning* of a myth, as is traditional from Milton to Joyce, so much as it is an escape from entropy by drawing on traditional narrative images to portray a world that is evoked subjectively by the artist or writer and then presenting such a world outside of its traditional context. The self-consciousness of the participants in cultural activities of this sort, I believe, is what gives them the sense of a rupture with the work of the previous few decades and that therefore motivates them to claim a Postmodernism that is opposed to Modernism, somehow replacing it.[15] If postmodernist arguments were fully valid one would expect the 1990s to intensify the currents of the 1970s and 1980s.

It hasn't happened. What we see instead among people in their teens, twenties, and early thirties is a generation in which education seems deficient by traditional standards, but the new generation appears determined not to decline, not to accept itself as decadent, not to fritter its energy away in a miasma of *haute cuisine* and nit-picking distinctions as so many postmodernists did, but to fend for itself and make its way. It is, rather, a premillennarian generation, complete with a premillennarian consciousness.

iii. The Premillenarian Sense of Art and Culture

Around us we see that the predictions that Buckminster Fuller repeatedly made in the 1960s—of a world of plenty when our main problem would be to use our leisure time well—are unlikely to come true without more work than we had anticipated. As for Marshall McLuhan's Fuller-related view of the positive role of media, this seems to have led to our mediocracy and to the more pessimistic view of media of, for example, Otto Gmelin, who argues that their power can lead, among other things, to a tyranny of the majority.[16] In our social and political life we see around us a world of violence and triviality, and we sense stagnation as the reality of our present. Violence and life on a low cultural level, media blitzes on behalf of nobodies, and poor products seem to be everywhere. Education alone is not the answer. Either one is trained for jobs that do not exist, or one finds that what one is best at seems undervalued by "the real world." The teachers appear either incompetent, locked into a meaningless world unto themselves, and out of touch with reality outside of themselves, or else they are prevented from teaching what we could best learn from them by over-structured and centralized programs or avalanches of paperwork. So be it. Yet there is a sense of an era drawing to a close, that the second millennium C.E. is drawing to a close, that one has but one life to live so it is up to us to make the next millennium better.

The last change of millennia in the West had a different historical sense from ours.[17] Many people expected the world would come to physical end at the time. The sense today is more that we are facing some sort of major transition, and that in some way we can turn this to our benefit. Faced with this transition, the Modernism with which postmodernist critics take issue seems less utopian than they say, more a matter of proposing model visions that may inspire patterns of thought that are appropriate to the next millennium. Talk with an intelligent twenty-year-old at this time and one will not find a nerd of the so-called "generation X" stereotype but a highly motivated person who is out to do some saving, of his or her own skin and world, and of the larger world, too, if possible. These are people who are comfortable with vision and principles and uncomfortable with the limitations of a market approach to life and taking no for an answer in the name of expediency. How to put this philosophy of life into practice is, of course, a question. But where there is a massive recognition of a need, it is likely that at least some effort will be made to fill that need. Such high-minded actions of the post-World War II period as the Marshall Plan, for example, seem more relevant than the knee-jerk conservatism of the 1970s and 1980s of the "Reaganbush" or Pat Buchanan varieties, with their sterile evocations of a mellow past that never existed.

Art is an appropriate part of how we survive, souls intact, in an impoverished world. I know a man, a good visual poet, who worked with the youth in the slum city of Newburg, New York. He had the youth making poems and art pieces, experimenting with art and finding their own way of doing things. He says it changed their lives and made them more hopeful than would otherwise have been possible, and I have no reason to doubt his word. If one can make a work of art which pleases one, then who knows what else one can make of a bit of one's world and finally of oneself? If we can discover that one can makes something somehow beautiful, what an amazement that can be. If in addition one can express oneself or the world one lives in, that is a route to satisfaction. One sees one's own potential. But, of course, simply accepting the given forms is of no particular use. One must find new ones.

The arts can heal. One thinks of the biblical story of the shepherd David playing to troubled King Saul and giving him a moment of serenity. However, though "art therapy" is now a recognized practice, healing has seldom been a priority among makers of art, and it is unclear as yet what forms will be most suitable. We must find these out.

Thus, for all that many great artists have been among the conservatives of their time, the sense that they were so because this was where their gifts lay is important in them. Thinking just of music for the moment, Palestrina, Vivaldi, Verdi (in his music, not his politics), Prokoviev, Barber, and Copland would all be examples of fine composers who were conservative. One senses they composed as they did not because they were unaware of other possibilities but because that was where their gifts and vision drew them. But if one's objective is to express one's situation and one's moment, then all the possibilities must be open, and this means the models from the past on which one draws are likely to be the innovative ones. Hence the current focus on Dada and Fluxus, for instance.[18] These are both recently transferred to "the past," in that their boundaries are known and no longer untested, even though there is not yet any consensus on precisely what they are.

In the situation of art that is in a dialectical relationship with the "real world" outside itself, the art work (as in both Dada and Fluxus, for instance) directly incorporates elements from daily living—treating the making of a cup of coffee as music, for instance. The purpose of this is not, of course, to shock or proclaim originality. If it were, the artist would surely propose to mix concrete and turds and fill the pot with that. Rather, it is to see something that many people experience every day in a new and aesthetic way, and thus it is very important that real water, real coffee, and a real stove (for instance) be used, not the illusions of them. In this way the overall experience of art will be enriched by one's life, and one's life will be enriched by art. This is called the "art/life dichotomy," and it is central to many of the arts of the twentieth century.

Another allegedly traditional distinction that breaks down in this light is that between popular (or folk) materials and their high-art parallels, while that between functional and eternal art is all but wiped out. The difference between kitsch and truly popular art lies in where each comes from. Kitsch and the art of the mediocracy are imposed upon most of us by commercial power and have no intrinsic value, whereas true folk and popular art are, instead, an expression of our predicament and of the situation of the people in any given community. High art was only "high" when it was the property of the milords. Climb a mountain, and it no longer seems so high; there are always further peaks, sometimes connected by a ridge or plain that was hidden from the valley. The separation of genres may come from Aristotle, but it is very convenient for the academics, who can use it to carve out little territories for themselves that have little correspondence in the world of living art. This would be fine if it were recognized as a convenient way of breaking down what would otherwise be vast and therefore vague and making it manageable. The problem arises when the separation of genres is made prescriptive, especially when it is made universally prescriptive: poetry shall never be visual, poetry and prose behave differently and are therefore not to be combined, this language is suitable for popular art while that is suitable for high art. We have all heard that viewpoint. Of course it can be masked as innovative: the academics venture into new territory and treat the world of popular culture as a new area for analysis. But actually the analysis of popular culture is by no means new, nor need it be separated out from the analysis of other culture, since our arts interpenetrate so much.

There always was another tradition in our Western arts which paralleled the Aristotelian purity of the genres in which one kind of work was cross-fertilized by another to make an enriched hybrid. Looking way back, for instance, to the fifteenth century, we see that the composer Guillaume Dufay based one of his finest masses on a popular song of the time, "L'Homme Armé" (The Armed Man). Shakespeare's plays are well known for their effective demolition of Aristotelian unities and purities. This lack of the unities the eighteenth century called "crude" even at the same time as, for example, one of its greatest composers, François Couperin, in his "Onzième Ordre" has a section called "Les Fastes de la Grande et Ancienne Menestrandise" (*The Annals of the Great Ancient Minstrelsy*) in which he both spoofs and revels in the rural folk music of his time. In the twentieth century the number of classical composers who have used jazz effectively in their works is enormous—Milhaud, Gershwin (who came, of course, from a popular-music background), Stravinsky, and so on. No matter that the jazz ceases to be jazz, the hybrid is effective as music and suggests further possibilities. Literally dozens of classical melodies have made our popular-music hit parade, from Rachmaninoff's *Variations on a Theme by Paganini* (a theme that became "Full Moon and Empty Arms" in the fifties) to Beethoven's Fifth Symphony (which became "A Fifth of Beethoven" in the seventies). Similarly, visual artists have used comic strips and newspaper clippings in their collages (one thinks of Braque, Picasso, Schwitters, or, more recently, Ray Johnson in his "motico" series), and popular cartoonists, such as Phillips in his "Strange World of Mr. Mum" strips that appeared until recently in the *New York Post*, have returned the compliment. American Pop Art was merely the commercialized and systematized version of this process; the best of its practitioners are interesting not because of the popular nature of their presumed subject matter but because of the interesting relation of their specific styles and their relation to their subjects.[19] As for the prestige accorded to popular art and culture, the main job of a piece of popular music, for instance, is to be popular, and there is therefore always a commercial element present that may (or may not) distort the actual value of a given work. Powerful forces must be brought to bear upon the market to make one feel "if you don't know this tune, see this movie, read this book, which has been heard by thirty million people, been seen by thirty million people, or sold thirty million copies, you are an irrelevant nobody." Isn't that a sort of snobbery of a new kind? It makes one wonder what would happen to a record company that tried to sell one set of hits forever more and did not change the market to sell new records: it would, in time, probably cease to exist. "New and better" is a marketing necessity, if not one for our serious arts, where the notion that beauty is eternal is at least a popular assumption.[20] This means that there is always a receding process when popular works are allowed to cease to be popular. Some are remembered and some not. Thus, "newness" is necessary for the company (whether or not the work is innovative in any way) as a selling point. The same is true of films or television or videos, and those who ignore the world of popular music or film appear to those who follow it as hopeless fuddy-duddies or irrelevant or snobs. This last assumes that the reason they do not follow it is because they feel superior to it, which may not be the case at all. Interestingly, in some places in the world the gulf between the innovative and popular arts is far smaller than in the United States and Europe. This is true of Brazil, for instance, where Caetano Veloso's hit parade album *Araçá Azul* (1973) has lyrics which are concrete poetry and where one of the main practitioners in that area, Augusto de Campos, is also among the most popular film critics in São Paulo.

But how can one meaningfully dismiss a poor kid's love of some unfashionable music, classical or otherwise, as beyond him or her? Must every black person confine him- or herself to rap or jazz? Must every Vermont farm kid listen only to country and western music or fiddling? Who says so? Only the mediocrats. Finding in oneself some affinity with a fine but unknown poem is a thrill many of us remember. Outgrowing it and finding some deeper piece is another. Thus, we need to have as much variety of artistic works available to us as possible, and we need the entry points to them. We also need to form a consensus as to how pieces can be received by us. How *do* we hear, see, and read? How *can* we hear, see, and read? How does the one lead to the other? To answer these questions we need an appropriate hermeneutic, a methodology for the interpretation of what we are experiencing. We need to know how to focus on the process of broadening our horizons.

Try these models, for instance: the "receiver" (we will use this instead of repeating "reader," "viewer," or "hearer") has his or her horizon of experiences, expectations, and assumptions. The artist has his or hers that the work expresses or reflects. While one is receiving the work, that is, actually experiencing it, the horizons fuse.[21] Afterwards the horizons separate again, and the horizon of the receiver has been bent and altered as he or she has experienced the work. Of course it may be further bent as the horizons re-fuse in memory. There is also the question, in performance work, of what happens when a performer reads a script or musical notation, or when the receiver sees or hears a stage performance of a drama or hears yet another performance of a musical work. But these are refinements of or supplements to the process.

The psychology of this process is, however, conditioned by one's expectations. In the late nineteenth century the sense that somehow out there a frontier existed that made many things possible helped to lend a characteristic optimism to the art works of an eastern-state poet such as Walt Whitman. Perhaps this sense of the imminent millennium conditions our sensibility and gives us, in spite of the rot in our socio-economic situation, with our falling per capita incomes and the gloom this entails, a sense that change for the better is possible. Perhaps it is simply that flowers have always grown well on manure piles. While the latter may also be true, the former seems more important at this moment.

iv. The Neoteric Fallacy and Hermeneutics

The term "neoteric," like the term "hermeneutic," has been with us for some time.[22] Thus, a modern coinage is not needed to fill in a technical gap in critical language. Nevertheless, it becomes a useful tool. While neoteric means "new" or "recent," it also connotes a *taste* for the new or recent, just as, for instance, "esoteric" suggests not just the exotic but a taste for it. If we think of our assumptions about artistic and scientific progress, we can note that in science a new hypothesis, once it has been proved, replaces an old one to the extent that the old one covers the same ground. Of course there may be territory outside that ground, but once the ground itself is covered, then the new typically replaces the old. In art, however, this is not true. A new technique expands the possibilities, but the old masterpiece or landmark is still an old masterpiece or landmark. The artist finds not just new forms but new meanings for old forms. Think of Ezra Pound's use of classical French or Provençal forms in his poetry. In 1927, when Arnold Schoenberg wrote his *String Quartet No. 3*, the rondo was a rather old-fashioned form; Schoenberg put an extraordinary one into his quartet. One thinks also of John Cage's mesostics that take off in a new way from a form developed in the third century or earlier. To assume that the new *replaces* the old, as some have said or implied, can be described as "the neoteric fallacy."[23] It is also a fallacy that may underlie the assumption of some postmodernists that the set of definends they ascribe to Postmodernism, even if this latter were a truly new movement, would make the set of values qua values less valid. Modern art did not *replace*, let us say, Romanticism in the absolute scale of works, any more than Romanticism replaced the Neoclassicism or whatever one wishes to call what went before Romanticism, except in the more limited sense that each of these tendencies replaced the earlier set as the modernism of its time. We are still free to love the Renaissance, the Baroque, the Neoclassics (or are they simply "Classics?"), the Romantics, the early Moderns, or whoever else we choose to love, and to us as receivers they are as wonderful and relevant as they ever were. Their horizons fuse with ours and speak not only of their own time but of ours as well.

Only if we happen to be artists and we try to use the old sets *as we have received them* will we run into trouble when we try to express our world; those older sets simply will not work for that, and we must turn instead to the quest for new forms, to the modernism of whatever moment we have found ourselves in. Yet, we may indeed be able to adapt this or that from what has come before along with this or that which we have invented. Schoenberg, an innovative composer and on the cutting edge early in the twentieth century, used to teach by analyzing works by Mozart and Beethoven from a century before.[24] William Blake, surely one of the most innovative artists and poets ever, learned his crafts by copying works of others, largely from the Middle Ages.

Who sponsors the neoteric fallacy? That is, why is it so prevalent? On the one hand, it is often borrowed from science, in which a new method usually does replace on old one. It is often borrowed from an aspect of an important strategy in the world of business, as has already been noticed and will be again. Why buy a plain cookie when you can get a new and improved one that just happens to cost more, a fine and trouble-free bed sheet when you can be induced to get a new-style form-fitted bed sheet that costs half again as much as an older, simpler one? This common business procedure has affected our critics and our academics profoundly. It has to sell books and make a market, so it says to the tenure-seeking teacher: "You must prove you are *au courant*. This new way of looking at Balzac or Schoenberg or David Salle makes all previous ways irrelevant." But why do we need the latest mode of looking at those things? What do they enable us to understand that we could not understand before? Have new facts appeared which can only be interpreted by the new modes? If they do indeed give us new understanding, if their insights are indeed the result of their new methodologies, then they are of value indeed, but even then one doubts that they replace so much as they augment the older methodologies and insights. For example, Shakespearean criticism has been with us rather a long time. Johnson, Coleridge, August-Wilhelm Schlegel, and many others have given us insights into Shakespeare. Along comes someone to decode hidden messages, to point out the patterns among the codes, in short to give us a structuralist analysis of, let us say, *Macbeth*. Next, along comes a young actress seeking to portray Lady Macbeth, and a director to direct her. Will they find the structuralist analysis has *replaced* the older studies? That is not likely. They may turn, for example, to Granville-Barker from earlier in the twentieth century. But for someone seeking truly to understand the world of *Macbeth* and how it differs from our own, then this person may well find the structuralist approach important and valuable as a method providing insight, not just because it is new, "in the discussion," as the literary-theory folks say, "in the discourse" as the fine-art theoreticians and rhetoricians say.

We have already noted the assumption of the neoteric fallacy in popular art/popular music, at least, but television shows and other trends and fashions follow a similar pattern. One sees the "new" movie in order to have cocktail-party conversation even if one seldom goes to cocktail parties. If it weren't for this, one would stress going to movies, new or old, which one simply had not seen before (and occasionally seeing other favorites again). That is how the neoteric fallacy has been drummed into us. But by becoming aware of this we can get a new perspective overall, can appreciate both past and present works by tuning into our horizons and truly expanding our worlds. In this way we can receive art works in such a way as to become ever a more whole person (William Morris's ideal for art). Through developing our own hermeneutic processes we can find ourselves in history and other areas of culture as well as art, can tune into the shifts to which we can become more sensitive by balancing our focus on our own horizons, those from the past and any others we can find in the middle. If we reject the past, even the immediate past, we are also rejecting the present. For what else is the present but a moment in the process of passing by? Thus, we must focus our attention on the process of becoming if we wish to see our moment in time as it really is and to expand upon that. Stripped of its bric-a-brac term, postmodern, the insights of some of the "postmodernist" critics are valid and useful. For instance, Hassan's list, already cited, which he applies to "postmodernism," can be applied to works that reflect the *Zeitgeist* of the 1960s and just before and after, such as Pynchon's *Gravity's Rainbow*. Right now a new modernism, a premillenarian one, is afoot. Viewed in this light, perhaps we no longer need to call any work from before 1900 "modern." Whatever threshold one chooses, by working with a continuity rather than a radical rupture, we can see the ways in which our time both is and is not unique, how we ourselves both are and are not unique.

II. Five Myths of Postmodernism

i. Preamble

TAKE AWAY A RELIGION'S MYTHS, and often it will wilt and die. In our cultural life, our trends and our fashions act much in the manner of a religion: the new trend debunks (or at least asserts itself) against the myths of the old trend, and, in so doing, creates its own.

So it is with the High Priests and Priestesses of Post-modernism (for example, Rosalind Krauss and the *October* crowd, Jean-François Lyotard, the artist Arakawa, and what seem to be at least six million professors of English or French literature), those who either accept or, more cynically, have found it advantageous to be identified with the myths of what they present as a new trend in our culture of the past forty years or so. But in doing so they have overstressed the novelty of the culture of these years, few of their myths are true or even necessary, and it is my contention that they have attempted to make a mockery of the real state of our arts, risking, as the folk expression puts it, "throwing out the baby with the bath water."

The culture of our moment in time (1989) is indeed a serious one, with high points that can compare favorably with the high points of that Modernism which overlapped and preceded it, but the encrustation of the new myths obscures its virtues and produces a curious jargon, not the least problematic term of which is "Postmodernism" itself. But the question of the validity of much of what is meant by that problematic term "post-modern" can only be dealt with when it is stripped of its inflated mythology, so that its contributions can be assessed positively and without its polemical content. So, onwards to the myths.

ii. Myth One: "Postmodernism is unique."

When "postmodern" came into use, it had to be on the assumption that it referred to one unique category that was therefore capable of being named (the issue of the disagreement over what that category was is a separate one, to be mentioned at the end of these reflections). Corollary to this and what was useful to its advocates was the assumption that what it referred to was a fixity, at least the style of a generation and perhaps of an overall tendency. By naming that referential category, the myth was created that it did. But does it?

All the main usages of the term "modern" in English date from the sixteenth century (in Italian, from somewhat before).[25] The term was used in the "ancients vs. moderns" controversy. To use "modern" for current art, a practice that dates from the eighteenth century, is a relative one, fading as some newer concept or style replaces it. Its utility as a term to describe the period of the great critic William Hazlitt in the early nineteenth century, for example, allowed him thus to name the artworks that reflected the *Zeitgeist* of his moment in history with its own ideas and styles, without his having to get too specific or defensive about the matter. It was a temporary category, to be replaced as time passes and the outline of a time and its culture emerge. Temporary it was: the term "romantic" came into use to replace what Hazlitt had called "modern." But what "modern" covers, what we perceive of it, and perhaps also the very essence of the work itself do indeed change.

One recalls a Fluxus performance work of 1961 by the Korean Fluxartist Nam June Paik. In it he grasps a violin by its neck, raises it ever so slowly over his head, then, at the peak, suddenly smashes it to smithereens onto a table in front of him. Of course the audience realizes, after the first few seconds, what is going to happen but watching it occur so inevitably is a thrilling experience. In the context of the classical music scene of the late 1950s, which was excessively intellectual and cerebral, the heyday of Post-Webernism in music and before the current wave of commercialist utilitarianism set in, the piece was delightful and a great refreshment. But seeing it again recently, twenty-six years later, I found that instead of being a positive work that clears the air, it had become a hideously negative statement of anti-art attitudes, so many of which we have around us today already. No doubt I have changed, but the climate of the art and cultural milieu has changed even more. It does not matter that Paik would not dream of doing the piece with a Stradivarius violin but only with a cheap, battered one; today we need every violin we can get. The joy of the piece is gone without it ever changing itself but with only an alteration in its context in the spirit of the times. So it is that works, once modern, change and seem now to belong to a past era. Yet, compensating for this is the way that once this happens the outlines of their contexts usually become clearer so that their true identities can begin to be seen, and a new name can come to be applied to them, with "modern" becoming the new catch-all term for what can not yet be named.

Elsewhere, in my *Pattern Poetry: Guide to an Unknown Literature* (1987) I have described over three-thousand years of visual poetry. What is striking there is that in some places and at some times, one has the sense that a poem belongs to the avant-garde of its era, to the cutting edge of its then modernism. This is true of the *carmina cancellata* of the Carolingian renaissance (poems, usually rectangular, in which a second text is "canceled out" from the first, which remains in the background, in such a way as to form a shape): it is also true of the early Renaissance shaped poems that follow the forms of the Greek bucolic pattern poems, and of most twentieth-century visual poems, from Apollinaire to the concrete poets and since. At other times the poems follow precedents and seem to reflect a very traditional way of working; they run counter to the modernity of their times. This would be true of the *carmina cancellata*, of the many

Figure 1. A carmen cancellatum composed by Hrabanus Maurus (784-856), and probably drawn by the scribe Hatto, representing the crucifixion, from "De Laudibus Sanctae Crucis" (ca. 835). See also cover illustration and note on p iv.

shaped poems of the late Baroque when the wealthy bourgeoisie would commission heart-shaped wedding poems or cross-shaped funeral ones from their local poets or printers. Fine works exist among these occasional verses along with other pieces that read like greeting-card verse. But although these occasional verses, the *carmina cancellata*, and the other pattern poems all belong to the same category, some are innovative and thus modernist in their times, while some are clearly not. The form is not what makes them modern; that comes from their perception and reception, and these vary.

Arthur O. Lovejoy, in his "On the Discrimination of Romanticisms" (1923), in tracing the evolution of "romanticism" found it necessary to use the term not generically, as had usually been the case, so that a plural would have been unnecessary, but as a term with a series of signifieds, so that the term really needed a plural if one were to refer to the whole series. Perhaps we should henceforth speak of "modernisms" if we are to refer to the shifting set of characteristics associated with that term. In such a context might one also speak of "postmodernisms?" For example, when the Impressionists were modern, the Post-Impressionists would be post-modern, or when the socialist Realists of the 1930s were modern, the abstract expressionists who followed them would be post-modern, and so on.

However, when Rosalind E. Krauss, an editor of *October* magazine and one of the best known of these High Priests and Priestesses of current Post-modernism, describes Rodin or his predecessors as "modern," as she does in *The Originality of the Avant-Garde and Other Modernist Myths* (1985), it could be argued that she is being nothing less than facetious since she knows full well that, while they were "modern" to their contemporaries, they are not to us. When, on top of this, she asserts a continuity of intention or style or virtually anything else from the Impressionists of the late nineteenth century through the Abstract Expressionists of the 1950s, she is truly stretching a point, as if one were to attribute some kind of spiritual kinship to Dégas, Kandinsky, and de Kooning because all worked in oil painting. Alas, she is not alone in her assumption, however. Incidentally, in her title essay she poses a similar problem with "originality," arguing that since the question is admittedly open as to whether Rodin's sculptures, the number of castings of which were occasionally more than the authorized number, are "originals," that this argues for his work not being "original" in the sense of extending the range of possibilities and being without obvious precedents, thus blending two distinctly different meanings of the word "original."

But, to return to "modern," New York's Museum of Modern Art has been with us long enough to have assembled an extraordinary collection of works of the past (perhaps) 120 years, little of it still modern. Should the museum give up its holdings? That would be administratively a disaster. Should it change its name? Perhaps, but that, too, could be awkward. The oldest of the Paris bridges is the "Pont Neuf," the "New Bridge." This seems to trouble nobody except a few tourists on their first visit to Paris. Presumably the museum will be like that, known as a museum of works many of which were once modern, but which, though they no longer so, are certainly of great interest.

I can remember, as a schoolboy, seeing in some English artist's writings of the 1880s, "postmodern" used as a means of establishing the validity of his own work vis-à-vis the French painters of the time. Since I was studying Cicero then, I thought to myself, "What a clever rhetorical strategy!" But, try though I may, I have never been able to find that text again. However, according to a letter of September 25, 1987, written to me by Kelly L. Tierney of Merriam-Webster, the dictionary publishers, Merriam-Webster's files indicate that the term was used by Arnold Toynbee in 1947 to describe the period of history since 1875 and continuing to the present, and that its use in architecture in its current sense dates from 1949.[26] In any case, even these two dates precede the starting dates usually claimed for post-modern art. The polemic current in "postmodern" remains, since the term, when used in a discussion, carries with it the suggestion that artwork other than that which one is calling "post-something" is now, somehow, out of date, or at least is no longer new. Rhetorically it is a trick that often masks a distaste for new or innovative art. Since that English painter of a century ago was, in fact, far less innovative than the Impressionists, the trick was clearly not lost upon him. But it often is just that when one looks through Jencks's *Post-modernism* (1987), Krauss's *Originality*, and the various "postmodernist" works about literature (those surrounding the cult of St. Samuel à Beckett, for instance), to see just what works the post-modernists advocate. On the one hand, the advocate of the post-modern often professes to lament the passing of an avant-garde, but, on the other hand, the tears are crocodile ones, and the work they present is usually very traditional, which had been with us all along, at least as an undercurrent, through the times of innovation and the various heydays of the modernisms. This has been true at least since Donald Sutherland's once much admired essay "Whither, Oh Avant-Garde" (ca. 1961), an early polemic for literary postmodernism, and it is clear in the similar arguments for Postmodernist music (George Crumb, for instance), performance (Laurie Anderson), visual art (Alan Feltus), and so on. There is nothing categorically wrong with conservative art, of course, but it need not be presented as replacing its opposite; that is a strategy that, in the long run, misrepresents and therefore both degrades and debases the great conservative artists of any age. As Harry Polkinhorn once told me, "Art is not a process of totalization; criticism is."

Art does not renew itself like medicine, with each new discovery replacing what went before it: rather, it proceeds by a dialectic of innovation and drawing new strength from its antecedents and roots in the non-art part of our culture, augmenting and supplementing the available stock of cultural experiences. One century's discard becomes the next century's treasure. Our histories are full of this.

Thus, we need our conservatives just as we need our innovators to monitor each other and keep the scene a complete one, so that all the artists—in music our Tallises as well as our Morleys, our Honeggers as much as our Iveses; in visual art our Audubons as well as our Turners—can contribute their best efforts according to their gifts and taste, in order that the *Zeitgeist* of our age can find its fullest expression, as we shall see after the next section.

iii. Myth Two: "Modern art is anti-woman."

> ... Does the concept of "avant-garde" necessarily imply political and philosophical as well as aesthetic preoccupations? Does it necessarily imply an elitist orientation? Can "avant-garde" be considered synonymous with "modernist" or "post-modernist"? Is "avant-garde" a Euro-centric, or at least a characteristically Western notion? Is it perhaps a characteristically "masculine" notion?

Poor grammar aside, these questions come from the prospectus to a summer program on the avant-garde directed by Susan R. Suleiman and co-directed by Alice A. Jardine funded by the National Endowment for the Humanities, which took place at Harvard University between June 22 and July 30, 1987. Among those who attended and wrote papers for the program were Professors Harry Polkinhorn (already mentioned) of San Diego State University's Calexico branch and Charles Doria (then) of Rutgers University, to both of whom I am therefore indebted for information. The prospectus shows more clearly than any other text I have seen a series of linkages among ideas common in many discussions of Post-modernism in its relationship to Modernism as viewed by what I have called the Priesthood of the former.

Especially among academic Marxists it is assumed that the artistic and political avant-gardes have a close relationship; this assumption is most lucidly expressed, perhaps, in Renato Poggioli's *The Theory of the Avant-Garde* (1968), which is still relatively current and is far less garbled Peter Bürger's more recent work on the subject, *Theory of the Avant-Garde* (1984), which depends for its arguments on many of the same false myths as Suleiman and Jardine's prospectus. The assumption, because it is so common, on the right as well as the left, should be treated as a myth of its own (see section five, below). Also, the notion that the avant-garde is to be equated, one to one, with "modernist" or "postmodernist" views or elites, and that it may well be illusory or at least undesirable to have an avant-garde today—this is the most complex issue of the five. But in order to handle it, as we will in section six, we must first deal with the somewhat separate issue of sexism and its relationship to our arts.

Although women are a statistical majority, at least in the West, art produced by women has traditionally been treated as minority art, of interest almost exclusively to other women, and, with the exceptions of dance and possibly of literature, not to be taken as seriously as art produced by men (or at least presumed to be for a male-organized audience, one in which the women were present but not voting). It is because of the assumption that this organization was somehow masculine that the question of sexism was raised in the form it was, asking if the very concept of an avant-garde, which relates to the military metaphor of advance troops coming before the main body, is masculine. To this one can simply say no, that, after all, feminists have been the avant-garde among women in general over the past century, fighting for political and, more recently, for social rights for women. Even the military metaphor of avant-garde itself seems more suitable for women today than in previous centuries, where women in military situations were so exceptional as to become legends (Jeanne d'Arc or Queen Boadicea, for instance), while now the women soldiers of Vietnam, Israel, or the various revolutionary groups are central to these armies' or groups' very strategies or existence. Women can be as devoted to war or peace as anyone else and in any way at all. For better or worse, the military allusion of "avant-garde" fits women as well as men nowadays. However, more crucial, ultimately, is the way in which Modernism is attacked by implication, through its identification with the avant-garde, as being somehow anti-feminist, an idea which bears with it the corollary assumption that Postmodernism is inherently more sympathetic to women's interests.

The evidence for modernist hostility towards women that was repeatedly brought up at Harvard was the distortion of the female figure in visual art, in many works of Picasso and in the "Women" series of Willem de Kooning (see Fig. 2). At Harvard almost all discussion revolved around French and occasionally Italian or American Modernism, with one reportedly disastrous incursion into German art (a presentation by a Harvard instructor on German Dada which dealt largely with the anti-dadaist *Die Neue Sachlichkeit* group), with contributions of Latin America, Eastern Europe, and all other countries being more or less ignored. Had Germany been more central to the discussion, the argument over this alleged hostility might, of course, have dealt with the works of Georg Grosz in his *Ecce Homo* series from the 1920s. Since none of the artists we have mentioned has produced any large body of homoerotic or homosexual art, another possible issue, that of alleged gay male hostility towards women, usually a different kind of myth, did not arise.

But does modern art, meaning here most art produced roughly between 1905 and 1960, really attack women or their image? Picasso has also produced many very sensual-looking women, notably the series on the pony-tailed woman of the mid-century (yes, I know her name but, except with portraits, I prefer to leave models anonymous). So, for that matter, did Grosz, particularly in later years. Nor were either of those artists notably different in their figure paintings from the works done by women artists at the same time. Rather, a different sort of view, a very different *Weltanschauung*, seems to be manifest. A vision of the world is depicted in each work and uniquely by each artist, a presumably new way of looking at things. That is the common denominator of all recent modernisms, I think. Women are part of the world, almost the world itself for some men. Thus, the woman is the perfect focus for their view of the world. Hence the many nude women in cubist or futurist art. Now suppose a male artist sees the world as being in a crisis. He has found many

Figure 2. Willem de Kooning (1904-), *Marilyn Monroe* (1954), oil on canvas. Collection: Neuberger Museum of Art, Purchase College, State University of New York. Gift of Roy R. Neuberger. Photo: Jim Frank. Gift of Roy R. Neuberger, Neuberger Museum, State University of New York at Purchase. This is an example of a modernist work in which beautiful painting employs bizarre descriptions of its subject. De Kooning's piece is one of the "Women" series, its subject a Hollywood actress proverbial for her beauty. While on one level indeed his image is made monstrous, on another, because of the torque, brushwork, and colors, the picture as a whole is very beautiful.

women beautiful (whether they wanted to be is another story). But the world has gone mad. What more natural way is there for him to epitomize this madness than to focus upon a demented view of the world, and especially of its women-folk? The artist's views on women are not known from how he has painted them, and one may even assume that he honors them by implication when he paints them with distortions in the context of a world vision in which there are other, equally obvious distortions. This explains, I think, the haunting whores of Grosz's series, painted during the postwar agonies of Germany, or the Willem de Kooning monster women painted following World War II. The artist seems to smash the stereotype with a sledgehammer, but also to assume that we will contrast these women with those that tradition has led us to expect, and that we will ask, "What kind of world is this one, anyway?" Had Grosz and de Kooning been homosexual, probably they would have painted the men they loved in the same way. What is revealed is not reification but distress, a very different matter.

Also, do the men necessarily fare any better in early twentieth-century art? Picasso's late cubist clowns or musicians, for all their decorative or even garish patterning, are not the sort of creatures whom one would like to encounter on a dark street at night; they look like thieves or con men, street people and drug addicts at the very least. Grosz's men are mostly suffering victims or callous and monocled generals and aristocrats. Are we to understand from this that Picasso is saying that clowns or musicians are decorative but nightmarish creatures, or that Grosz sees all men (or himself) as forever victims or exploiters? Rather, is there not a social message in the Grosz work, that this is how the world is, which you, as viewer, are to compare with your own vision of how things should be? The issue, of course, of whether political art is or is not possible is a separate one, but Grosz's vision, though negative, is presumably intended positively, reflected through the harsh lens of satire.

Finally, familiarity changes how a work appears to us.

Picasso's cubist women may have looked ugly because of their distortions when they were new to someone. But that same person, with time, may well come to value even the look of the same painting. It can reveal a subtler level of beauty than a more photographic vision would have. This is why it is dangerous to accuse Picasso or any other artist of bad intentions too quickly (or perhaps at all). We have a common way of describing this changing of appearance. We say, "This piece grew on me. I found it ugly at first, but then I saw it differently." Most of us have had that experience at one time or another.

A new wave of feminist activity began in the 1950s, roughly contemporaneously with what is known as post-modernist art including literature. Thus, in this literature and art a self-conscious pro-woman outlook is often implicit. But even in what Jencks calls "late modernist art"—art that is chronologically recent but that does not match his own criteria of what constitutes post-modern art—one finds the issues of feminism dealt with and its contributions recognized, in the works of Meret Oppenheim, Elaine de Kooning, Marisol, or Carollee Schneemann, to name four recent and distinguished women artists who cannot properly be called post-modernists.

Summing up the problem that is inherent in our mythographic question, however, the way the question is formulated confuses vision and literal appearance, as did the reporter who asked the great modernist writer Gertrude Stein, a feminist throughout her life, why she had added the third rose in her poem that goes, "A rose is a rose is a rose." Her answer? "I know people don't talk like that. But I think that in that poem a rose is really red in literature for the first time in two hundred years."

What we see when we see a painting (or what we read when we read a poem) is one thing. What we see in it is another. We project into it from our experience, and to mix the two processes is to miss the point.

iv. Myth Three: "The avant-garde is a myth today."

> C'est nous, artistes, qui vous servirons d'avant-garde: la puissance des arts est en effet la plus immédiate et la plus rapide. Nous avons des armes de tout espèce: quand nous voulons répondre des idées neuves parmi les hommes, nous les inscrivons dur la marbre ou sur la toile; nous les popularisons par la poésie et le chant; nous employons tour-à-tour la lyre ou la galoubet, l'ode ou la chanson, l'histoire ou le roman; la scène dramatique nous est ouverte.
> —Henri, Comte de Saint-Simon (1825)

> I am devoted to the idea of burying the avant-garde.
> —Rosalind Krauss, at a conference in Iowa (1981)

The idea that the avant-garde is over, non-existent, depends, like the other myths of Postmodernism, on the idea that there was only one avant-garde, presumably that of the late nineteenth century, which was supplanted by Modernism, or, in the political variant of this theme, that it led to the modernist revolution and, in due course, it died away, so that what is called today an "avant-garde" either is an imposture or has only the trapping of an avant-garde and is therefore not worthy of serious attention. Thus, Professor Krauss seems to be trying to freeze a moment of the past, and to wish to bury the avant-garde, as if it were a corpse. Naturally, the corpse objects. Professor Krauss seems annoyed by the "corpse's" protesting; thus, the characteristic shrill tone of her writings. But, returning to our discussion, let us take up these two versions of the myth one at a time.

The quotation from Saint-Simon is, according to an article in *American Historical Review* 73 #2 (1967:343), the first known usage of the term.[27] It appears in Saint-Simon's last essay published in his lifetime, in the collaborative *Opinions littéraires, philosophiques et industriellles* (1825:341-42), in a dialogue among an artist, a "savant" (perhaps we would say a "pundit"), and an industrialist. Clearly the image is of a military vanguard. But while Saint-Simon's use of the image with reference to the arts is precisely that to which we are accustomed, it is important to note here that Saint-Simon's date is roughly a half-century before the heyday of the Impressionists and their followers, which is the period to which the scholars of Postmodernism are usually referring when they allude to an avant-garde of the past. Saint-Simon is, therefore, referring to some other, unspecified avant-gardes, probably the Romantics. If so, then there are implied at least several avant-gardes, and the habit, which one finds in Krauss's work and which Doria and Polkinhorn reported to me from Harvard, of referring to the avant-garde of early twentieth-century Modernism as the only valid one, is parochial and excessively narrow. It is simply not what the term means to most people. Also, we should at least note that there are avant-gardes of medicine, of computer design or any other technology, as well as of business.

To pursue a different direction for a moment, let us grant that the characteristic spirit of the 1980s has been rather utilitarian, one which looks for function in all things, prizing quick results and immediate success and tending to take popularity as a major indicator of quality. It, therefore, tends to favor standardized popular art more than, let us say, the 1920s or the early 1960s did. Thus, it seems that there is no room at the moment for an avant-garde, that it, like highbrow taste for specialized matters in any area, is relatively repressed. Yet is that not, precisely and especially, exactly when the image of an avant-garde is most applicable? In the 1920s, with the acceptance of experimentalism in all areas of culture, what one was seeing was actually the waning of an avant-garde phase, as what the avant-garde had stood for became widely accepted. The arts of the 1920s had their avant-garde or heroic phase at the beginning of the century, with Fauvism, Cubism, Expressionism, Imagism, Vorticism, Futurism, Dadaism, and perhaps a few other "isms" as well. These simmered, under attack, then suddenly were discovered to be of more than passing interest when the 1920s found that they suited their *Zeitgeist*. In fact, the arts of the 1920s that did not have roots in the avant-garde of earlier decades (Neoclassicism, late Constructivism, Bauhaus, *Die Neue Sachlichkeit*, and *Gebrauchskunst*, this last becoming "Functionalism," or, in music, the Objectivism of Nadia Boulanger and her circle), are the avant-garde, in a sense, of the reaction against formal experimentation that later became predominant in the 1930s and 1940s, this last in turn generating its new avant-garde that, again, was experimental and flourished in more recent decades, into the 1960s, in which the experimental mood is but a climax of an earlier avant-garde of the 1940s and 1950s — Black Mountain, John Cage and the first generation of Cageans, and so on.

What was unique to the 1960s was Pop Art and their new, more self-referential version of Neoclassicism, what a recent exhibition at Bard College called "Neo-Neo-Classicism," which is what Charles Jencks, at least, seems to be equating with "Postmodernism" in his book *Post-modernism* (1987),
On the other hand, the more hidden, struggling avant-garde of today, appealing for the moment to those who are able to find it but not yet known to those who lack this skill (*de facto* elitist or "highbrow" if not, probably, highbrow or elitist by preference), this avant-garde is indeed with us, now as always, doing its innovative magic outside of our academies and, as yet, our recognized media. For example, a whole new wave of desk-top publishers has appeared to make new styles of poetry available, and these seem to be quite different from what we knew twenty years ago, or from what the "language" poets (an avant-garde of the 1970s[28]) did ten years ago — more intimate than these last, I think, often using visual effects interestingly. In music one finds any number of composers working with the various possibilities of comput-

ers, producing results on simple Macintoshes or PCs that, two decades ago, would have required mainframe computers and million-dollar synthesizers. Also, every large city has its art gallery today that bucks the received taste of the moment and that is more professional and systematic than the more underground "alternative" spaces of the 1970s. Thus, the conditions are ripe for the next surfacing of an avant-garde.

Before turning to our next myth, I would like to say a few words in connection with elitism and highbrow taste, because these are truly germane to the very idea of an avant-garde. There are two kinds of elitism. One is a belief that there is an elite or natural aristocracy of some kind that comprises the few who are truly capable of appreciating a serious cultural communication. This is not, of course, a democratic attitude, and those who believe in a democracy are properly uncomfortable with such an attitude, usually described as "snobbish." The other is the elitism that comes from the idea that this is an imperfect world, that our education and experience are wanting, and that in such a world it is simply not realistic to expect everybody to be able to discern, equally well, the more arcane points of cultural experience. There is a fortunate elite, such a person feels, who can do so, an elite that normally does not coincide with the worlds of privilege, social, fashionable, moneyed, or even educational (since education is assumed to be flawed), and this elite has the moral obligation to share its findings and experience, to share and to test them, as it were, on the world outside itself to see if they can make their way to ever larger numbers of people, or if they cannot to look for something else that can. This is the natural world of the trend-setters, of those who perform not by fashion but by consistently sharing their findings, the "research and development" function in cultural experience. The concept of an avant-garde is inherent in such a model. We might call this the "highbrow" elite, since it is a total meritocracy with quality the sole criterion in the long run,

gerous, and where small, informal galleries to show innovative work are all but unknown, except for Poland, it is a
relatively risk-free way for the artists to communicate, to
share ideas and keep their spirits up, to form new groups and
contacts towards that hoped-for day when they, too, can
surface to a larger public. It is small and hard to press; in a
regime that closes the mails to all but standard communications, the art will arrive by some alternate means. Even if one
destroys the artist, enough works have gone out into the
world to point towards what might serve as paradigms for
the next artist who comes along. If an artist works unofficially
in Romania or Bulgaria, for instance, to acquire the means to
actually execute a work of art—glue, inks, paints, canvas, or
fine paper—represents a major triumph of organization.
What the work says, by existing, is "He (or she) did it. Here
I am!" Thus, in the context of the East-bloc countries, mail art,
existing and circulating and providing a network among
unofficial artists, is far more important than it is here. It is
avant-garde: it points in the direction the artists propose to
move when the opportunity arises. Even if we take the idea
of revolution metaphorically, and refer to this or that technological or other non-political revolution, the basic principle
still holds that the artist, the avant- garde artist at least, has a
role to play in finding the uses of a particular technology.

In the 1960s, a concern with ecology spread across the
land. Some artists made Earth Art, which had its avant-garde
moment and which still continues. Artists have experimented
with computers in programs like the one at Bell Laboratories
in the 1960s, and all kinds of innovative work came out of that
situation that could not have been anticipated by the engi-
neers on the premises. It was at least technologically, if not
spiritually, avant-garde work. The model still exists: give an
artist access to a new technology, and new potentials will
appear that are innovative and, usually, in some sense avant-
garde. So it continues, in ways that a WFM can never understand if he draws only on the Marxist canon as interpreted by

his or her colleagues, as opposed to being implemented by a whole community of people, some of whom happen to be artists.

vi. Myth Five: "Criticism is the art form of the future."

> Il faut de la réligion pour la réligion, de la morale pour la morale, comme de l'art pour l'art.
> —Victor Cousin (1818)[30]

> But Professor de Man, what is the erotic of your theoretical literature? To whom does it offer pleasure? Why should a non-specialist read it?
> —Dick Higgins to Paul de Man at a theory lecture de Man gave at Bard College in 1983

Now let us offend everybody. Let's propose an oversimplification of the past twenty or so years in criticism; it is, however, a formulation that can be polished and adjusted to the reader's need.

In the thirty years leading up to the 1960s, criticism of the arts, at least in the United States, was almost all of the sort called "practical" or "pragmatic criticism," a term derived from the Latin *praxis*, meaning "practice," and not necessarily from "pragmatism," the philosophy associated with William James and others. The theory underlying this criticism, when it received attention at all, was often mistrusted by the communities of artists, critics, and the cultural public alike. The critics, with the exception of the New Critics, worked intuitively for the most part, and the critics assumed that their task was to explain what artists did, be they musicians. painters, or writers, usually with reference to the biography of the artist, to Marxist or religious theory, to Freudian or existentialist philosophical or psychological principles, and so on, either totally accepting or rejecting one or another of these reference points. The idea that the technicalities of a theory underlying all this might have intrinsic interest seemed alien or suspect. But in the arts of the 1950s and 1960s, there was enormous ferment. New forms and media were generated for which previous modes of criticism and previous evaluative categories and sets of dichotomies were inadequate. Pairs like classical-romantic, Dionysian-Apollonian, objective-subjective seemed to break down when applied to Abstract Expressionism and its offshoots, dodecaphonic and aleatoric music, happenings and Pop Art, chance, concrete and sound poetry, and the like. These appeared as if by spontaneous generation all around the world. Nobody could explain why, and, at the time, few even wanted to. Most academics chose to ignore them or to misrepresent them; the WFMs preferred to denounce them as well. The world of commercial art media (galleries, museums, publishers) could neither co-opt nor deal with the new forms, so they went along with the academics. Something had changed; Modernism had extended itself into a new direction.

In the 1960s a new focus on formalism began to be prominent, as in the writings of Meyer Schapiro in art, or in the formal-structural focus popularized by H. Marshall McLuhan. Even my own reintroduction of the "intermedia" concept was of this sort, since it defined new art forms by their relationship to already existing ones, ignoring subject matter. Also similar was the criticism that grew out of the linguistics of Noam Chomsky.

But none of these was enough. They did not offer a satisfactory balance of form and meaning. It was in this context that structuralism came into prominence. This was a linguistic approach based on the work of Roman Jakobson and Ferdinand de Saussure, a method of treating subject matter formally, by handling it technically as if it were grammar. Literature and visual art, at least, could be treated this way. To structuralism was added (and almost appropriated unto itself) a second focal point, semiotics, which had been with us at least since the seventeenth century (the earliest use of the term I know is in a scientific work by Ernst Friederich in the seventeenth century.[31] The resulting brew looked more scientific than humanistic, and as such it acquired some of the prestige of science, although how scientific it actually was or is is a moot point. As an approach it offered insight into strongly mimetic works in which style was not a primary consideration, into the seventeenth-century French classics, or into the realism of Dickens and his contemporaries; arguably its most spectacular achievement is Roland Barthes's *S/Z* (1974), an analysis of a short story by Balzac); the analysis is book-length, the story a short one. But, especially in its American form, structuralism was cumbersome; the scientific trappings it offered depended too much on the materials they revealed or colored by concealment. A new approach was needed, and it was found by avoiding the problem of offering insight into specific works of art, by working up a critico-theoretical approach that was based on the language of theory as such, called "post-structuralism" or "de-constructionism." So it came about that there was created an enormous gulf between the best innovative arts of the time and the critical context that surrounded them. The unspoken formula was that there was now a need for "criticism for its own sake," to parallel "art for its own sake," that much misunderstood formulation of Victor Cousin's which was very popular 150 years before (Cousin's formulation served as an antithesis to Benthamite Utilitarianism, Comtean Positivism, and German Idealism). When works of art came into the discussion at all, they were almost always from periods up to World War II, and the early part of the century was treated, as we have already observed, as the only valid modernism. The art of the 1910s-to-1930s avant-gardes was treated by misprision, by the selection of a few atypical masterpieces. These were presented as typical. René Magritte, an exceptional surrealist, became the subject of endless theoretical discussions. The highly exceptional career of Marcel Duchamp was treated as if it were the norm, because it did, in fact, offer interesting paradigms for the theories of the 1970s. Duchamp's urinal of 1917 and Andy Warhol's Campbell's soup cans, because they were the opposite of a Vasari, craft-oriented paradigm, were presented as the norm of Modernism, thus creating the illusion of an end of art, to which normative post-modernist works, with their bland look and their intellectualist complexity (I am thinking of Arakawa here), were supposed to function as a release from the presumed dilemma. Such art, of course, was subservient to theory, and the real game in town was supposed to be — you guessed it — Criticism.[32] Yet, unlike the situation in scientific theory, no consensus was possible. Critics were professionally committed to disagreeing on what Postmodernism was or why.

This brings us to the present, to 1989. The supporters of Postmodernism can now offer a closed system with a language that is self-referential (it leads to itself). They can offer a historical view, "art is dead" (or is it "art history is dead"?) supported by misprision and incompleteness, one that runs parallel to the current academic philosophers' chant that "philosophy is dead," to the historians' arguments that "history is dead," and perhaps for those who must teach these things they are dead indeed: at least it is professionally catchy to say that they are. However, for those who live them and experience them, they are not dead at all. But be this as it may, in this context post-modern art critics can denounce those artists who do not fit into their Procrustean bed as "late" modernists (suggesting some kind of decadence or, as Gilbert Murray characterized the decline of Greek religion in late antiquity, a "failure of nerve"), and they can attack their own colleagues who do not toe the official theoretically oriented line as supporters of a "new pragmatism" (which, not being clear on their Latin, they usually confuse with philosophical pragmatism à la James). To support their theories, should they wish to provide examples from outside the magic circle of their language and theory, they can defend a whole body of art, good or bad alike, as "postmodern" and thus presumably somehow more relevant than more demanding art. This is comfortable for the vested powers in the culture industry, so the world of fashion goes along with it.

But it is boring and, in the long run, unsatisfying. More than the usual reason, economic anxiety, it is why so many young people who, in the 1950s and 1960s would have involved themselves in the ads, turned away from them in the 1970s and 1980s, producing the much-maligned "yuppie" culture. The yuppies are the heirs to the patrons of nineteenth century salon ad; they like their ad to be pretty, with just enough suggestion of newness to titillate them (and no more), and they also like theories that justify this. But art comes from material, including intellectual material that has nothing to do with theory: it balances red and the look of a plant, including what we know about plants; it structures the squeak of chalk on a blackboard with the sound of a violin in a matrix that suggests something about the reality around us. The sense of a poem interacts with its words to provide an overall effect that is synergistic, greater than its parts. It relates what we know with what others have known in different cultures and times and places and situations, expanding our horizons, giving us threshold experiences and glimpses into other worlds, preparing us to deal with our own world in new ways.

Can theory as such offer this? If not, can it still be art?

That is the reason I asked my question, given at the start of this section, of Paul de Man, one of those who introduced structuralism into the United States and who was identified with the post-modern aesthetic. He seemed troubled by my question, which had evidently not been asked of him before, and replied that he asked of theory only that it be true. "True with reference to what?" I asked, and de Man was silent, perhaps realizing that the same answer might have been given by a religious fanatic who was asked about why anyone should read his or her sacred text. Later de Man was honest enough to remark that he was still thinking about my question. But not long after that he died.

However, I wonder if my question could be answered by anyone. Let us suppose that criticism can imply an erotic of "the exquisite working of the mind in collaboration with the senses," as an editor, Joan Burns, phrased it in a letter to me. Is it not, then, only secondarily criticism, but primarily art? This new question suggests the long-term resolution of the art/criticism dichotomy. But it is with the short-term assumption that we must deal first here, that because criticism can be aesthetically satisfying it can in and of itself replace art in the central position. But is criticism the most efficient way of combining mind and senses? Is not art more appropriate a means to do this? If so, and if there is a difference between joining art and replacing it, then the assumption remains problematic.

vii. Some observations

> Human history is riddled with mistakes or "wrong turnings." ... [But] when innovation seems deadest and humanity most settled in its ways, that signals the moment of the avant-garde's joyful, giddy return ...
>
> —Charles Doria in an unpublished paper (1987)

> There are as many "modern periods" as there are human epochs.
>
> —Octavio Paz, *Children of the Mire* (1974)

Not all myths are false, of course. An important part of our culture deals with our myths as archetypes or even prototypes, as links between our experience of what we see and what we believe or feel. Some new approach to myth has even been central to the arts in our time, and myth is central,

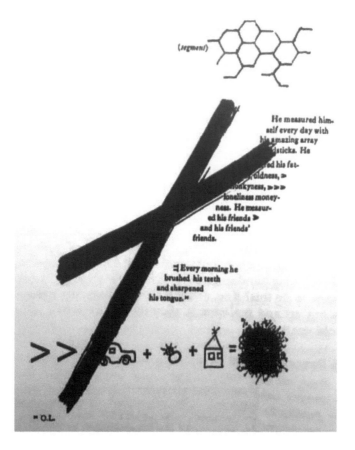

Figure 3. Ruth Laxson, from *Measure-Cut-Stitch*. Atlanta, GA: Press 63+, 1987. Laxson's artist's book synthesizes verbal narrative, visual image, and even, at times, melody, in order to achieve a poignant whole. In no way does this work resemble Futurism, Dada, Surrealism, Abstract Expressionism, Concrete Poetry, Fluxus, or any other recognizable avant-garde of the past, nor does it fit the criteria of Postmodernism or even "late Modernism." What is it, then? It is unmistakably an avant-garde work, replete with possibilities for future works to use and develop in other directions. Instinctively, one recognizes that this is so even if one cannot verbalize why.

for example, to Ihab Hassan's particular version of Post-modernism, as laid down in *Paracriticisms* (1975). But the myths I have dealt with here are the fictions and hypotheses that appear to be inherent in post-modernist approaches taken as a group, though they may not be found in all works associated with those approaches. The function that, in practice, they serve within non-native Post-modernism is to allow the person who believes in them to proceed as if the world of innovation had ended and, while lip service continues to be paid to the new, mostly it is treated as if it were an advertising slogan, and handled with suspicion. The normative post-modernist, as we can call him or her, warns that innovative arts, especially of the "modernist" (that is, early twentieth-century) variety, suggest utopianism, and that this might be dangerous. In a lecture at Williams College in Autumn 1987, Rosalind Krauss told a story of some architecture students at the Massachusetts Institute of Technology in 1968 who were frustrated by the contrast between the ideal conditions for which the "modern" architecture they were taught seemed directed and the actual world of building codes, cost calculations, and so on. So as a sort of protest against the implied utopianism of these conditions, the students filled the hall where their projects were supposed to be shown with detritus and odd materials, old tires, sheets of plasterboard, parts of posters, creating a sort of mad eclectic assemblage. Krauss seemed to suggest that these students were somehow being post-modernist in their approach and that her heart was with them. But wouldn't the students have done better to give some attention to changing the conditions in which their architecture was to exist? The allegedly utopian earlier architects did.

Ironically, if one takes Heinrich Klotz's *Post-modern Visions: Drawings, Paintings and Models by Contemporary Architects* (1985) to speak for the field, architecture is the one art in which the non-native post-modernist descriptions of Post-modernism seem fairly accurate. Perhaps that is because it is only partly a fine art. The rest of architecture, like the decorative arts, belongs to other areas. Revealingly, the original title of Klotz's work was *Die Revision der Moderne: Post-moderne Architektur*, thus implying a modification rather than a more radical opposition as is usual in American discussions, and which avoids the formal conservatism associated with normative post-modern positions. But attempts to apply the same criteria of post-modern architecture (wouldn't "revised modern" be a better term?) to fine art have been a disaster, even for Charles Jencks, whose *Language of Post-Modern Architecture* (1977) is something of a landmark. His new *Postmodernism: The New Classicism in Art and Architecture* (1987) simply proposes a return to 1920s Neoclassicism; his distinctions between the old and new classicisms are utterly unconvincing. What the normative postmodernists have done is to make a position suited to the characteristic spirit of the 1980s, which is the most exclusively conservative or even reactionary decade of the twentieth century. But as I argued in my fourth section, above, what shows is the result of a trend that began some time ago, and, in fact, the counter-trend is present, though still hidden, while the avant-garde continues its work under the surface, following not fashion but function and need.

This is the significance of the quotation from Doria, cited from his unpublished essay "Permanent Change: The Meanings of the Avant-Garde," which he wrote for the Harvard seminar discussed in section three. All the myths attributed here to normative Postmodernism were to be found there, with the resulting discussions being so deadly all through the summer one would receive reports in letters on what an awful seminar it was, lacking anything like a dissenting opinion. What does one do? The artist can simply shrug, ignore the voices of media and fashion, and tighten his or her belt yet again. But a serious person who wants a full and contemporary life, a sensitive critic or observer, or a lay person who wants to know well the only art that he or she can ever know at first hand, the art of one's own times, such a person deserves a more suitable mix of values and materials than the normative post-modernist can offer. The mix is, as already noted, based on the interaction between form and content, which is never a closed system. Since there is always such a dialectic taking place, the process goes on even when it seems not to. The art works thus engaged in that process are the modern ones of their time (hence the quotation from Octavio Paz), and this too is true even when it seems not to be. For example, the sixth century was not a hospitable one for the arts in the Merovingian Frankish kingdom. The national economy had all but collapsed, literacy had declined terribly, and there was little leisure for cultural pursuits. But that was the very time when Venantius Fortunatus developed the *carmen cancellatum*, when Gregory of Tours developed the art of the Medieval chronicle, and when Merovingian book illustration showed the way to the master-works of the following centuries. We can see these as important innovations now, but it must have been far less obvious at the time.

So what is one to do? First of all, one should refuse to play the word games that are locked into much of postmodern criticism, particularly deconstructionism. To participate is to become involved in a closed and sterile system.

Secondly, one should mistrust, even more than in the past, the art works which are praised by the culture industry; they are selected because they fit into a world picture that is at least problematic and probably largely false. If they are excellent, it is probably not because of reasons usually offered in their defense (for example, the works of Marcel Duchamp).

Thirdly, to find out about things, one should focus on factual material as much as possible, saving the theory that goes with it for later, perhaps for some time in the late 1990s.

Fourthly, one should especially mistrust the critic who plays word games to the extent to which he or she does so. Even if we accept that there is a good deal of validity in a good deal of the insights offered by the normative postmodernists, it is the insights we need, not their names. A new set of criteria (or a modified old one) is what is called for. Renaming "post-modern" something else would not make for a new mix. One sees the names "neo-modern," "neo-avant-garde," "late modern" tossed around as alternatives, but these solve nothing. My own conclusion is that it is simply too soon to make up new names for the most current work, that it should be called, simply, "modern," while what was, until now, called "modern," that is, the arts of roughly the first half of the twentieth century, now needs a new label. This was the case 150 years ago, when the arts of the early nineteenth century, previously called "modern," came to be described instead as "Romanticism." What might such a term be? "Stylism?" "Visionism?" "Self-cognitivism?" That would depend upon where one wished to focus attention, and it would depend on having some consensus. The best that one can do for now is to point to the need for attention to the problem, so that a consensus can be formed in due course. That, however, although it is related, is also a different matter from the one at hand, and it will require the efforts of many many people.

Figure 4. Dick Higgins. *Agrippa and the Decline of Oxford* (1988). Acrylic on canvas. Courtesy Emily Harvey Gallery, New York. The head at the right is a portrait of Marcus Vipsanius Agrippa (63-12 B.C.E.), Augustus Caesar's chief collaborator. The map of the Roman Empire is based on one made at Oxford in 1883, allegedly showing the Roman Empire in Agrippa's time, but actually it includes three important errors and is more accurate for the reign of Trajan over a century later. The whole painting is an assemblage of paradoxes used for lyrical effect.

III. Mediocracy

A FAIRLY OPTIMISTIC ARTICLE by myself appeared in 1970 that later became a pamphlet from a small press, "Towards the 1970s." A good deal of what it said would happen did, in fact, occur. Dance achieved a new centrality, there was less formal and more content innovation in poetry, visual and sound poetry became normative, performance art was established, and music continued to progress towards the ancient Boethian concept of *musica speculativa*, which had been more or less ignored as a possibility in Western music since, say, Cerone's *El Melopeo y Maestro* of 1613. The 1970s may have been a mess politically, but they were not too bad for the arts. Masterpieces were made, but that is another story.

Now we are faced with a very different situation and a frankly decadent decade, one in which the very taste for excellence seems to have disappeared. Since that taste is what allows the surfacing of innovation in art, innovation has become hidden, as if marked by some cosmic rubber stamp "FOR SPECIALISTS ONLY." We are living in a mediocracy— rule both by the media and by and for the mediocre, to the benefit of the pseudo-cultured and to the detriment of the common people who are, ultimately, the rest of us. This is not just a conservative period: political conservatism may or may not be accompanied by cultural retrogression, just as political liberalism is no guarantee of artistic innovation or progress. Our educational deterioration, so much in the newspapers, can only partly be explained on economic grounds. Our liberal arts courses are taught by certified and professionalistic hacks, and they have only themselves to blame that the young, who usually are inclined to take chances, won't take a chance on their curricula. This causes the young audience to decline, and the older sophisticated audience cannot regenerate itself. The infrastructure of our arts has, thus, begun to deteriorate to an alarming degree. But before we can look at this, we must look at the media aspect of the situation.

Many things can, of course, be covered by the term "media, from oil or acrylic paint to "poetry" or "music" or "intermedia" to the mass media. But when the emphasis on mass media became so overwhelming during the 1970s, a certain deterioration of the will to do the best work possible took place, since such things are inherently out of bounds for media whose job is not to present the best work available, but to sell soap or other "product." You sell more soap when you reach more people, and art that imitated, while pretending to exploit, the exploiting media, actually was exploited by it, in a sort of perversion of McLuhan's dictum that the medium is the message. The prestige of the media was such that at least *resembling* the media was a way to appear modern; thus, the prestige of video art. Video art had existed in a positive way in the 1960s, and people such as Stanley Vanderbeek or Nam June Paik in the USA or Michael Morris in Canada (now in Berlin, Germany) did exciting work, but in the seventies this art medium lost its soul (at least for now), and now it is, par excellence, the domain of the grant-guzzling mediocrat. Just now there seems to be a direct proportion between intelligence and the degree to which a person ignores television of *any* kind, art or otherwise. We need activism, and TV is passive.

I cannot speak to the rise of women in art, which seems to be a result of the women's movement; most women's art appears to be for women, and that is something I am not. But I can observe that most—not some but *most*—of the best new thinking in the arts just now is being done by women. Perhaps one can also point to an unusually large number of fine male and female artists who are openly homosexual in their subject matter, presumably a result of the gay liberation movements. That seems healthy, since it was missing or repressed for so long. As for black, Latino, Asian, and Native American liberation movements, their priority is not, at the moment, in the arts; it may be that at some point this will be part of their need, and they will help lead us out of the mediocracy. We shall certainly welcome them then. We need their fresh perspectives, too.

In the past and even into the 1960s not only was there more private patronage for the arts than today, both individual and from foundations, but also commercial outlets — book publishers and stores, art galleries and theater producers, and so on — could take chances which have become impossible in 1983. Twenty years ago you could go to places like the Castelli Gallery and see the superstars of the day. In 1983 you go to the Castelli Gallery or to the Mary Boone, one of its latest clones, and all you see in "product," plain and simple. You might as well stay home. Literature is in an even worse situation. Our large publishers are parts of conglomerates that look to the bottom line before all else, so the editors are understandably afraid of taking chances. It is many years since a serious book got a major award. Guggenheim grants used to come to independent artists almost as a matter of course. In 1981 and 1982 about 95% went to academics; perhaps only an academic could afford the secretarial time needed to fill in the forms, but, more likely, the judges and the panels assume that there is no life outside academia. That does not bode well for our arts, since much if not most of the most valuable art works have always been done in inaccessible places, outside of the academies and official art centers. If not exactly underground, it has usually seemed *outside*, somehow, until at last by persistence and sheer accretion of interest, they are suddenly seen to be mainstream.

As for public funding, today in a sense it is not insignificant. But, in scholarship and broader culture, our National Endowment for the Humanities (NEH) grants seem more designed to keep the mediocrats in power in Washington and in our universities than to fund cultural research which really *needs* doing. Doubt me? Get the NEH pamphlet, "Research Materials Program," that contains the grant application forms and look them over critically. One must make a *social* justification for all grants (even art history grants that benefit the public in the long run, but seldom in the short), must provide twenty sets of Xeroxed applications and substantiating materials, must work up budgets more suited to team projects than individual ones, locate panels of experts on whom the NEH can call to verify the respectability of one's project (at least there's some little justification for that one), and then one must *normally*, it says, find matching funds. The result is to send all the scholars scurrying to the same few sources of matching funds, taking time away from their research and delaying it. Abolish the program? Of course not. Expand it, reform it, and make it more professional and less professionalistic. National Endowment for the Arts (NEA) grants are better, but not by much. There, too, the tendency is to overstress accounting and to create teams where individuals might do the work better. All of this creates the necessity for someone we need but should not: the professional fund-raiser, who gets a commission out of the grant and who speaks the language of the mediocrats. Somebody has to pay the fund-raiser, and in the long run it is the public, by way of inflated budgets, wasteful overheads, and, worst of all, worthwhile projects that are not done. The best artist or scholar is seldom the best fund-raiser.

Where are conditions any better? Try Canada. There the population is just over one-tenth of the USA's, yet Canada has about the same number of first-rate writers as America, not per capita but overall. Is there something magical about the Canadian soil? That's doubtful, much as Canadian writers like to praise "the Canadian experience." The Canada Council, however, has been run well by peer review for the past twenty years or so, their literature program has been particularly well managed, and now the Canadian people are benefiting from it. Their music scene is also, in proportion, better than ours, and, though their visual arts have problems (mostly an inadequate private sector), it is not too bad. The system is an elite one but is benign and responsible to the people in the long run. It works. We could learn from it if were we not so narcissistic. The fact is, art doesn't just arise; it develops where it is wanted.

Of course a great deal of magnificent work is still being done by Americans, but it is seldom seen in America. At no time since the 1920s have so many American artists been living in Europe. No longer is it because Europe is cheaper or more "cultured" as a whole. Today it is because one sees more professionalism there than here among the people who run the cultural organizations, thus creating the matrix for important things to happen for a large public. Our professionals are more "professionalistic" than serious; they have degrees but neither knowledge nor understanding. Great museum shows can happen in Europe that include recent arts but that could never happen here, for instance, the "Für Augen und Ohren" show in Berlin, on the interfaces between visual arts and music over the centuries and up to the present. There was competence at every stage. No way could that happen in America, not even in New York. Our arts personnel have degrees but not expertise; they simply would not know how to put together such a large-scale conceptual undertaking. Mediocrats cannot handle such things. In Europe the museum directors have faces and personalities, while ours are merely spokespersons for boards and panels. When nobody rules, nothing worthwhile gets done. Even the art collectors in Europe have more genuine taste and information, so, if you want to see the best of American art from the 1960s till now, you must go to Berlin, Aachen, Cologne, Darmstadt, or Vienna. Our museums get only the second best. Who loses out? The American people, of course. It is, after all, our art, our culture. But while the Europeans know us and, above all, our language, which gives them access to those of our works and ideas they find valuable, rather few of us make regular use of even one of the European languages, which means that we are usually cut off from those of their works or ideas that *we* need.

Even if we did know a European language, usually we have very little theoretical grounding in our arts training. In

Germany, art history is a *required* subject in all academic high schools. The long-term result? The German art scene is currently the best in Europe. Think about that. In American high schools our students are given, at best, a few hours a week to splash some paint around. On the higher levels our art schools teach art as craft, like basket weaving, not as a mesh between craft and culture, and we Americans usually make perfect idiots of ourselves (with some exceptions) when we discuss these things. Ever seen an American artist (or even, usually, an American critic) on a panel with European colleagues? It's usually pathetic. The American chatters about what Bill and John and Joan are doing, while the Europeans discuss cogent ideas cogently. Not that the opposite would not be an equal danger, namely, too much theory, too little practice. That happens, but it's rare. More usually the American retreats into our current favorite myth: the Myth of American Originality. It goes, "Only Americans can do original work, because Europeans are too weighted down by tradition." What makes it seemingly tenable is that Americans only see some token amount of first-rate European innovative art, Beuys, for example, among the Germans, while Vostell or Diter Rot, who have had major museum shows in most European countries, have yet to have major American museum shows. Not that we need be Europe-crazy; our best artists are as valuable as those from Europe, our art scene is by no means the worst in the world, and our best artists usually have access to the necessary ideas from Europe or *both* Americas. But our public and *most* of our artists have become distressingly provincial since the great days of the 1950s.

The result of all this is, of course, a terrible move away from excellence, among our artists, writers, and public, not to mention even our composers. I could go on in this vein for some time, pointing to the inadequacies of our poets and readers, to our theater which has dwindled away to insignificance from the fervent years of the 1960s, to our dancers who know their bodies well but not the dance. In music the situation seems to be slightly better, but not much. But I would rather use what space I have left, after this bleak picture, to say what I think needs to be done.

First of all, we have to scrap the mediocrats' approach. We have to reward excellence without going to a superstar mentality, and we have to take care that at all times all the possibilities are covered. We must use, not just learn, languages beside English. We must start with a healthy degree of skepticism, questioning our myths and the status of the beneficiaries of the mediocracy in these 1980s. We must recognize that elites have their uses, in producing real expertise and professional innovation. We must scrap our dependence on panels and boards where a succession of individuals can function better (let someone pick something that he or she *really* wants to fund, not just something that nobody has too strong an objection to); the role of panels should be to evaluate the performance of directors in the long run, not to assume the directorial role. Being democratic at every stage of the process robs people of the excellence they deserve, and that is *not* democratic. Particularly we must be skeptical, in education as well as the arts, of those whom the mediocrats have rewarded with academic degrees that only perpetuate the mediocrats' control. We should depend *much* more on the obviously gifted amateur: great artists, critics, and scholars are usually of this kind. A college should be ashamed, not pleased, if more than a certain percentage of its teaching personnel have Ph.D.s, not only in the arts, and for an arts organization to list the Ph.D.s of its staff is a guarantee that it cannot be relied upon for professional perspective. "Back to basics," the current educational reform slogan, really means "back to what the mediocrats say is basic" and is a move towards even greater mediocrity. Basics should be what actually is basic to our cultural and art needs, which is a knowledge that no Ph.D. can guarantee. All that a Ph.D. means is that someone has successfully dealt with the mediocracy through some years of graduate school, which may qualify such a person for being a fund-raiser, but it means just that many years of insulation from the actual art or intellectual community outside of academia.

We must cultivate a taste for excellence wherever it is encountered. We should avoid art works that are merely *au courant*, knowing from bitter experience that art works shown at such galleries as I have mentioned as examples, or touted in the mediocrats' (advertisers') art magazines are probably going to bore us to the point of tears, that books praised by the *New York Times Book Review* are likely to be published by the big corporations and to be rather silly in the long run. We should cultivate our tastes and perspectives, make these worthy of our dependence on them, and throw out most of the cultural bric-a-brac we have accumulated—dull books, hollow art, respectable but unplayable phonograph records and cassettes—and allow ourselves more depth. We should look for small, interesting-sounding concerts or performances and avoid those which some critic liked but one knows one won't, look among small and often local art galleries for those that buck the institutional taste, and support the organizations that sponsor such things. Often we will pay more, but we will get more satisfaction.[33] We need not go to the extreme "underground" unless we want to; there are excellent things for all of us, if we will but search them out. Better to be an honest, self-determined highbrow than a bored, pretentious middlebrow. "Classic" need not be a put-down term as it so often is just now. We are the ones who decide anew, for every generation, what is and what is not a "classic." We do this every few years except when the academics and, now, the mediocrats are in control. Those are always the dullest of times, in any case. In our education we do not need what Thomas Carlyle called the "dry-as-dust" experts; we need ourselves, communicating directly with past and present, bearing in mind that the present is the only time we will ever know at first hand, so the present arts are our living heritage, for better or for worse. It gives a certain thrill to recognize one's own voice in a present art work that only the greatest voices of the past can match, so we must inform ourselves enough to recognize that voice.

But as for the arts of these 1980s, they are, frankly, an expression of the current mediocracy and inferior to the arts of the 1950s, 1960s and 1970s. So who cares where they are going? Their only interest is not intrinsic but projected historical; we can look for the germ of a better 1990s in them, for the potential for new ways and forms of seeing and hearing and thinking of things. Great changes are needed now, as always; and great works will hopefully happen in due course. But we must now create the enabling structures. We must not simply accept what art we have (it's no worse than what we deserve, if we do) but must earn the arts which we want.

IV. A Book

A BOOK. Consider a book.

Before one can consider a book, one must consider what it is to have a text. A text is an array of words on paper, or, if not words, other things that are to be read. One can have a text with no words at all—music or visual entities or symbols.

But when we are talking about art-an art book, the art of language and not just information to be used for something other than the experience of being oneself-one must have a self or selves. One need not dwell upon it. But we are all complexes of past experiences and knowledge, each unique unto itself. One need not ask oneself, at the outset, "What is this self? Who is this me that I am being?" One needs no particular ego to experience art. But one does bring a certain horizon to the experience of a book that is its own past and complex of tastes and non-tastes, desires and non-desires, beings and non-beings. When a ship moves towards a horizon, that horizon always recedes, no matter in what direction one moves. The complex of what one knows and what one does not know and what one knows without consciously considering it, that horizon is always in motion. The text that is a work of art brings its horizon to us. The horizons intersect and interpenetrate.

Authors make texts when they offer us arrays of words that generate horizons that interpenetrate with ours, when they displace ours in the course of this interpenetration. The author is supremely unimportant while we are studying a text. If we want to know about apples, if we want to study why apples are as they are, *then* we must study about apple trees. But when we are hungry, we do not study about apples. We eat them. So it is with texts and authors. When we are hungry to experience our horizons in motion, the author is beside the point; here it is the text the author has made that is important. For us it is our experience of the text that we are living with, not the text the author thought he made. When

Samuel Richardson wrote *Clarissa* he thought that he was making a series of morally exemplary letters—prudish, perhaps. Instead, he created what we experience as one of the most erotic novels in our language, erotic in its curious horizon of dwelling forever upon the sexual innuendo. Lately most criticism has dwelt upon the linguistics of the text, upon the structure and *langue* and *parole* and semiotics of the work. But judged as experience, that is relatively unimportant, since it is the effect of the style that is so crucial, the phenomenon of the generation of the horizons of Clarissa and her circle and how they fit and do not fit with ours. Same with Gertrude Stein, whose focus is upon the language *of* her horizon and ours: it is displacement. A structuralist and a semiotician would go mad trying to explain why Stein works when "it" (her work) works. For us, enjoying the displacements of our horizons of language by hers, there is no problem. We each have our own horizons, our own hermeneutic for this (our own methodology of interpretation). I can document mine, and each human being who reads Stein can learn to document hers or his. But the gut feelings that the work generates, the emotional and connotative and phatic elements, these do not come solely from what she says but from the process of matching how she says it with our own horizons.

A text can be spread over space without becoming a book. We can write it on a scroll and experience it as never-ending, unbroken. Most texts seem to have been written for experience upon scrolls—perhaps their authors think of life as scrolls. In point of fact, of course, scrolls have their own interesting qualities, their physicality and their unique continuity.

But a book, in its purest form, is a phenomenon of space and time and dimensionality that is unique unto itself. Every time we turn the page, the previous page passes into our past and we are confronted by a new world. In my *Of Celebration of Morning*, my book *qua* book that uses these ideas most purely, I even called each page "world 1," "world 2," and so on, through the eighty pages. The only time a text exists in a solid block of time is when we are no longer reading it, unlike, for example, a single painting that is all present before us when we consider its presence physically. In this way a book is like music, only experienced moment by moment until it, too, is past and remembered as a whole. But the space of the book, even when it is not self-consciously shaped and patterned (as in visual novels or concrete poetry or comic books), is part of the experience. *Alice in Wonderland* written out by hand is a different work from *Alice in Wonderland* set in type; set in Baskerville, even, it is a different entity from what it would become set in some barely-legible but beautiful "Old English" blackletter face. It is, as it were, translated when it is changed from one face to another, just as surely as if it had been paraphrased into another language. All literature exists only in translation for this reason—it is displaced from the author's intention, displaced visually by being presented to us upon the page, displaced by us conceptually every time we experience it by reading it, displaced according to our horizons at the moment. One time we read a text with passion, one time coolly, one time in a desultory way, one time with great attention to the characters and gestalts generated by the text, another time with our eye on the horizons of our language and the text.

The book is, then, the container of a provocation. We open it and are provoked to match our horizons with those implied by the text. We need not consider ourselves to do this, but the more vivid our horizons and the more vivid the gestalts and horizons in the text, the more vivid the displacements and coincidences of these horizons. Therein lies the true pleasure of the text, the true erotic of literature. Criticism that ignores this does so at its peril. It may be fashionable for a moment, but it will die. Great criticism always keeps its eye on the horizons of work at hand and so, like Coleridge's lectures on Shakespeare, always exists upon three horizons of time—its subject's, the critic's, and ours. Perhaps that is the crucial difference between criticism and poetry. The former, for example, has three horizons, the latter has two to offer. Not that "the more the merrier," of course. Two horizons can be plenty.

But the book that is clear about what horizons it can offer up for our experience (whatever nonsense its author may have intended it to be) is well on its way to matching its horizons with ours and is, thus, on the track of potential greatness.

There is no need to bother with the rest.

V. The Naive and Its Function in Meaning

MY NEIGHBOR KNEELS when he tends his cows. I have photographed him doing so. If I show my photograph to most observers, they will think he is worshipping them, but not so. To the great frustration of his wife, who must wash his dirty work pants, it is a habit he picked up long ago, and he's reached an age when he is unlikely to change. Alas, if I tell my friends the truth, the photo becomes far less interesting. It loses its emotional impact.

So it is with the critics. They argue the meaning in art of this or that but never ask themselves, why should an art mean anything? Can art mean anything? Or the negative, which in this case is an antinomy: can art mean nothing?

This leads to the usual ambiguity of attitude: if I like a work, it is meaningful; if I do not, it is meaningless (or vice versa.) Yet, if I dislike it, isn't that also a form of meaning? Thus, the critic fails to distinguish between the meaningful character of a work, a potential object-language, and the meta-language of his own attribution. Put differently, the meaning he sees in a work, whether intellectual or emotional, lies in his own head: the work itself may or may not have any meaning.

But nobody ever loved a poem because of its meaning alone, because what it said was right. An essay, perhaps (especially if one agreed with it). But a poem—its impact comes from its ability to provoke meaning, not from any intrinsic meaning it may have. To understand a work is, therefore, to misunderstand it, to receive the provocation that it offers, and to attribute that provocation (a response) to something inherent in the work.

The poem is—and the same holds true of music, I think— a test, therefore, and a provocation. The most naive listener says: I do not understand it. What he does not understand, in fact, are the ways he might react to it.

The next-to-most-naive listener is the ideal one. He is

most deeply provoked but does not have the coolness of connoisseurship to inhibit his natural responses.

The less naive listener, the connoisseur, is jaded in his response because he only allows his response to a token level, enough to determine for him the character of the work. After that his cognitive opinion is allowed to take over. The work is transformed into his opinion of it, by a sort of mental and emotional clinamen.

The least naive listener, the absolute expert, the professional, even his response must be subsumed and schematized according to his image of himself as critic and professional, according to the system of roles and functions he has built up (usually for teaching or for journalistic purposes). He is dead to the work. It is merely a name, a conventionalized sign.

Wittgenstein, in the *Blue Book*, for instance, is among those who have pointed out how we think in signs, and so we do. But the response is far from being automatic as the response of a typesetting machine to the correct number of holes in its controlling tape. The semiosis of morphemes and transforms in the literary arts is in a constant dialectic with the life and communications of the listener (or reader, or viewer; heard poetry is merely my paradigm: I am speaking of all the arts).

But far from a cumulative sophistication being built up by an enormous quantitative exposure to an art, exhaustion sets in. The professional cannot afford to admit exhaustion, so he or she carries on in some purely analytical way, according to a cognitive scheme he or she has devised. Were the listener to act less cognitively, he would be free to become refreshed by adding to his experience some work that was unfamiliar or that was incapable of being or becoming familiar (or as nearly so as possible). Work of this last sort is rare. Yet it was to attack the progressive ossification via connoisseurship that, for instance, testing structures and chance operations were applied to poetry by Jackson Mac Low and myself, among others. The dancerly dance is always deadly, but the dance of life is not. There must always be something, in a work, that is incapable of being known and about which the listener remains naive in order for the work to provoke a strong positive or negative response. The non-response, the safe one, involves less of our selves, but it is at our very great peril that we hide there. That way lies depersonalization and professional hebephrenia. The cognitive approach, therefore, with its characteristic self-imaging and "professional cool," is a dead end.

Art is possibly, then, an experience, but it is modified by its recognition as art, and this act of recognition (which replaces the concept of the creative act in older systems) is precisely where the artist (who would otherwise develop all the negative characteristics of the cognitive professional, and the worst artists usually do) places his own emphasis. If what he or she did became too familiar, a cognitive effect would take place. Thus, to avoid it, the artist must always work with something about which he or she is naive. The poet, therefore, cannot repeat himself; the composer cannot keep on grinding it out in the style that made him or her famous — even if he wanted to — without simultaneously committing an act of destruction of his or her most vital self. Finally, the artist can only accept his or her own identity in a similar state of motion, in an ongoing process of movement into the unknown, for if he or she did not stress this, his or her own cognitive image would take over and the joy in work would die.

The strangeness of the familiar — about that there are never any experts. Yet it is there that the most powerful aesthetic provocations and simulations lie. Too strange? The work would be decorative. Too familiar? The process would become cognitive. To work with the concrete, then, including the specific and precise abstraction that is really part of the concrete, requires that the artist remain naive about these. Far from the artist teaching, in his work, the way an expert teaches a subject, the artist shares those things that strike him in his naiveté. The subject of the work teaches the artist, and he merely shares the experience.

Since such a system requires that the artist continually explore, it also follows that the artist, working in *terra incognita* on his map, must always deal with what is to him or her an avant-garde. A prisoner's first sonnet is an experiment, but his twentieth is not. To maintain his involvement he must, therefore, move to other forms, as all artists must. For the listener, the first experience of the work is apt to be the most profound; any further experience of it, to match the initial experience, must have some equal revelation of some area in which the listener was previously naive (for example, a conductor's unorthodox but successful reading of a symphony). Provocation, to succeed, requires naiveté.

VI. A [very short] Autobiography of Originality

IT IS HARD TO SAY where I came from. Certainly my parenthood is uncertain, and I've always thought of myself as something of a mongrel. I have always belonged to many worlds, and the world we live in now is always suspicious of such divided loyalties. I seem to pass in and out of fashion the way a weaver's shuttle moves across the loom, always moving from in to out, from warp to woof. In any case, it seems to me that my history does not begin with conception but with perception, whatever the reaction to me may be. I suppose I had a childhood, but it is part of my suspended consciousness, to be recalled as needed, but seldom needed. At some point I was noticed. That's that.

In the course of a long lifetime, whose documented early career begins with one or another of the "Pre-Socratics," whoever they may be, I have met up with some interesting characters—in fact, that has been the most exciting part of my lifetime—and I would like to tell you about a few of them and how they have perceived me.

Plato was an odd duck, I recall. He seemed to prize me in his practice, at least, so long as I was official, authorized by the councils of his faculty. His *Republic* seems more like a model for a university than a place for people to live their lives and careers. He was, however, terribly jealous of me. He banned the artists from his republic mostly for their dallying with me; they might upset his system of government, or even seize the university president's office. A jealous lover is always hard to take, and that's what this guy Plato was to me.

Then there's Aristotle. I loved him, but he ignored me. He does not even mention me in his *Poetics*. Imagine! Well, there was nothing improper in our relationship, I assure you. I am feminine in most languages, especially in Europe. But, of course, "Hell hath no fury like a woman scorned," and I had my revenge—on his children. Those who take the Aristotelian line—from Aquinas to T.S. Eliot—are doomed, finally, to be deadly: I don't go with them. His values repeat themselves endlessly and become mere stock in trade. They tend to be neo-this and neo-that, neo-classic or neo-romantic, but when they claim their family in Aristotle's lineage, they become neo-ists, endlessly repeating what has already been done, usually long after it needs doing.

Of course, the Arabs followed—they always do. They followed Aristotle like they followed the crescent. I didn't like that. I hid from them.

The Carolingian Middle Ages were an interesting time for me. Officially they banned me from the front door, while allowing me in the back one. On the one hand, Hrabanus Maurus' *De Laudibus Sanctae Crucis* (ninth century) seems to allow me no room, yet its poetry is the-same-but-different from earlier square-shaped poetry. Its canceled forms, its little monk staring at the gigantic cross in the Vienna manuscript, staring *past* it in the Vatican one—who knows which way Hrabanus wanted it (see Figure 1, p. 25)? But it is a powerful statement of my way, and gives the lie to those who say that old visual poetry or intermedia are good for tricks but beside the point.

Then there were people like Giordano Bruno at the end of the Renaissance. Bruno was a syncretist. He tried to know everything from every time and every era, and to fuse it together somehow. The Roman Church (not really catholic) got jealous and burned him as a heretic. Bruno didn't think he was a heretic. In fact, when he was arrested, he had returned to Italy to become (he hoped) an advisor to the Pope. His eye was on the past; his mathematics is Mediaeval, and his thought a fusion is based on ideas he had found elsewhere. But their combination? That's where I come in. His *De Imaginum, Signorum et Idearum Compositione* (1591) is a sixteenth-century semiotics (among other things), though as every official Barthesian can tell you, there was no semiotics before the twentieth century. Bruno saw everything as alive, not just people and plants but rocks, the earth, and ideas as well. Touch a thought or a thing: it is alive. Well, maybe that's a dangerous heresy to some, especially Aristotle's friends whom Bruno battled at Oxford. Ah, those English! They always fight me.

The historians tried to derive me. It was the only way they could describe me. They pointed at my name: "origin" plus "alita." That is, if you go there, you are at your origin. A quality of being an origin is what they said I meant, though I wonder if that is what I mean today. The fact is, that may be what I once meant, but I've gone beyond my name. You seldom take me apart, do you? The linguists, forever running after the historians, just simply abused me, confusing what I *might* mean with what I *do* mean. But, then, ah well, it's their occupational hazard. So don't confuse me with my name.

The scientists understood me differently, cumulatively. They saw that this piece from here and that from there made a useful composite of me; each vision of me, if it was real, replaced the one that came before it. The out-of-date was then no longer to be consulted, except in learned histories of science.

The artists misunderstood me. That's natural, because every art work that is fresh to us is somehow a deliberate misunderstanding and misrepresentation of something that's come before. I'd like to start an Institute for Creative Misunderstanding, and all the best of critics and artists would be members. But art moves in clumsy ways. The modernists were quite awkward. They always aimed at me and jumped, and most of the time I had to move out of their way. Jumping is no way for grown human beings to try to get around! Walking works better. But those modernists, they seldom saw that. Jumping here, jumping there, they also tried to use the scientists' notion that every jump made all the older jumps obsolete. But that's silly, isn't it, that neoteric view? Each art expresses its time, monolithic like the nineteenth century, flexible like our present crazy moment. Each time is necessary in the progress of things, and so all the expressions of these times as art, they too are necessary. Every child deserves a voice, and every moment its say. Anyway, I can't be aimed for, only found to be around. Aim for me and I'm a cheap and artificial whore. It's my pleasure to pose that way anyhow, sometimes anyway. But I'm a perfect audience. You'll always find me on the spot when something new needs to be said, danced, played, painted, performed. Why? Because new messages need new languages. Discover a new language that is natural (not one that you've made from fashionable, received, but perhaps wrong notions), and I am always there. It's art where I "hang out," as the teenagers say, not artifice. In fact, artifice is where I'm not.

You'll find me all over, not just where the learned authorities point. The Americans imagine I'm particularly American, but that's their myth. I was born speaking Japanese as well as English, singing Rock as well as Mozart. I wander; at one moment I'm at one concert, and then, when it is imitated enough, I get bored and leave. Life attracts me: its echoes don't.

I am a problem and proud of it. I'll never settle down.

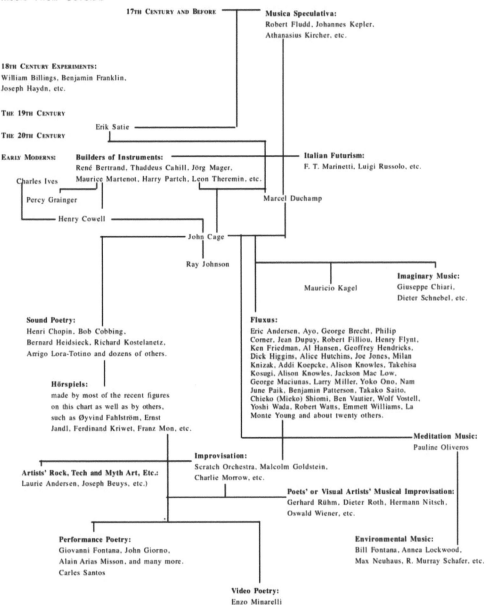

Music from Outside

17th Century and Before — **Musica Speculativa:**
Robert Fludd, Johannes Kepler,
Athanasius Kircher, etc.

18th Century Experiments:
William Billings, Benjamin Franklin,
Joseph Haydn, etc.

The 19th Century

The 20th Century

Erik Satie

Early Moderns: **Builders of Instruments:** — **Italian Futurism:**
René Bertrand, Thaddeus Cahill, Jörg Mager, F. T. Marinetti, Luigi Russolo, etc.
Charles Ives Maurice Martenot, Harry Partch, Leon Theremin, etc.

Percy Grainger Marcel Duchamp

Henry Cowell

John Cage

Ray Johnson

Imaginary Music:
Mauricio Kagel Giuseppe Chiari,
Dieter Schnebel, etc.

Sound Poetry: **Fluxus:**
Henri Chopin, Bob Cobbing, Eric Andersen, Ayo, George Brecht, Philip
Bernard Heidsieck, Richard Kostelanetz, Corner, Jean Dupuy, Robert Filliou, Henry Flynt,
Arrigo Lora-Totino and dozens of others. Ken Friedman, Al Hansen, Geoffrey Hendricks,
Dick Higgins, Alice Hutchins, Joe Jones, Milan
Knizak, Addi Koepcke, Alison Knowles, Takehisa
Kosugi, Alison Knowles, Jackson Mac Low,
Hörspiels: George Maciunas, Larry Miller, Yoko Ono, Nam
made by most of the recent figures June Paik, Benjamin Patterson, Takako Saito,
on this chart as well as by others, Chieko (Mieko) Shiomi, Ben Vautier, Wolf Vostell,
such as Øyvind Fahlström, Ernst Yoshi Wada, Robert Watts, Emmett Williams, La
Jandl, Ferdinand Kriwet, Franz Mon, etc. Monte Young and about twenty others.

Meditation Music:
Pauline Oliveros

Improvisation:
Scratch Orchestra, Malcolm Goldstein,
Artists' Rock, Tech and Myth Art, Etc.: Charlie Morrow, etc.
Laurie Andersen, Joseph Beuys, etc.)

Poets' or Visual Artists' Musical Improvisation:
Gerhard Rühm, Dieter Roth, Hermann Nitsch,
Oswald Wiener, etc.

Performance Poetry: **Environmental Music:**
Giovanni Fontana, John Giorno, Bill Fontana, Annea Lockwood,
Alain Arias Misson, and many more. Max Neuhaus, R. Murray Schafer, etc.
Carles Santos

Video Poetry:
Enzo Minarelli

Figure 5. Chart suggesting the historical context of outsider music,
especially of Fluxus, which is, of course, as much a part of visual art
and literature as of music as such. George Maciunas had made
about seven *far* more elaborate charts than this, showing the context
of Fluxus up to 1978, when he died. However, as not all of Fluxus
is music, not all of outsider music is Fluxus, either. The tendency of
music to show different facets of itself when viewed from outside
or when made by musicians who are acting as outsiders is the main
point of this article.

Section Two
Pages from the History of Intermedia

VII. Music from Outside

i. What "Music from Outside" Means

SOMEWHERE IN HIS *PARIS DIARIES* the composer Ned Rorem wonders that there was, in "classical" music, no phenomenon of amateur music akin to naive, folk, or primitive painting—art by amateurs or at least non-professionals. While Rorem goes on to speculate that this is because of the highly technical nature of traditional music, the fact is that, though he was scarcely an ill-informed person, very little scholarship has been brought to bear on music that I will call "music from outside," reviving a concept developed in the 1950s by Colin Wilson, since "amateur" really means "lover," and, hopefully, most professionals love their art. But an outsider here would be a person who had no professional commitment to the technical traditions of art music, who chose to experiment with its very nature or assumed functions, and whose position outside these technical traditions allowed for a certain objectivity about the possibilities. The outsider might or might not be technically trained, would presumably not be naive on his or her own terms, and might or might not use folkloric traditions in order to extend the range of possibilities.

ii. The Historic Tradition

Actually there *is* a rich tradition of outsiders' music, but knowledge of it has not been generally available. In Greek musical theory, two-thousand years ago, the overview of music was of three sorts: *musica humana*, *musica speculativa*, and *musica mundana*. The first was ordinary, performable music. The last was the "music of the spheres," the music of the forms beyond the material world, only perceptible to

78

those whose souls were suitably in harmony with these forms. But *musica speculativa* (from the Latin *speculum*, mirror) was the music that reflected reality in some way. It might or might not be performable, but, even if it was, its point was in the conditions of its existence. While Boethius did not originate this idea, he codified it in his *De Institutione Musica,* and his text remained well known through the Middle Ages, the Renaissance, and on into the seventeenth century, where it appears to have been an inspiration to the experimental musical thinkers of the time, such as Robert Fludd, Athanasius Kircher, and Johannes Kepler.

Fludd's musical work is the least well known. Robert Amman's "The Musical Theory and Philosophy of Robert Fludd" is almost the only study of it. But Fludd was influenced by the microcosm and the macrocosm, by the idea that all things reflected or even implied their larger context. He based many of his ideas on the monochord, an ancient instrument of unknown origin, in which a string is stretched over a sounding board; although it was usually used to demonstrate the effect of tuning and musical intervals, Fludd and others used it as a way of reflecting the divine proportions associated with Christian Platonism (see Fig. 6).

Fludd attacked Kepler, who replied in kind, but the two thinkers had more in common than they probably realized. Kepler's theory was, as was appropriate to a great astronomer, a sort of projection into the microcosm of the celestial organization of the universe. It has been discussed in the abstract by many writers, notably by the late D. P. Walker of the Warburg and Courtauld Institutes. But it has also been applied as a system and realized on a phonograph record by two physicists from Yale (see Figure 7).

Kircher was a Jesuit always on the edge of unorthodoxy, much given to speculations about ways of experiencing reality. He proposed that a sphere be constructed in which the audience might be surrounded on all sides by musicians, and in this way, if suitable music could be composed for the environment, a parallel would be made to the earth in the

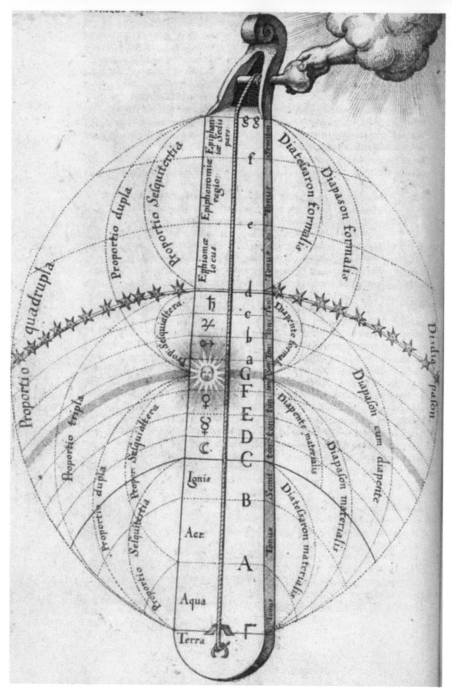

Figure 6. This diagrammatic picture of a monochord shows it as a microcosm corresponding with the macrocosm of the universe. It comes from Robert Fludd's *De Utriusque Cosmi Maioris . . .* (Oppenheim: Johann Theodore de Bry, 1617). Fludd viewed the universe as a musical instrument that was played by the soul of the world.

THE HARMONY OF THE WORLD

A Realization for the Ear of
Johannes Kepler's
Astronomical Data from
Harmonices Mundi 1619

Realized by
Willie Ruff and John Rodgers

Figure 7. Willie Ruff and John Rogers (Yale University). *The Harmony of the World*. Kepler, LP 1571. According to the ideas of the great astronomer Johannes Kepler concerning the harmony of the spheres, the planets could produce six-part harmony. Here we see the cover of the only recording we know of the work developed out of Kepler's musical ideas.

cosmos. Kircher also invented a composing machine, the *arca musarithmica*, which, alas, has not survived if, in fact, a working model was ever actually built.

Also to be noted in this context is Pietro Cerone's *El Melopeo y Maestro . . .* (1613). Mainly a manual for playing and composing for the lute, its final section gives an account of composing with chance and other unusual techniques, a "guide to musical chaos" that is a poetic overview of the relation of music and existence, and also the work gives numerous examples of graphic notations, to which we shall return in a moment. We might take Cerone's work as summing up most of the material we have discussed until now.

However exciting these literally *speculative* concepts of music may have been to the Baroque, they did not appeal to the more neoclassical eighteenth century or the empirical mood of the next two centuries. Nonetheless, music from outside the prevailing traditions did not entirely disappear. In the first place, it did not disappear altogether. For example, living in the isolation of colonial America, the inventor Benjamin Franklin wrote an extraordinary "Quartetto" for three violins and cello, mostly on open strings, in which one can almost hear the prevailing world view of the intellectuals of the time (it was not necessarily Franklin's) being expounded, with its Deism, its vision of the universe as a sort of gigantic clock set in motion by a Divine Clockmaker. One might note here that America could not afford to support professional composers, so that most of the gifted composers of the time supported themselves by other work, such as William Billings, a tanner by trade, or Justin Morgan, a schoolmaster and the developer of the morgan horse. Such composers were less susceptible to professionalistic pressure from their peers than composers living in more cosmopolitan milieus.

Music was also judged a suitable medium for works by certain artists better known for their work in other areas. For example, the social philosopher and writer Jean-Jacques Rousseau wrote a charming one-act opera, *Le Divan du Village*, that reflects Rousseau's idyllic concept of rural and primitive life. One can almost imagine Marie-Antoinette and the elegant ladies of the French court affecting white muslin gowns, staging an amateur performance of Rousseau's piece on the grounds of the palace at Versailles instead of merely playing at being milkmaids.

The nineteenth-century artists had a distinct taste for extending their work; the more universal the artist's formal concerns, the greater the artist. Perhaps it was inevitable that some of the characteristic artists of the time should try their hands at writing music. Thus, a Romantic literary figure such as E. T. A. Hoffmann, best known to the English-speaking world from Jacques Offenbach's opera *Les Contes d'Hoffmann* (*The Tales of Hoffmann*), wrote a fairly considerable body of music, some of it recorded. Friedrich Nietzsche, as a young man, wrote both songs and keyboard music. While Hoffmann's music is not first-rate in any respect, and though Nietzsche's music is really immature salon composition, nevertheless it indicates the seriousness of his musical interests even before the famous relationship with Richard Wagner. On the other hand, the American late Romantic poet Sidney Lanier, an accomplished flautist, wrote a number of works for that instrument, and his music is no less appealing in a hot-house way than his rather ripe poems. As for Wagner, not only is he a "polyartist" (Richard Kostelanetz's term for an artist who is active in more than one medium), but in his work one finds the composer expanding his purview into many non-art areas, not only writing his own libretti and but also developing the theory of the *Gesamtkunstwerk* or overall art work, one in which a single artist is responsible for all aspects of the conception in order to present a unified vision, even, in Wagner's case, taking on the additional burden of being some kind of spokesman for the Germanic race (as if there were such a thing), with truly tragic results. For this last we should not blame Nietzsche; when he realized where Wagner was heading, he split with him.

There was also another, less grandiose way to be a polyartist or to combine the different areas of one's art experience in one work. This was to fuse them conceptually, making visual poems, sound poems, and "graphic" (visual) notations for music. I have documented the first of these areas extensively in *Pattern Poetry: Guide to an Unknown Literature,* which provides short chapters on the last two areas as well (see Figures 8a and 8b).

For graphic notations, there are numerous examples of heart-shaped and, even more, circular notations from before modern times. An example of a late Gothic one by Baude Cordier (fourteenth century) is "Tout par Compas," which has been recorded and printed many times. Also, Cerone's *El Melopeo . . .* (1613), already mentioned, presents numerous examples of chess-shaped and cruciform graphic notations, many of them by Ghiselin Danckerts, a Dutch Catholic composer of the Reformation who fled to Italy and worked mostly in the Sistine Chapel in Rome. Perhaps the most prolific pre-modern composer of all of shaped notations is, however, not from the Baroque or earlier, but is the great symphonist Joseph Haydn, many of whose canons for chorus have circular notations—about 32 works in all (see Figure 9).

Turning to the early moderns, by the time the twentieth century came around, we see that the knowledge of earlier experimentation had become obscure, but the impetus to expand the available concepts of music had become normative as part of each composer's presentation of his or her musical vision. Thus, although Charles Ives, composer of radical vision that he was, never made any works that encompass more than one medium, his musical notations strain at the very fabric of the possible within our traditional system of writing down notes, and his younger colleague, Henry Cowell, had to work out new systems for writing down tone clusters and multiple rhythms. The Australian pianist and composer Percy Grainger also composed some (then) unperformable, unnotatable pieces that have subsequently been realized and recorded. Grainger worked with Cowell on several occasions, but the results of their collaboration have not been made generally available.

THE TEARES OR
LAMENTACIONS OF
A SORROWFVLL
SOVLE:

Compoſed with Muſicall Ayres and Songs, both for Voyces and diuers Inſtruments.

Set foorth by Sir WILLIAM LEIGHTON *Knight, one of his Maieſties Honourable Band of Gentlemen Penſioners.*

And all Pſalmes that conſiſt of ſo many feete as the fiftieth Pſalme, will goe to the foure partes for Conſort.

LONDON
Printed by *William Stansby*, 1614.

Figures 8a and 8b. William Leighton, canon with bass from *The Teares or Lamentacions of a Sorrowfull Soule* (London: William Stanley, 1614), title page, recto and verso. From a microfilm in the collection of the James William Gee Library, East Texas State University, Commerce, Texas. This piece, printed twice in Leighton's work, is fairly typical of circular notations, from Baude Cordier (15th century) through the Baroque. It was probably intended to stand alone at the start of the book, since Leighton's lyric only appears on 4b, but then it was repeated for decorative purposes on the title page. The music is theoretically endless, reflecting the proverbial endlessness of a circle, which seems to have appealed to the composers of the time. Circular forms are by no means the only ones. Cruciform notations were also popular, the best-known to the English-speaking world being one by Thomas Morley.

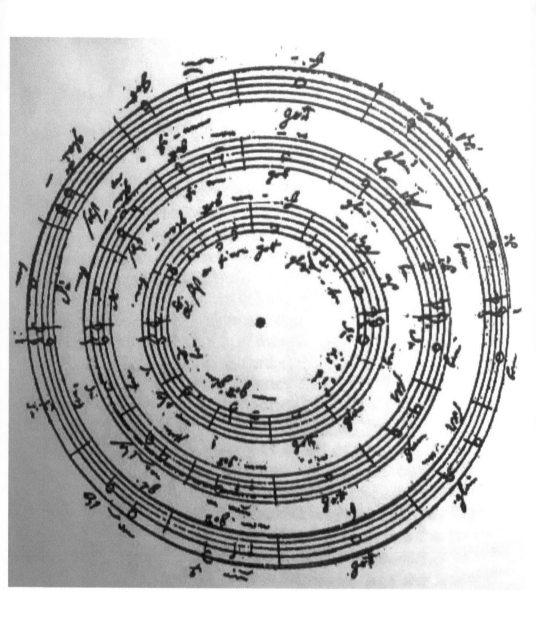

Figure 9. Joseph Haydn. Manuscript of the first of the *Geistliche Kanonen* (Hoboken XXVIIa, no. 1). It is said that Haydn's canons were made because he was too poor to afford wallpaper. Given the complexity and subtlety of the compositions, this seems doubtful or misstated.

By the mid-century it had become almost commonplace for a composer that he or she would have to use some special means of notation to indicate fully how a given piece was to go. At the same time, musical instrumentation had been expanded to include numerous sources of sound that had been either condemned previously as noise or unavailable for technical reasons. For example, the Italian futurists had a program of systematically pushing the frontiers of art. As part of this, Luigi Russolo and others set out to create musical instruments of their own that were more suitable than the traditional ones for the expression of a truly modernist spirit. The resulting instruments—barkers and roarers and suchlike, generally classed by the composer as "intonorumori"—have all been lost or destroyed, but not before they were recorded and photographed.

In Russia both before and after the Revolution similar experiments were made. A comprehensive documentation of this was part of the *Für Augen und Ohren* exhibition in Berlin and Paris in 1980-81, organized by René Block, whose catalogue is a useful tool for researching the materials on this. Leon Theremin, for example, made an electronic device originally for building security but which became the musical instrument known as the theremin, used in Hollywood movies of the 1930s to create an eerie atmosphere. Theremin also collaborated with Cowell in building an instrument, the "rhythmicon," used initially to demonstrate complex rhythms but later as a percussion instrument in its own right. This highly technical approach to extending the musical frontiers leads ultimately to such (now) contemporary approaches to music as those of Max Neuhaus, as much electronic experiment and sometimes fine art as music. The current project of this highly skilled percussionist (Neuhaus was first known for his recordings of works by Karlheinz Stockhausen) is to develop a new emergency signal for large cities such as New York.

The dadaists and surrealists did rather little with music; there was a dadaist fox-trot, but Breton and his circle had the impression that music was necessarily a kind of opiate, producing appetites it could not satisfy. However, as the influence of the surrealists waned, visual artists became active in music. The collagist and correspondance artist Ray Johnson and the composer Earle Brown collaborated on music for dancers in the late 1950s, and Johnson made a memorable "Funeral Music for Elvis Presley" on magnetic tape around 1958. Even artists of a more traditional hue, such as Jean Dubuffet, were composing music by the 1960s, some of it available on record.

The voices became a roar by the 1970s. On the one hand, there was a popular trend towards visual artists not so much expanding their art into music as reveling in the pop music of the time. This genre was (and is) called "artists' rock," and is best known from the works of Laurie Anderson, though even Joseph Beuys tried the genre for his political song, "Wir wollen Sonne Statt Reagan."

On the other hand, musical improvisation, an obvious feature of jazz, became extremely popular in the 1960s among classical musicians. In Tokyo the Ongaku group and Cornelius Cardew's Scratch Orchestra are both examples of this. Visual artists also got into this area of work. For example, Gerhard Rühm (trained as a composer and pianist before he became active as a poet) made a number of recordings, usually called "Selten Gehörte Musik" (Seldom Heard Music), with other artists such as Diter Roth or Hermann Nitsch, or with writers such as Oswald Wiener. Each of these others has also made music and recorded it, such as Nitsch's massive *Requiem*.

Yet another sort of music—perhaps the most striking of all—is the music of chance pioneered by what Irving Sandler has called the "Duchamp-Cage Nexus." Marcel Duchamp made a few musical experiments as part of his process of exploring his world rather than creating it. In the recorded examples, he can be seen, on the one hand, as acting in the tradition of *musica speculativa*, and, on the other, as being close in spirit to the concerns of the late nineteenth-century French composer Erik Satie, many of whose musical structures depend on time patterns quite outside European traditions, but also whose overall *geste*, as shown in his writings, is one of experiment, of objective fact and science concealing any distinct personal expression, and of a mode of humorous focus for his ideas which masks his serious concerns. Duchamp in the "Green Box" notes: "Classify combs according to the number of their teeth." Satie's "Memoirs of an Amnesiac" suggests that he should only eat white things, that he, Satie, should not be considered a musician but a "phonometrist." He goes on to describe "phonometry" in an amusing series of neologisms, concluding with the remark that "the future belongs to philophony" (literally "love of sound"), a serious prophecy. The reader must struggle with these paradoxical statements, often skirting the issue of meaninglessness, as some sort of proto-Zen koans in order to discover their significance for what is, finally, art. If the dadaists and surrealists, in the main, ignored music, at least two of their marginal figures, Duchamp and Satie, affected it (see Figures 10 and 11).

Among the key techniques employed by Duchamp is chance. Never does it take on a mystique, and never is it systematized as such. But it is present in perhaps a majority of Duchamp's mature works and readymades on some level, now in the pattern of the broken glass in the "Big Glass" (anticipated in a painting a few years before), now in the traces of paint applied by cork to a canvas (see Figure 10).

It is unfair to John Cage to locate his compositions purely in the field of chance simply because he has systematically used correspondences among unrelated arrays of numbers or other sequences in order to structure his materials at hand. He has, after all, done other things—the graphical musical notations do not all use chance (see Figure 12). In Cage's work, chance is an aspect of a larger concern, "indeterminacy," better described in his interviews than in his essays. However using chance *as if—as if* it were reasonable, *as if* it were the guiding principle of all existence (even Cage knows it's only one of them, though an important one)—and apply-

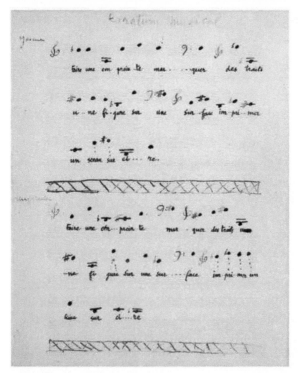

Figure 10. Marcel Duchamp. "Erratum Musicale," from *La Marie Mise à Nu* (1913). Duchamp's only actual musical composition, its text reads:

Yvonne:	Faire une empreinte marquer des traits une figure sur une surface imprimer un sceau sur cire.
Magdeleine:	Fair une empreinte marquer des traits une figure sur une surface imprimer un sceau sur cire.
Marcel:	Faire un empreinte marquer des traits une figure sur une surface imprimer un sceau sur cire.

The main attention here seems to be literary, based on the mystical number three and on the word play. The music is made by using a funnel, a toy train with open cars, and balls to be put into the funnel; the balls bear a number that represents a note on a chosen instrument. The balls fall through the funnel into the cars as these pass below. The balls are then taken out of the cars, and the numbers are transformed into notes. With great diligence the composer and flautist, Petr Kotík, made a realizaion of this work that was recorded on *The Entire Musical Work of Marcel Duchamp* (the record also includes a "Musical Sculpture" from notes, but this is not a composition).

However, Duchamp's importance to music does not stem from this composition, which is very slight, for all its Rube Goldberg charm, nor from his originality in using chance as such (see Figure 6 below), but from the larger aspects of his *geste* and his inquiry into chance, as disccused in the main text.

Otro. Aduiertan que Iuſquin, entre ſus Miſſas, hizo vna parte
con el Canon: *De minimis non curat Prator* : adonde (como de-
ximos) va cantando ſolamente las notas Breues y Semibreues,
dexando à parte las notas, que ſon de menor valor: mas no ay de-
ſpues otra ſegunda parte, que vaya diziendo las demas notas intermedias, como aqui ; con que
viene à ſer la inuencion mas ingenioſa, y mas acepta.

Enigma de la ſuerte, ò de los dados. Num. XXXXI.

PAra dar occaſion al eſtudioſo, que pueda conocer eſta manera de Canones ſecretos y no
ordinarios con mas facilidad, pongo eſte otro Enigma : y le ordeno aſſi.

CASVS VBIQVE VALET

Declaracion. Solo con ver el dibuxo de aquella mano y dados, y con ver aquellas pauſas
aſſi à ſolas, ſe entiende que poner ſe pueden aqualquiera parte ; aſſi al Tiple como al Tenor,
que

Enigma de la mano.   Num. XXXVIII.

ALTO.

Chi vuol ſaper di queſta mano il canto,
L'ordine ſegua de gli abbachiſti ſegni :
E ſe deſia tener tra tutti'l canto,
Stia ſuegliato nel dar i valor degni :
Tenendo conto con le dita alquanto,
Si vederà Signor de i vari pegni.
L'indite vno moſtra, tre l'anellare,
Il lungo due, e quattro l'auriculare.
Per più chiaro parlare,
Se li verrà in mente Longa figura,
Vna parte tacere, l'altra cantare,
Diuerrà ſol per trouarſi à miſura,
Se'l tutto aſſicurà con lieto core,
Felice lui, felici gl'anni, e l'hore.

Figure 11. Pietro Cerone. "Enigma de la suerte, ò de los dados,"
from *el Melopeo* (1613). This text describes how chance was used
to compose music in the Renaissance and early Baroque; the
work was not obscure but was one of the main guides to the
techniques of lute-playing and musical composition in its time.
Haydn often used chance to select the opening chords of his
works, and Mozart wrote a tractate on composing with dice.
Forgotten in the nineteenth century, such techniques are crucial
to the Duchamp-Cage nexus.

ing it to elements of a work in order to disconnect them from our assumptions, taste, and prejudices, is very much in the Duchampian spirit.

Others have, of course, picked up on this contribution. It has been used by many other artists for their own purposes, for example, in poetry by Jackson Mac Low and myself. Mac Low uses chance in many of his works to atomize his language and to extend the possibilities of his vision; this is close to Cage's practice. On the other hand, other poets have explored matrices of various kinds—mathematical or crystalline—and have found chance useful as a process of testing and filling these in, much as tables of random numbers are used in science. No one method of using chance is, of course, the correct or valid one, but all are in some way indebted to the Duchamp-Cage nexus of our recent arts.

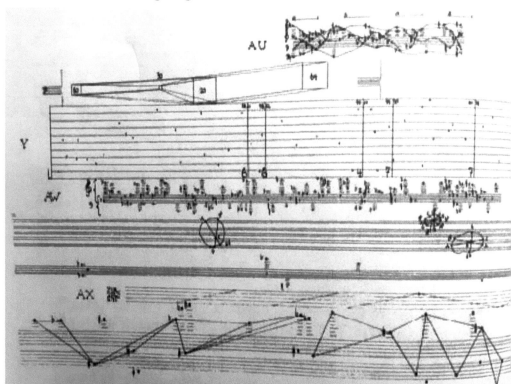

Figure 12. John Cage. Page 38 from the *Concert for Piano and Orchestra (1957-8),* an example of one of Cage's works in graphic notation. Copyright © 1960 Henmar Press, Inc. Reprinted by permission of Peters Editions, Ltd., London.

iii. Intermedia and Fluxus

The notion of intermedia—the conceptual fusion of two or more previously defined areas of art or concern—underlies many recent developments in art. To treat it historically has been done enough, but rather little has been documented about its use in music and in hermeneutics. This latter must wait, but not before we note how the intermedial interest seems often to feel, to the artist, as an imperative to try out new fusions, and to a public (or receiver of a work) as an approach offering an ingress to a previously mysterious work. The viewer asks, "What does this resemble?" and works out a sort of averaging that demystifies the work. But the intermedial nature of works has no traditional vocabulary, so it is hard to develop into a depth criticism as yet. Still, when one sees some of the performance notations of Giuseppe Chiari or Dieter Schnebel or Mauricio Kagel (especially the "instrumental theater" works; see Figure 5), one notes at first that they can be performed, and then one wonders whether they *have* to be realized in real time in order to be experienced. Isn't this or that work mostly an academic hypothesis? Then one tries them out, Chiari's "Gestures for Conductor," for example, and one finds that one is entering areas of aesthetic concern that had previously been inaccessible. One explores the gestures of conducting and finds that they have their own choreography, that one finds oneself becoming a sort of dancer or watching another performer become one.

The situation is the same with many Fluxus works. George Brecht proposes that we consider:

•   **at**   **least**   **one**   **egg**

This piece by George Brecht epitomizes the laconic concentration of Fluxus "events." Originally intended for use in private rather than public performances, such pieces were mailed out by the artist in small envelopes; the events were collected and published as George Brecht's *Water Yam* (New York: Fluxus Editions, 1963).

One must suggest to the reader of this piece that he or she now do just that—consider "at least one egg." Get a few eggs together. Don't just name the act; collect them, look them over, and do something with them.

What happened? When we do this in fact—and not till we do—we enter the art-life intermedium. Where before it seemed as if there were an art and life dichotomy, now they somehow fuse (see Figure 13).

There are many kinds of Fluxus works, but most are intermedial. For "pure Fluxus," one must look to the pieces of the late fifties and early sixties. But just as Max Ernst did not die with Dada, so the Fluxus artists did not end with the self-consciously defined Fluxus "tendency" ("movement" is a problematic term for Fluxus). All the original Fluxus artists have changed and evolved to do other work; only a couple of them, like Tomas Schmit, have repudiated their early work.

Fluxus has its expressionistic side, best known perhaps from the works of Nam June Paik, Joseph Beuys, and Wolf Vostell (Figure 14). For example, Nam June Paik explores the intermedium between the world of advanced technology and the world of art expression. Even in his recent graphics, the image is often of a television set, and a tear. Even in works like these the Paik of the early performance pieces, dumping buckets of water over himself, is still present, for all the more subdued quality of the recent pieces. In other words, traces of their Fluxus pieces are still to be found in recent works of most of the artists who were involved in it. Wolf Vostell's music, like Paik's, is imagistic and expressionistic in intention. It works best when it is most maniacal—screeching, crucified creatures in his homage to Hieronymous Bosch, the *Garden of Delights*. Joseph Beuys was only active in Fluxus in 1963 and perhaps 1964. But the freedom he got from his work

A Contribution to the Art of Music.

    Since Music has to do with _____ (anything) _____

    then if you take a(n) _____ (anything) _____

    and a(n) _____ (anything) _____

    and put them together

    you will get music.

    Repeat four more times.

Figure 13. George Brecht and Robert Filliou. "The Mystery Game," from *Games at the Cedilla* (New York: Something Else Press, 1967). In this little Fluxus piece, the act of composing becomes what is performed. Copyright © 1967 Something Else Press, Inc. Reprinted by permission.

Danger Music Number Seventeen

Scream! Scream! Scream! Scream! Scream! Scream! (May 1962).

Figure 14. Dick Higgins. From *Danger Music* series. Each piece in the series exemplifies some kind of danger—to the artist, to the performer, or to the members of the public. The problem in this piece was to see how much expression could be put into a minimal unit. A good way to perform this work is to turn all the lights out and scream as loud as one possibly can to the very limit of one's endurance (more than six times). Published in Dick Higgins, *foew&ombwhnw* (New York: Something Else Press, 1969). Copyright © 1969 Something Else Press, Inc. All rights reserved. Reprinted by permission.

there—its usefulness in freeing himself from the professionalistic traditionalism of the time—was useful to him long after. Similarly, the Danish composer Henning Christiansen was only a "Fluxcomposer" for a short time in the early 1960s and produced no important Fluxus pieces. But when Beuys and Christiansen collaborated, as they did on various performances that are recorded, the result is an intermedial collage of ritual and half-remembered song ("Loch Lomond," in the *Scottish Symphony*, for instance) that is striking if not always aesthetically satisfying.

Philip Corner (Figure 15) was the composer of several important early Fluxus works, such as the notorious "Piano Activities" in which a grand piano was taken apart at the Wiesbaden Fluxus Festival in 1962 (the first). Actually, this piece was mis-identified; the real "Piano Activities" is a different, far more sedate work. But there is another piece, the "Work of Destruction," which could have been used to dismantle the piano. The sounds of the dismantling, however, were very beautiful at times, belying their inherent violence. Many of Corner's early pieces are in a collective book called *The Four Suits*. As for his more recent pieces, most are either gamelan works (a different area of his music), or they focus on one or another isolated sound or class of sounds, metallic sounds, for instance.

My own work usually enters intermedia between art and history or geography. George Maciunas, the artist who designed and named Fluxus more than anybody else, used to say that my pieces were "neo-Baroque theater." Perhaps he was right. Theater did indeed monitor my sensibility, though what was performed suggested games or rituals more than dramas. In recent times I have found myself making two-dimensional surfaces in acrylic on canvas; since I am working with found images in books, this is an appropriate medium for me. Whether or not they are "painting" or some other kind of graphic is not for me to say. But I feel the traces of the early Fluxus works in these paintings.

Alison Knowles's work (see Figure 16) has always been

Prelude

before an action   from the first move
                     made in the directiion of the
action

                     to the last moment
                     up to the point of acting on it

                     :the whole step of this process

                     —at every stage within it

                ......wait on it......meditate on it......

for public
for work
for self

Figure 15. Philip Corner. "Prelude," from Philip Corner, et al., *The Four Suits* (New York: Something Else Press, 1965). Copyright © 1965 Something Else Press, Inc. All rights reserved. Reprinted by permission. Typical of Corner's works of the early 1960s, he says what is intended to happen (and why), rather than simply presenting materials. Not all his pieces are this interior or conceptual, of course.

imagistic, from the "Bean Rolls" and "T Dictionary" of the early 1960s (this last is in *The Four Suits*). Characteristically, she focuses on one kind of material—beans, words beginning with a "T," tuna fish sandwiches, or Native American traditions associated with moons. She uses these images or materials to produce new syntheses in areas that are seldom seen as related.

Milán Knizák has used death, decay, and destruction in a positive way, fusing it with his art and musical experience to establish a continuity between the first and later of these areas. For example, a broken record, formerly discarded, is patched together with similar parts from other records, resulting in a sculptural whole. One can only speculate on the sound that would result if the piece could be played on a phonograph!

Of course, one could go on and on talking about the various Fluxus artists' particular intermedial and fused areas and images, especially their music, both in their work of the time when Fluxus emerged and today. But it would be redundant. More to the point is to mention a few artists who were not involved in Fluxus but who are exploring other aspects of intermedia.

Such a person would be Pauline Oliveros, a composer and musician whose recent work explores fusions of the world of spiritual reflection and sound. Her pieces are in no way "New Age," which is usually very conservative work. Instead, they deal with sound as such, often the breath as such, sometimes the dream as such, and the matrix into which these things fall is what is meditative. Her best known series of pieces is, incidentally, "Sonic Meditations." She has also recently done several important light-spirited and even humorous pieces, such as the "horse spiel" (from the German *Hörspiel*) works. These are usually for radio, for example, the *Dream Horse Spiel*, which collects images about dreams and horses in many cultures, but they have been performed live as well, and they use associations with the four elements.

Another interesting intermedial performance artist is

Three Bean Events

Find something remarkable. Bring it out and add it to the beans.

Deliberately spill the beans.

Place a bean on one another's head. Protect it with a hat all day.

Figure 16. Alison Knowles, from *More by Alison Knowles* (New York: Printed Editions, 1979). Copyright © 1979 Alison Knowles. All rights reserved. Reprinted by permission. As described in the text, Alison Knowles' work is usually imagistic (there are exceptions). Here she uses beans. Simple pieces like these can be used to fill any amount of time quite refreshingly, and can be used to explore the art-life dichotomy at the same time.

mask a wire cage

portray a metal pole

unleas a rubber hose

_____

as a man steal magic

as a woman sell fleas

Figure 17. Benjamin Patterson, from "Seminar II," from Philip
Corner, et al., *The Four Suits* (New York: Something Else Press,
1965). Copyright © 1965 Something Else Press, Inc. All rights
reserved. Reprinted by permission. Patterson's musical and
performance pieces are usually very playful and often involve
toys or working with found materials from daily life. This piece
has not, so far as we know, ever been performed in public,
though it could be. The two parts of the piece are inteded to be
compared by the performer(s) while performing; thus, either
could be what is actually done—the more narrative the second
part, or the more concrete and object-oriented the first. But what
would the audience see? How could they best witness the entire
process? Better they should be "let in on the Act" by giving them
the text to follow with, so they can imagine what they might,
themselves, perform.

Wind Music

1
Raise wind.

2)
Be blown by wind.

3
Wind at the beach,
wind in the street,
wind passing by a car.

Typhoon

1963

Figure 18. Mieko Shiomi. "Wind Music," from Ken Friedman,
The Fluxus Performance Workbook (Verona: Editions Conz, and
Bergen, Norway: El Djarida, 1990), p. 46. Copyright © 1990
Fluxus, Ken Friedman, and the individual artists and authors.
Reprinted by permission. Mieko Shiomi's compositions, such as
"Wind Music," are among the purest and most striking Fluxus
pieces in their concentration and definition of some principle or
concept and their penetration of the art-life dichotomy. A piece
like the above could be taken as a sharing of a life experience—it
sounds as though she is documenting things that happened—or
proposing a life action (something off-stage in any traditional
sense). For example, "Raise wind?" How might one perform
that? By making a magical ritual? By saying a silent prayer? Yet
a truly thrilling indoor performance might be arranged by
bringing a jet engine on-stage, starting it up, and allowing
oneself to be blown over. The possibilities of this piece seem
endless.

Carles Santos, a virtuoso pianist but who is also a skilled vocal artist and sound poet. With the composer Charlie Morrow, he once staged a "sound poetry boxing match," hired a gymnasium, bought tights, robes, and the rest of the paraphernalia, and each artist built up a team of attendants. Then, before the public, they matched voice and notion instead of indulging in fisticuffs. Santos' works often fuse literary, pianistic, vocal, and even costume and choreographic elements. For example, in one piece the pianist is approached by a young woman in a dragon costume who crawls all over him and then goes away. The sounds that result are, of course, an important part of the piece, which otherwise is a lovely, lyrical, and traditional one.

iv. Whither Now?

It is dangerous, of course, to predict the future, since one will probably be wrong and because it might cause the public to ignore some marvelous development. But one can at least point towards three of the areas in which this outsiders' sound or music-based art is thriving: 1) sound poetry, 2) hörspiels, and 3) work that is based on new functions for sound art.

Sound poetry, intermedial poetry in which the acoustic element is the dominant one, is not new.[34] But writing it down or publishing its texts could only result in the production of a notation, not in a definitive performance of what the artist meant to achieve in it. Thus, its full development had to wait for the arrival of recording media, and this in fact took place. Marinetti and other futurists made sound poems, as did Kurt Schwitters and Raoul Hausmann among the dadaists (or near-dadaists). The recorded anthology by sound poet Arrigo Lora-Totino (see Figure 19) and the cassettes accompanying Henri Chopin's *Poésie Sonore* document the early modernist sound poem very well, as well as sound poetry up into the 1960s, when the widespread availability of tape recorders and studios caused a large increase in the number of artists

(se s'usasse la registrazione su nastro dell'autore, l'evento potrebbe essere commentato da due azioni simultanee: a) travasare acqua da una bottiglia ad altre, ciascuna di foggia diversa; b) esecuzione d'un concertato di 'musica liquida'; gorgoglii, sciacquii, gocce che cadono eccetera)

Figure 19. Arrigo Lora-Totino. "Verbale 1987." Beginning of second section ("lento assai," rather slow) of *Fluenti Traslati: Concertazione Drammatica in Quattro Tempi* (Naples: Edizioni Morra, 1988). Reprinted by permision of the author. Lora-Totino is a performer of futurist works as well as of his own sound and performance poetry. This section opposes synonyms and ant-onyms. Lora-Totina has staged it with the action of an endless pouring of water form one bottle into another of a different shape, 1981-87.

and poets making sound poetry. Chopin and Bernard Heidsieck edited a magazine in Paris that included recordings of sound poetry, and there were seven records produced by Sveriges Radio in Stockholm (now very scarce) in the 1960s that document the festivals of sound poetry held there. Another important journal is *Stereo Headphones*, published by Nicholas Zurbrugg, formerly from Britain and now located in Brisbane, Australia; it, too, publishes both texts and records.

Sound poetry today is basically of two types: works in which the voice is explored by technological means, using recorded amplification, alteration, or even computerized modification, and the more live, performance-oriented, "real time" sound poetry (see Frontispiece), some of which uses notation and is known as "text sound," a subgenre that allows the artist to work with the audience directly by giving it notations to perform. Chopin's own work is of the first type, as is Richard Kostelanetz's *Invocations*. Heidsieck's *Autour de Vaduz* uses a notation but is performed by the poet over a recording of himself reading the text, while Britain's Bob Cobbing is an example of a poet who blurs the distinction between performer and spectator by giving the audience copies of the score and asking it to read along with him. But sound poetry today is evolving into new areas using other technologies. Oliveros's *Dream Horse Spiel*, already mentioned, could be considered a sound poem that would have been impractical to assemble except with the aid of a computer. Enzo Minarelli, calling his work *polipoesia*, has explored the mixture of video imagery with live and recorded sound, and these new areas are by no means exhausted.

Hörspiel, literally "hear-play," is the usual German word for what we call "radio drama." The German radio dramaturgist Klaus Schöning and others have developed the concept, at WDR (Westdeutscher Rundfunk) in Cologne and elsewhere (not just in Germany), of *neues Hörspiel* (new hörspiel), meaning "acoustical, usually non-narrative literary work to be heard." Since this concept is not covered by previously existing terms in other languages, most have borrowed the word *Hörspiel* to cover *neues Hörspiel*, which is a little confusing but, until a better term comes along, it is all we have. Obviously, there is no hard and fast line between the hörspiel and sound poetry, but hörspiels can be performed by groups of people and are more akin to drama than most poems would be. John Cage's *Roaratorio* is a major hörspiel, and major ones have been composed by the visual poets Franz Mon, Ernst Jandl, and Ferdinand Kriwet. Most of the living artists mentioned in this article, Mauricio Kagel, for example, have by now composed hörspiels, though they have never been performed in the United States, where the absence of appropriate high-quality but non-commercial broadcasting facilities has made their production almost impossible. However, in April, 1989, there was a series of evenings at New York's Whitney Museum devoted to live performances of hörspiels, thus increasing their independence from radio broadcasting. Perhaps their future will be in the field of recorded sound, cassettes, for instance. This would be interesting for another new form of hörspiel, the "mini-hörspiel." Most older ones were full length—ideally in multiples of a quarter-hour duration. But the concert format suggests the development of short works so that more people could be represented on an program, perhaps a program devoted to a specific subject.

There are also new fusions, new intermedia, being explored by the outsiders. Mathematical art is old, but Henry Flynt, Christer (now "Catherine") Hennix, Ladislav Nebesky, Bern Porter, and many others have explored it, and there is a whole anthology of mathematical art or poetry available, edited by Ernest Robson and Jet Wimp. Music has always been close to mathematics; one can only speculate how this will affect music.

The field of text-music translations—music that literally interprets a text—is very new when it is worked on a large scale, for all that Johann Sebastian Bach used the notes B-A-C-H to provide the theme for part of *The Art of the Fugue*. We do not know of anyone focusing on this area besides the Canadian Robert Racine, but there may well be more.

The final new area for outsiders' music is based on new

musical functions. For example, there are numerous instances of healing music in traditional societies, music associated with the healing arts. In New York City in 1987 there was performed a whole concert of this sort of music, and there are now books on the subject and several recordings. Whether or not it works aesthetically or with healing effect it is too soon to tell, but the model seems to hold promise.

R. Murray Schafer, one of Canada's finest composers and not precisely an outsider, has written a notable book, *The Tuning of the World*, in which he discusses the sounds of nature from an ecological or environmental perspective. Schafer's musical work does not seem to have developed a practice based on his ideas of this sort, although he has made amazing and original theater performances and calligraphic works. Schafer's ideas provide the background, conscious or not, for other recent works, such as some pieces by Max Neuhaus, already mentioned; for certain works by Annea Lockwood, who has recorded and used water sounds; by Joe Jones, who has made a piece in which the growth of a plant causes sounds to occur and to change over time; and by Bill Fontana, who has, for instance, recorded the sounds of the Berlin subways and played them through the sidewalk gratings in another German city, Cologne. Particularly a work like this last is not so much dependent on the aesthetic experience of the sounds as on the concept of the movement of the sounds themselves, from one city to another, and on the sensitivity this movement encourages. "How do the sounds of the Berlin subway differ from those of the Cologne one?" The receiver can hardly avoid the question.

These last areas are only beginnings, of course. Like most beginnings, they may be frail. But it would seem unwise to dismiss them as impossibilities, simply because they do not measure up to the achievements of the modernisms of the bulk of the twentieth century, now ending. We do not know where they will lead. But we are not just Modern or Postmodern today. We are beginning things; we are *pre-millenarian*, and it is up to us and those who come after us to determine what that means.

Figure 20. Eric Andersen. *Solplænen (Solar Plane)*. Presently
under construction in Copenhagen and due to be completed in
1997, this hemispherical construction by the Danish Fluxus
composer Eric Andersen will be ten meters high, will have grass
on its surface, and will revolve so that it always faces the sun. Its
interest is as much scientific as aeesthetic.

VIII. John Cage: Perception and Reception[35]

i. Introduction

ONCE THE WORLD WAS VERY YOUNG, in the 1950s, and new art forms and ideas such as concrete poetry, happenings, and what became Fluxus were springing out of the air like jackrabbits from a magician's hat. The master magician of the time was John Cage, seldom taken seriously by the same press that today lauds him as if the whole of Modernism began (and perhaps ended?) with him. He lived on very modest means, rounded out his income by selling wild mushrooms that he had gathered in the woods, and devoted himself to his art and to his friends, as now. But then he had the time to see them whenever he chose, and he lived for the next conversation, the next dance, the next concert (not only his own).

Today there is a sort of patina of fame on the man, but this patina is not a healthy one. Patina is becoming to things, but not to people or ideas. It blinds us to the message of the man and to his work. The messages are not quite the same, as I would like to point out. The time has come to do some sorting out, to work out some access to the work that is not dependent on his own delightful presence because, face it, some time within the next decades we will no longer have that presence, and we must be able to deal with the work without it. Even apart from this, the work has been with us long enough, and there is enough of it, that it would be our own loss if we failed to digest it, to learn to respond to it in an appropriate manner.

ii. Cage's Theory of Cage

Cage has given us a large body of work—music, poetry, graphics, both musical notations and prints, including some amazing concert programs that are, like the Polish cubofuturist type compositions—intended only as useful and striking posters, but poems in spite of themselves—and, of course, there are Cage's theoretical essays and lectures. The styles used in these essays are often so striking as to give the pieces themselves the quality of poetry, but, for the moment, it is the overt content of those texts on which we should focus, even though the styles often imply their content. To deal with the styles is a worthy matter, but it must wait for another occasion.

The theoretical position Cage has proposed since the early 1950s is not precisely that of his earliest work, in which the oriental inputs, both Japanese and Indian, show more clearly. It seems as if it had come out of nowhere, though perhaps with some devious connection with Zen (some observers, like Arakawa, seem to blame Cage for not being authentic Zen—but, then, that is a claim Cage never made for himself). The position is found most clearly in the book *Silence*, only supplemented by his other collections, which are largely poems, especially acrostics in homage to his friends and to those elders whose work he most admires. The position is then summed up in the writings of Daniel Charles, especially the interview book Cage made with Charles, *Pour les Oiseaux,* and in the collection of materials that he and Richard Kostelanetz judged relevant to his work, *John Cage*, which therefore stands as a sort of autobiography by samples and examples.

This position, in its barest outline, is not hard to sum up:

1) Art is in the piece, in the material; when it leaves the artist, it has a life of its own, as soon as it is published or performed (though it doesn't exist until it is one or the other of those things).

2) The use of randomizing means, "chance operations," is to allow the work to exist at a maximum remove from the artist's tastes or prejudices, and from the accidentals of the artist's moment in time.

3) In the case of performance pieces, including music, the performer is a co-creator with the composer. Therefore, since the performer is working with sound, he must, above all, listen, and must work with sound rather than with his own

experience. Thus, raw improvisation is not appropriate, and a notation is needed as a means of bringing the performer outside his own accidentals or incidentals.

4) The listener (or reader or viewer—what some people call the "receiver") is in a sense the co-performer, perhaps even the co-composer. This receiver is the person who experiences the whole thing, puts it together, and, in this way, incorporates it into his or her own existence.

5) The art work is not a thing, not a static object; rather, it is the process of interaction among receiver, performer, and composer. All three are equally important, equally indispensable, but the composer is only an initiator in the last analysis and, after the performance the work exists at one flash, a memory, finally independent of the time it took to reveal it. The composer is like a watchmaker who, once the watch is in use, should stand out of the way. The watch is now telling the time for all kinds of purposes unknown to the watchmaker. So it is with the composer; his work is done, and, if anything, he now becomes simply a well-informed receiver, a member of his own audience.

Paradoxical, isn't it, then, that Cage is treated in the manner of some Romantic creator, idolized and thus dehumanized? Just because he shares his initials with Jesus Christ does not mean that he need be made part of the god-head. If his achievement means anything, it is that such idolization is blinding and irrelevant, a true violation of the spirit.

In learning, as we therefore must, to live with the work, we must meet it on its own grounds. First of all we must be quite skeptical about whether this theoretical position is, in fact, appropriate to the work or whether it is even the best theoretical approach to Cage's individual pieces.

There is a historical precedent for this shift of theoretical perspectives: the Impressionist painters. These thought they were capturing light; their approach to their work was cool and technical, focused on light and color theory as they saw it. Had this been all it was, they would have been forgotten today. Instead, the generations that came after them saw their work with new eyes, grasped its implications for composition, and moved onwards through the ground they had staked out for their own purposes, onwards to abstraction and to non-representational art. So it is, I think, with Cage's work. But before getting on with this, let us make two short digressions.

iii. Two Short Digressions

Moving our understanding of Cage away from a focus either on the man or on the theoretical positions he has offered us is not to say that these are not wonderfully important in their own way; they are simply not the only possibilities. The theory is a work in its own right, and the man has shown many an artist how to be an artist in a utilitarian world, how to survive being ignored or mocked and yet to live on a very high cultural plane indeed. At the University of Wisconsin at Milwaukee, at a performance conference in 1977, those of us who were lucky enough to be present saw an example of this. There were a lot of philosophers on hand, mostly Heideggerians, and some of them undertook to ask Cage highly technical questions, while others attempted to answer on his behalf, as if he could not possibly be trusted to speak for himself. Finally, Cage simply raised his hands and began to answer the questions—in perfect Heideggerian! It was unimportant to ask him where he had learned that form of discourse; perhaps he had done so when he studied with Daisetz T. Suzuki at Columbia University, who was, after all, trained in Western philosophy as well as Eastern, or perhaps he simply read deeply in it as part of living a holistic cultural life. The point is, he knew it. It was part of his world, of his cultural environment, and so he picked it up.

This is one of the examples he has set for us, part of the integrity with which he has absorbed our times, filtering out only the normative, neo-Benthamite utilitarianism so typical of the pettiness of our own moment in history. There is no waste in Cage's mind, no need to bother with hierarchies of what one does. If a thing is there, it is to be understood. This is a position of integrity, transcending the usual fashions—very rare in our time—and it is this that gives Cage his uncommon moral strength. It is of intrinsic value, since Cage has so often been proved to be right about art, people, and ideas. Anybody can be quite original. I have even made a satirical performance piece that causes the performer to be extremely original, but also ridiculous. However, most originality is seen, later, as mere eccentricity. Cage has been more prophetic than most people. But prophecy is not what his work is about.

Another small digression: what we need most from Cage is his work. Nobody else can do that. Lots of people can be charismatic, can recollect what it was like to study with Arnold Schoenberg or Henry Cowell, can be helpful on panels and platforms, can lend their names to worthy causes, and so on. But nobody else can think Cage's thoughts or can make one of his pieces. By dragging the poor man all over Kingdom Come, whether at his time of life or twenty years ago, we intrude upon him, and we waste him. We also reduce ourselves to the level of screaming groupies, mistaking his autograph for the signature of his ideas.

Recently there were an exhibition and festival at a college near my home about Black Mountain College, where Cage and other fine artists taught, and which died out in the mid-fifties. The survivors were roped and tied and trundled out onto parade, Cage among them. No doubt this was thrilling to the young college students. "Gee, two and a half tons of surviving artists!" But was it good for them, as studying the works and ideas on display in the college art gallery was? Didn't it create too personal a focus? Would it not have been better for them to attend some substantive discussion of the Black Mountain experience? It is a pity that the survivors, including Cage, did not have the nerve to stand aside and say: "No. My priority is my work and those things I really want to do. Not all the pennies in the piggy bank, not all the mistakes of detail or unimportant errors you might make and that my presence might help prevent, not all of that can keep me from my game plan."

Really, we must learn to do better by our best and senior artists than treat them as public monuments! You can catch a tortoise, can kill it and paint its shell in brilliant colors, make art of it, and even sell it. But what is best for the tortoise? Surely, to wag its tail in the mud. If we want to know about tortoises we should let the tortoise wag away, and the wise tortoise does just that. It does not teach itself or control how others see it. But perhaps that is too much to ask.

iv. Starting from the Work

Digressions over, I return to the main point: most Western art assumes a creator. This creator makes something or other inside himself or herself—a model, an intention, an idea, an image, a construction of notions or words or sounds—and then releases it in some way, with expression or persuasion, focusing either on that expression or on some other purpose (didactic, mimetic, religious, or whatever). Cage, by his work with chance and with processes outside himself, minimizes this sort of creation. Neither is working in this way unknown in art works of the past. For example, it is found in the West in the work of many folk artists, in the eighteenth century in some works by François Couperin, among the moderns in Duchamp, and in any artist who has made *objets trouvés*, in the works of the anonymous fresco muralists of the twelfth and thirteenth centuries, in the pattern poets who used magical ciphers as their art forms. In other words, it has its venerable tradition, but it is rare from the Baroque to the 1950s.

When one hears *Music of Changes* (1951), *Fontana Mix* (1958), *Atlas Eclipticalis* (1961), *HPSCHD* (1967-9), or — — — —*circus on* — — —(*Roaratorio*, 1979), all of which use chance and interact with some reality around them, it seems to me that what Cage is really doing, as opposed to what he is usually said to have done, is to perceive something and then to embody it. He starts by being a receiver in the hermeneutic sense, witnessing some process of existence, and then embodying the process in a work. This is, of course, a far cry from the usual ways of filling some straightforward commission, of sitting on a pine bough and waiting for inspiration, of making something that other people will presumably want or need enough to buy, those ways in which we are used to thinking of as how artists act. Perhaps visual artists have always started by noticing things. Picasso said the good ones did and the bad ones didn't, and so he drew his exquisite late minotaur drawings—almost cartoons but not quite—about the problem, making his point in vivid and memorable satire. Perhaps this is also why, for many years, it was the visual artists who understood Cage best, not the musicians, and certainly not the poets. Cage's poetry was all but ignored, printed but seldom "in the discussion." Why? Once he defined poetry to his class as "the principles of music applied to language in space." Such a definition might delight a visual artist or musician, but it would be anathema to a typical, professionalistic poet in his gray flannel suit or brand-new Levis awaiting tenure at some university. As for the musicians, they were simply not used to Cage switching some portion of the roles of "creator" and "receiver" around. Cage has written little, if anything, explicitly about this, and yet somehow it seems as if it will stand forth as one of his main contributions, something we will see and feel in his work intuitively without having to read about it.

The relationship between Cage's work and reality we can call "Cagean mimesis." Cage is of the generation of artists who, for the most part, did so-called "abstract expressionism." These artists most frequently rejected in their art the imitation of the static forms they saw around them; for this reason they allegedly rejected mimesis. But often they represented something about the world they felt—their realism was simply not photographic in any sense, though a few did photography, focusing on forms that in some way resembled their paintings. Cage took this a step further. He asked himself what reality was, and then demanded of his art that it behave as reality did. He asked that it resemble Nature, not in her passive form of being, *natura naturata* as Samuel Taylor Coleridge quoted it from Joachim de Fiore's *Liber Figurale*, but in her active mode of being, *natura naturans*. Other artists, Coleridge among them, just talked about such things: Cage showed us how to do it. The hidden symbolism in Cage's work is not formal but is part of the subject matter; "of what is this work symbolic?" is the implied question Cage seems to be asking of the implied receiver. For example, there are no repetitions in the typical Cagean piece. This goes with Cage's view of reality; it is chaotic, characteristically random. It is the principle that he, following the physicist Werner Heisenberg, calls "indeterminacy." It focuses upon a certain aspect of reality at least. No matter that there are other aspects of nature in which repetition and structure are characteristic — the shapes of healthy animal cells (cancerous ones would be more random and irregular), crystal lattices in mineralogy, for instance. These are static, *natura naturata*. Bach — Cage's pet peeve among composers (he once threatened to make a piece using Bach during which insurance salesmen would pass through the audience selling policies) — might be compared to a composer of cells or lattices. The vision Cage has perceived is the vision of the craziness that so often enriches our lives, the positive side of the unpredictable. This is what he shares with us and, if we hear his music correctly, what we will draw upon in years to come.

Finally, there is the social side of this. Cage's perceptions are inseparable from his views of human relationships and, on the macroscopic level, of society. He gives the fourth bass fiddler a graphic notation. It is different from any other music any other performer is playing in the concert. Nobody has done that before. Usually the fourth bass fiddler is just a cog in a system run by the conductor, who is at best a benevolent dictator, at worst a domestic tyrant. For the first time in his life the fourth bass fiddler sees the eyes of the world upon him.

He can't merge his sound into that of the whole, doing only as little as he thinks he can get away with before the conductor notices. For once the fourth bass fiddler is as important as the first violinist or trumpeter, is invited to rise to the occasion and to act nobly, to take the consequences for his actions in music as he, perhaps, might in his private life, and to contribute his utmost by offering his skill in good faith at the service of the piece.

This is how Cage's work is, in a major way, ethical and political. It exemplifies some spirit of generosity, perhaps of democracy, which can be admired by people of many different commitments, not just to other anarchists, as Cage has so often described himself being. The act of making music—or of reading his poetry—becomes a paradigmatic one. Some element of ethical and social consciousness on the part of the receiver must be involved in discovering Cage's perceptions in a given work. Cage's intentions are not particularly important. What counts is what we make of the process, assuming only our good will. One is reminded of Immanuel Kant's categorical imperative, which also, at its basis, relies upon good will, and Kant lies behind Coleridge, also a theoretically and philosophically inclined artist, whom Cage, curiously, resembles. Can we use the work, that is, its process, to make our thoughts and feelings more harmonious? To become closer to our own real nature? One is tempted to say, "to our Buddha nature," but there is no need to go so far from our Western traditions in order to understand what Cage is doing. Cage may have drawn some of his ideas from Japan, but, as I remarked earlier, he took them away to his own space, and, in the process, they were assimilated and translated, if not necessarily transformed.

Thus, if a work is not to be a mere face of a dead jewel, if we are to accept as aesthetically valid if not logically binding the Cagean vision of a world without repetition, then it also follows not only that each work of art must create its own form, one that is neither repeated nor imitated from previous art works, but that its way of doing this must be unique. His art is always beginning, never just continuing. Cage does not demand that all art do this, but he makes it a characteristic of his own art. We, his audience, may or may not be concerned with the ideas he has placed behind this process, but we may well enjoy the vision of a sort of endless metaphysical primavera or spring, one in which beginning is all that ever happens, up to the moment of cessation, which is the other thing implied by such a vision—after all, the piece won't remain in performance forever, even if, in some sense, it projects out of the edges of its canvas or its moment in time. Birth and death are quite enough subject matter for his focus.

This also implies a sort of anti-historicism in the sense that it inherently rejects precedent. The musician will ruin the performance if he alludes on some predetermined basis to pieces he already knows. This would, of course, be all right, if the musician were performing on a radio, and if the radio were monitoring some music that simply happened to be in the air at the time. One can't predict what a radio will monitor, if anything. It may be silent, as Sidney Cowell, Henry Cowell's widow, recalls was mostly the case in the now-legendary first performance of *Radio Music for 1-8 Radio Players* (1956), which happened too late, at the end of a long concert, to pick up much music from the broadcast waves. But radios are a medium, and they do not choose what they play. On the other hand, the musician who, in playing Cage, decides to play some phrase that is recognizably from Richard Strauss, for instance, will break the whole fabric of the piece; the phrase, however beautiful in its original context, will sound startlingly wrong and, ultimately, it makes fun not of the piece but of the musician himself. The musician will seem not to be witty but to be copping out. The best Cagean musician, on the other hand, becomes less of a willful entity; he or she seems at one with the surrounding sound environment, contributing whatever is played out of a spirit of generosity, invisibly filtering out only any music he happens to have known all his life. This musician becomes more like a medium than a performer as such; the work happens through him or her more than that he or she performs it. In this way the musician, paradoxically, becomes somehow more than he or she was.

v. Thank You, John

Is this too much to ask of a musician? Has it happened— meaning to achieve the kind of music he has said he intended, or that I have described—that Cage has failed and has made just another kind of traditional piece, dependent for its success on the glamor and charisma of the participants? Perhaps, but I do not think so. Of course, it will take many years before the verdict is in on this matter. The subject cannot really be discussed until the middle of the next century, and few of us who ponder this today are likely to be on hand for the discussion.

However, the nature of the pieces is to be as they have been made: they are less subject to a tradition of interpretation than, let us say, Tchaikovsky's *First Piano Concerto,* the beginning of which the composer intended should be calm, lyrical, and jewel-like, but which almost all performers make as loud and grand as possible. Why? Because with most of the pieces each musician's realization is different, deliberately so. The musician is very unlikely to imitate his predecessors. Thus, no repetitive tradition builds up. One need only compare the various recordings of Cage's keyboard pieces—the different realizations of the *Amores* (1943) or the various sets of *Variations* (1958-66), for instance—to see what I mean.

Finally, Cage's very effort is of interest—a noble endeavor, indeed, designed to bring us beyond the limits of our mental noses and into the world of the fragrance of sound itself, to be synesthetic about it. That effort is bound to be some kind of landmark, whatever else becomes of it. One is reminded that Friedrich Schiller's "Ode to Joy" with its paean to human brotherhood, set to music in Beethoven's *Ninth Symphony,* never prevented any wars or even colonial conquests, but, as a vision of better possibilities, it worked and haunted the whole nineteenth century.

Furthermore, having attempted to perform in a Cagean way has an irreversible tendency to lodge in the ongoing consciousness of a musician, to affect him or her permanently. After playing a major work of Cage, when a pianist then plays Mozart by some open window, he finds himself passively watching his fingers while his mind relates actively instead to the traffic noises of the street, to making counterpoints with automobile motors or with birds. It is as if playing Cage opened windows in the other music one had played. So it was with myself as a very young man, and so it seems to be with many another young person who has tried to mix the two. Just as Bach sounds different after experiencing Mozart, Mozart after Mahler, Mahler after Debussy, all of them sound beautiful but different after Cage, even after those great pre-chance works of Cage's, such as the *Six Melodies for Violin and Keyboard* (1950), the *String Quartet in Four Parts* (1950), the *Sonatas and Interludes* (1946-48) and other keyboard works, some for prepared piano and some for—what should we call it?—"unprepared piano." We did not know that it was "unprepared" until we heard the prepared one; that is what I mean by our consciousness changing from knowing Cage's pieces well. After all, those early pieces do not use chance, but they do use structural means which seem found, perceived, invented rather than composed. Cage's use of chance merely brings to a head a current of his work that had gone on since the earliest percussion pieces, since the *Imaginary Landscape Nos. 1 to 3* (1939-42) (there are others of these, but they are different), or *First Construction (in Metal)* (1939).

It takes a great deal to change the ears of modern receivers. Our children have heard more kinds of music than Mozart heard in his whole life. We have access to more works than many a musicologist did at the beginning of this century. Perhaps we are not jaded, but we are certainly in danger of becoming so. Thus, suddenly to have among us an artist whose aim in his music is somehow to let us hear things freshly and simply, whose poetry activates space in ways that invite us to rethink how lines mean things, who challenges us to join him in composing what he has seen, to look hard at the world around us and ask, not what we can make of it but what it wants to be—this is a gift indeed. It does not matter, finally, to what precise extent the attempt is successful: art need not succeed to make its point. The attempt is more important.

One can only say, as Sidney Cowell did in a beautiful anecdotal radio work she made for Cage's seventy-fifth birthday celebration in Cologne, after knowing Cage for some 54 of those years, and recollecting moments in her and Henry Cowell's experience of him— "Thank you, John."

IX. Early Sound Poetry

IT IS NOT SURPRISING that early sound poetry from before 1900, to choose an arbitrary point to begin this exploration, is less commonly found than early visual poetry, of which some 1,400 or so examples exist. Sound poetry, in order to become an art form, tends to need the option of not simply a sophisticated audience, but also the various possibilities of potential recording. Before 1900 the rarity of graphic printing techniques needed to realize complex notations—offset printing and camera work—combined with the lack of recording processes—phonographs and tape recorders—meant the potential sound poet would have to depend on more or less improvised notations. In our discussion we will not deal with ethnopoetic sound poetries—chants and the various similar options that were and are available to people operating under the most non-technological conditions. I have discussed these ethnopoetic materials in my article "Points towards a Taxonomy of Sound Poetry" (1981:49-59), and Eugene Jolas's "From 'Jabberwocky' to 'Lettrism'" (1948:104-20) also covers some of this ground. Our discussion will deal, rather, with sound poetry as a conscious art form, distinct, for instance, from nonsense poetry. It is the intermedial form parallel to visual poetry, which lies between visual art and poetry; sound poetry lies between music and poetry, and depends upon this acoustic element for its formal and aesthetic sense.

In this way sound poetry is somewhat different from some kinds of nonsense poetry, since the category includes materials that have no correspondence with the normative world, which is not true of all sound poetry. That is, there may be considerable sense or logic in the acoustic structuring of a sound poem, while much of nonsense verse deliberately rejects logic or sense except in its own universe. In fact, nonsense verse tropes upon the conceived contrast between what we know and what we are hearing. But this is a semantic element. In nonsense verse, the ludic spirit is inherent in this contrast, as in, for example, Noam Chomsky's famous example of an "illegal statement"—"colorless green ideas sleep furiously"—in which each idea that is introduced is, in some way, at odds with what went before it. The Chomsky remark may have some poetic value of its own, but that value is semantic, dependent upon meaning of some kind.

In sound poetry, on the other hand, the sound generates its own sense through its patterns and by their reference to our experience. The most obvious area of this sort is in onomatopoetic lyrics to songs, such as the animal imitations in *Le Marriage Forcé* (1671) by Marc-Antoine Charpentier (ca. 1635-1704), or the Marinetti-like imitation of battle sounds in an early chanson, in "La Guerre: La Bataille de Marignan" (ca. 1549) by Clément Jannequin (ca. 1500-ca. 1555). Such musical works extend the onomatopoeia of the lyrics, but they are not really sound poetry until they can exist as autonomous pieces, apart from the music that goes with them.

In the great cultural fermentation that took place in the sixteenth and seventeenth centuries, with the sense that the old forms were dead or dying and long live the new ones, at least some speculation was devoted to the making of new forms we would call sound poetry. The pieces had a name, "tautograms," and they were often made by the same poets who did visual poetry, thus the relevance of my earlier theoretical digression that points out the analogy between sound poetry and visual. For example, sound poetry passages appear in the *Pegnesisches Schäfergedicht* (1644), in Harsdorffer (1966), composed as a collaboration between Georg Philipp Harsdorffer (1607-58), Sigmund von Birken (1626-81), and Johann Klaj [Klajus] (1616-56), such as this passage by Klaj: "Die kekke Lachengekekk koaxet/krakkt/ und quakkt." This onomatopoetic passage evokes a similar passage in "The Frogs" of Aristophanes (fourth century B.C.E.)—"Brekk kekk koax koak . . . " Basically, in the *Pegnisisches Schäfergedicht*, poets meet in some undefined rural situation, in a pastoral setting, and share the fruits of their poetical experience. They perform their poems for each other, they offer each other *poèmes d'occasion* that are visual pieces — garlands, cups, and the like — and they make poems relating to the rural environment in which the action of the poem cycle takes place. This is not far from the world described in Ruth Katz's essay "On 'Nonsense' Syllables as Oral Group Notation" (1974), which correctly points out the function of nonsense passages in musical rituals of all kinds. But its purpose is ultimately different, since it is self-consciously concerned with exploring new artistic means. The world of magical incantations and such-like is, again, another similar but different area, as discussed in Alfred Liede's massive *Dichtung als Spiel* (1963, 1:256-78). The purpose of magic is not to provide an aesthetic experience but to cause something to happen, in which the aesthetic element may be a part but is not the major purpose of the performance of the magical event. The appearance of sound poetry is not unique, however, to renaissance and baroque Europe. In India, for example, such interludes constitute a recognized genre in Sanskrit literature, the "yamakas," which can be translated roughly as "chimes" (per Jha [1975:45-52]). A discussion of this genre in relation to Western poetry is in Lienhard's "Enigmatisk vers och carmina figurata i sanskritdiktning" (1983). Also Tuwim (1950:5) gives an example from the Kavya Darsa of Dandin (seventh century C.E.).

One thing all these pieces have in common is that they are notated for performance, with little responsibility given to the performer, as in modern sound poetry. The earliest extant example is by Quintus Ennius (239-168 B.C.E.), in the *Annals* (ca. 201-168), fragment 109, printed in Warmington's *Remains of Old Latin* (1967, 1:36): "0 Tite tute, tati tibi tanta tyranne tulisti!" By stretching the grammar, one can translate this as: "You to yourself, Titus Tatius the tyrant, you took these terrible troubles!" But the point of the outburst is not its semantic sense but its madcap sound. The vowels vary, but the consonants do not: this is the very essence of a "tautogram." The genre did not disappear with the ancient world, however. A long piece in iambic hexameters by Hugobald the

Benedictine (ninth century) appears in Juan Caramuel's *Metametrica* (1663, sec.193:106-7), in which all the words begin with "C" and in which musical sense is high while semantic is minimal. Iacobus Nicholai de Dacia (late fourteenth century; see Figure 1) provides another example in his *Liber de distinccione metrorum* of 1363 (in Iacobus [1963:150]), a series of very playful meditations upon death:

> Morsterit, hunc refit/hunc grauat/hunc cauat, hunc populatur;
> Hic ruit/hic luit, hic tacet/hic iacet, hic lacrimatur;
> Hunc rigat, hunc ligat/hunc secat/hunc necat vicere diro;
> Hunc tegit, hunc regit/hunc vocat/hunc Iocat ordine miro;
> Hunc tremit/hic gemit/hic olet/hic dolet, iste senescit;
> Hic latet/hic patet/hic meat/hic screat, ille putrescit;
> Hic abit/hic stabit/hic riget/hic piget vitro manere;
> Hic strepit/hic crepit/hic cauet/hic pauet ista videre;
> Hunc vorat/hunc forat/hunc petit/hunc metit ense cruoris;
> Hunc capit/hunc rapit/hunc plicate/hunc fricat vngue furoris.

Another example, by the Portuguese poet Manuel de Faria e Sousa (1590-1649), appears in the "Century II" in Askins (1983).

> Procuras, Pecador, Pan provechoso?
> Para prepetuarte Paz procuras?
> Pretended pot Pastor primas pasturas?
> Pides para passar Panal precioso ...

On the one hand, here, we have the alliterative; on the other hand, note the interplay between the P's, R's, T's, and S's.

A short bibliography of such pieces appears in Canel's *Recherches sur les Jeux d'Esprit* . . . (1867, 2:141-44), but the largest collection and discussion appears in a work already mentioned, the *Metametrica* (1663) of Juan Caramuel de Lobkowitz (1606-82). Caramuel is best remembered as the Cistercian monk who was in charge of evaluating the condition and repair of buildings belonging to his order. In this capacity he traveled throughout Roman Catholic areas of

Europe. One of the great experts of his time on church architecture, his books on this subject are still consulted occasionally. However, the *Metametrica* and its sequel are utterly different from his other books. The *Metametrica* is both a poetics and an anthology of interesting language art pieces. Beginning with a traditional description of language and a normative Latin grammar, the *Metametrica* develops speculations on language and linguistic art, proposes a new language (that is monosyllabic like Chinese but that uses a simple grammar like that of English), and suggests all manner of new visual and sound poetries. Additionally, the *Metametrica* proposes cylindrical poems that would have no end, spherical and cubical poems, and so on. He even includes a simple tautogram of his own—"Lex, rex, rex, spes, spes ius . . . " (1663, sec.518:np).

During his time at Rome, Caramuel was part of a circle that may have included Andreas Bayam, a Portuguese monk from Goa in India, who made a book of heart-shaped poems (see Bayam [1624]). Another book by Bayam, the *Panegyricus sine Verbis* . . . (1629) gives instructions for an elaborate wordless performance. The circle definitely included Francesco Passerini (1612-95), who included Caramuel's chessboard-like poem, "Ama Fama," in his *Schedarium Liberale* . . . (1659:177) along with a nonverbal poetic maze (216). More work has to be done on this circle, clearly; the only available discussion is by Giovanni Pozzi in his *La Parola Dipinta* (1981:90). Another collection of pieces of this sort is in the anonymous *Das ABC cum notis variorum* . . . (1703, 2:210 ff.). Elsewhere in Europe similar pieces were being done. For example, Hermannus de Santa Barbara (seventeenth century) includes a long tautogram that starts, "Salvae scriba sacer supremae, slusiae sedis . . . " in his *Carmelo-Parnassus* (1687:1-14).

At the other conceptual extreme, using extremely informal structures but a non-semantic language, are pieces like the following, "A lo mismo," by Luis Gongora y Argote (1561-1627) in Gongora (1921, 2:242-43):

Algualete, hejo
Del Senor Alà
 Ha, ha, ha.
Haz, vuesa merc:
Zaiema i zalà,
 Ha, ha, ha.
Bailà, Mahamu, baila
 Falala laila
Tana el zambra la jauena
 Falala laila
Que el amor del nenio me mata,
 Me maita
 Falala laila.

1. Aungue entre el mulae il vaquilio
 Nacer en este pajar.
0 estrelias mentir, 0 estar
Califa, vos chequetilio.
2. Choton, no Ioiga el cochilio
De quel Herodo, marfuz,
Que maniana hasta el cruz
En sangre estaras vermejo,
 Algualefe, hejo
 Del Senor Ala,
  Ha ha ha.
1. Se del terano nemego
Oies, vozanzed, el rabia,
Roncon tener io en Arabia
Con el pasa e con el hego.
2. Io ester xeque. Se commengo,
Andar, monteca, seniora,
Mel vos e serua madora
Comeras senior el vejo
 Algueiete, hejo
 Sel Senor Ala,
 Ha, ha, ha.

This poem, composed around 1615, is not specifically a tautogram, like the Latin pieces discussed. Rather, it is a type of sound-based improvisation. The poem evokes an Arabic milieu, not just by the references to "Señor Ala," or the Arabian reference, but in its other exotic sounds as well. It attempts to evoke as much as possible without depending overly on the sense of the words. It also prefigures one of the best known early pieces of our own century, "Le t'aime (kikakoku)" by Paul Scheerbart (1863-1915) from the *Roman de Chemin de Fer* (1900). What both pieces share is a sort of glossolalia or talking in tongues. The speaker seems inspired and, by releasing himself from the need to mean anything substantive, the language starts to live a life of its own. This is true on the intuitive level of those few surviving pieces from the American Shakers, a community that rejected art as a godless distraction from the spiritual life, but which individual Shakers continued to perform, albeit feeling guilty for their own frivolity. A few Shaker pieces and descriptions of others, which were performed for themselves at quiet times of the day in private, not just as public rituals, resemble sound poems, described in Andrews (1967:72).

Finally, there is a sort of hybrid sound poetry that is neither formally tautogram nor improvisation, but that treads the fine line between sound poetry and the semantic, a sort of highly refined nonsense poetry, written as it were in an invented dialect. This is the case with an interesting genre of material that has come down from late medieval France, the "fatras." Here is an anonymous, untitled fatras from Porter (1960:160), quoted from the (Paris) "Bibliothèque Nationale Nouv. Acq. No. 4237, ff. 29r and 29v."

Item autre taille de fatras ents
Or gardes mieulx vos gelines
Que Rembourc ne fist son coc.
       Fatras
Or gardes mieulx vos gelines
Que trois grues orphelines

N'ont fait l'asne de l'Escot,
Qui a encusé par signes
Le premier cop de matines
Qui s'endormait en un noc
Et quant il fu mat d'un rot
Il abatises volsines,
Puis leur vendy par racroc
Son chat plus de trois poitevines
Que Rembourc ne fist son coc.

Again, what is striking here is not the nonsense but the sense. The same is true of such pieces as the sections in an invented German by Andreas Gryphius (1616-64), in *Die gelibte Dornrose. Schertz-Spil* (1647), or the similar passages in made-over French in the "tragicomedy" *Oriselle* (first performed in 1631 and published in 1633) by a certain C. Chabrol, of whom not even a first name is known. Turning to more familiar ground, made-up language was certainly common enough—it was done, in the nineteenth century, by Goethe and, at the end of our period, on a larger scale by Stefan Georg, who invented a hybrid romance language named "lingua romana" and wrote a few pieces in it.

But the sound poem in the nineteenth century is not so intriguing as the fatras, the Spanish piece, or the tautograms. There are Victor Hugo's djinns and trains, the "Chanson du Rayon de Lune" of Guy de Maupassant (1850-93), or that school-child favorite by Robert Southey (1774-1823), "The Cataract of Lodore," in which an enormous chain of participles describing how water might behave is used to evoke the water's passage. To quote but a fragment, from Southey (1884, 2:69-73):

... The cataract strong
The plunges along,
Striking and raging
As if a war waging
Its caverns and rocks among;

Rising and leaping,
   Sinking and creeping,
 Swelling and seeping,
   Showering and springing,
 Flying and flinging,
 Writhing and wringing,
 Eddying and whisking,
 Spouting and frisking,
Turning and twisting
 Around and around
With endless rebound;
 Smiting and fighting,
 A sight to delight in;
Confounding, astounding,
Dizzying and deafening the ear with its sound . . .

This may not be first-rate poetry, but it is not altogether far from its earlier heritage in the tautogram. Thus, though it cannot be said that sound poetry was really common before our century, the few surviving pieces do not deserve their more or less total neglect. One thing we shall never know, of course, is the style of performance intended to go with the pieces, especially the tautograms. These seem designed for performance, not merely for reading to oneself. But how was it done? The old books of poetics do not go into any great depth on tautograms, even when they mention them. Was one to perform in a subdued manner? A formal one? A personal one? What was considered appropriate? What were the styles of performance that were used for them? It would be wonderful to think that there might have survived, in some attic, a description of a performance by Caramuel or Bayam. It is the missing element in our coming to understand these old pieces. One can hope for such a discovery, because until then it is as if we were confronted by only a part of the thing, like the shell of a sea creature after the animal has gone.

X. The Golem in the Text

ANY OLD POEM CAN HAVE ITS MUSIC, just as any poem that is drawn, written, printed has its look. The study of this is "ekphrasis," and it is a useful area of inquiry, one that is being widely investigated today. Recently there was an issue of *Visible Language* devoted to it, and several of the panels at this summer's *Word + Image* conference at Zürich include papers on the subject.

But not all poems are illuminated by being described as "visual poems" or "sound poems." These terms should be reserved for pieces in which the work is as much visual or acoustic as literary or even all three of these, works that are truly intermedial. But among the intermedial poetries one sees that the works do not all behave the same way. A visual poem, whether a modern piece or a thousand-year-old pattern poem, is like visual art: it is seen all at once, one can let the eye return to a part of it, and though, like a painting, it can be read, there is always the potential for simultaneity, for seeing it all at once. It approaches, though it never quite achieves, an independence of time, perfect instantaneity. One sees its visual part when one first sees the text; the words seem somehow to fill the text in. The interaction of the two is usually easy to identify.

Sound poetry, on the other hand, needs *time* to reveal it— time to hear it and, like other poetries that are *not* intermedial, time to let the words enter the mind, by the eye and the ear, letting eye and ear penetrate into oneself, slowly discovering whatever is the essence of the piece. Thus it is that with a sound poem, a poem in which the sound or acoustic element is as much a part of the work as its semantic sense, it can be difficult to feel close to a notated work in which there are scored complexities, where the eye is asked to use its esemplastic, image-making function to deduce the presumed sounds of the piece. The reader tends to see the notation as a visual entity, to admire it and say to himself or herself, "This looks interesting. I will come back to it later when there is more time." Of course that moment seldom comes. Thus, one might offer a caveat to the poet who is making a sound poem that requires a complex notation of some kind—words scattered on a page, multiple voices to be sounded together, unfamiliar sounds and pitches—that he or she should not think of the notated version of the piece as the definitive one, while at the same time it should be clear that a notation can be useful if others are to make realizations of the poem, to see what they can bring to it, things the poet may not have thought of. Such works, it should be mentioned here, are known as "text-sound" pieces.

But let us think of a great traditional dramatic performance; more or less any will do. What the actor or actress does is to bring out something already living in the text, letting it come alive in some new way. The words are not just themselves. The performer may be a bore apart from the performance. But the performer is a medium, and the words are haunted by a ghost who comes to possess the performer, a sort of golem perhaps, who takes over and consumes the text. Olivier as Henry V, Brando in *On the Waterfront*, here the haunted actor is greater than the sum of his parts, than either Brando or Olivier (actors but mere mortals) or the simple character (a cipher on a page). The magic comes from the phenomenon of haunting, of the interaction between the performer and the piece generating a new identity. The process of haunting takes us beyond what we had thought were the possibilities of a story or a poem and into a process of comparing what we see with what we had imagined.

Think also of a puppet, especially of a complex one, a marionette. We see the doll limp on the wall. What might it do? Then it comes to life. We compare what we see with what we know and what we imagine; the puppet comments by its terms of existence on what we know and what we imagine. This is why puppet theater is so useful for satire. It is also why, for a puppeteer, the essence of puppetry, like that of dance, is movement. We can see from the limp puppet what the thing looks like, but the art begins when it moves, when it does something unexpected, with graces and styles we could not have anticipated.

Thus it is also with sound poetry. The poem can have a non-semantic text, but its structure may rest with its sound; no, it *will* be with its sound. A poet can read his text and try to make it completely unstructured, but in vain. It will always be the poet's voice and the time of the performance. The poet cannot make the piece have happened the day before, nor can he or she suddenly become someone else reading it. Even if the poem is performed by a mechanical sound system—a tape recorder or a record—it is still being performed by a tape or a record. Thus, a truly unstructured piece is not among the options with a sound poem.

But the sound poem can do something else that is not obvious until one stops to think about it a while. That is, it too can play upon its nature as performance and do what the drama performances have been mentioned as doing. That is, it can generate a golem from within itself who can possess the performer in the mind of the listener.

This golem need not be a frightening creature. I prefer the word to "ghost" as being less loaded with supernatural associations for most of us. A golem is, after all, a homunculus in Jewish folklore, endowed with life by its maker. I can cite two examples of the process.

Meredith Monk's "Song from the Hills," a vocal piece, was performed in Milwaukee by her in 1977. In it she includes the sounds of cattle calling and street selling from long ago, digested and made her own. Her normal voice, both for speaking and singing, is rich and mellifluous, as those who know her records can attest. But here it was consistently tiny, nasal, shrill. What happened is that the piece we heard less as text ("Mikni minnikminni . . . " is not semantically rich) or music (as an *a cappella* piece with sliding tones it was not traditionally musical) than as a delightful process of character revelation—not Monk's character but that of a spirit, a golem—that lived only in her piece. What did its appearance suggest? A child, a rural spirit, a farm person by turns, someone half remembered but somehow familiar. One hoped the piece would last long, so one could watch the golem exist.

Another example is found in any typical work by Henri Chopin when he performs it live. He uses non-representational sounds of voice and microphone, and usually works by playing at least two tracks of highly complex recorded sound—often electronically manipulated and usually quite loud—over which he works, using voice and microphone, exploring the possibilities that can be generated. To help the audience concentrate on what he is doing, he works in semi-darkness with a spotlight on himself. He happens to be a small man, but he has great intensity. The result is that he seems to grow and grow and grow, to become a giant, and, because of the seriousness of his manner he suggests a vampire or a threatening spirit. The process by which this spirit emerges from his performance can be quite terrifying. Noticing the emergence was not akin to the naive viewer of an abstract painting, let us say, who says: "Oh, that piece of paint reminds me of my dog," because simply pointing to the possible resemblances holds a viewer in close connection with his or her memory and blinds him or her to what is actually being said, thus producing banality. Why? It is because the process is non-mimetic, based on something the performance artist, in this case Chopin, is actually doing. The emergence is inherent in the effective live performance of the material.

Of course, other personae can emerge from sound poetry, too, but these two brief examples will, I think, suffice. Something surprising about the appearance of these haunting golems is that they have been so little commented upon, for all that they are so obvious. After all, sound poetry is a form of performance poetry, like dance, drama, and puppetry. It is not just a hybrid of abstract acoustics and words but is art work in which the artist must take the responsibility for all the possibilities offered in a given piece. The artist is, among other things, an explorer of potentials. This or that element of a work can do this or that, and the artist, in realizing the work, brings out some of these.

XI. The Origin of "Happening"

IN THE LATE 1950s all the avant-garde arts tended increasingly to fuse, as artists explored new media. Visual artists such as Allan Kaprow made extensive collages, using machines, mirrors that reflected the spectators, and, ultimately, live performers. Kaprow realized he needed a term to describe what was obviously developing into a new art form, and he called it a *happening*, because, as he later told me when I asked about it, "I didn't know what else to call it, and my piece was something that was just supposed to happen naturally." Precisely when the term was first used is unclear; probably it was employed in April, 1957, when Kaprow gave a demonstration of one of his collage performances for a group of fellow artists, students, and critics at the farm of the sculptor George Segal near New Brunswick, New Jersey. The first public use of the term, however, was in the Winter 1958 issue of *Anthologist*, the undergraduate literary magazine of Rutgers University, where Kaprow was teaching at the time. In it, some of Kaprow's students published the scenario for a very ambitious (and still unperformed) happening, "The Demiurge," above the text of which appears the caption: "Something to take place: a happening."

Not long thereafter Kaprow became involved in setting up a cooperative art gallery in New York, the Reuben Gallery, most members of which had already become known through their associations with the earlier Hansa Gallery. Many of these artists, once Kaprow had blazed the trail, went on to do happenings themselves, notably James Dine, Robert Whitman, and, later, Claes Oldenburg. Kaprow's first happening in the new space, "18 Happenings in Six Parts," described in Michael Kirby's book *Happenings* (New York: Dutton, 1965), caused a sensation in the art world, and the form was widely imitated by such diverse artists as Jean-Jacques Lebel in France, Wolf Vostell and Joseph Beuys in Germany, and T. Kube in Japan. Others coming from different backgrounds saw how Kaprow's term at least partially described their work, and so, even though they did not use visual-arts collages or environments for their performances, they did not hesitate (to Kaprow's delight) to use the term. Thus it happened that musical composers such as Benjamin Patterson, Nam June Paik (now best known for his video-synthesizer sculptures), and I called what we did *happenings,* at least for a while. Other artists did analogous works, but used different terms in order to differentiate themselves from their colleagues: *orgiastic mystical theater* (Hermann Nitsch), *kinetic theater events* (Carrollee Schneemann), *total theater* (Ben Vautier). But the public quickly came to call all such performances *happenings*. The term also began to appear in odd places. Jack Kerouac refers to me in one of his writings of the time as "the Happenings man." Some off-off-Broadway theater productions took advantage of what seemed to be a faddish new term by promoting themselves as happenings.

Because so many artists of various kinds were doing happenings, there appeared to be a happenings movement, and careless writers throughout the 1960s tried to define one. However, the differences among happenings artists were as striking as their similarities. Within the happenings format there was room for the ultra-precise and controlled works that I did, for the lyrical but still very controlled imagistic style of Kaprow and the visual artists, and for the almost unbounded imagistic improvisation of Jean-Jacques Lebel and Al Hansen. This last kind of work caught the journalistic eye; thus, the public came to think of all happenings as wild, irrational free-for-alls, so that by the mid-1960s most happenings artists had either to qualify their use of the term or to find another one.

A complete bibliography from the heyday of happenings would be quite extensive, but the primary texts can be mentioned briefly. My book *Postface* (1964) was the first, followed by Michael Kirby's *Happenings* (1965). Kirby, now the head of the School of Performing Arts at New York University, also edited a "happenings" issue of the *Tulane Drama Review* (Winter 1965). His book deals only with happenings by visual artists associated with the Reuben Gallery, but the magazine includes other sorts of happening, especially "events" (a genre of mini-happenings pioneered by George Brecht, Bob Watts, and others associated with the Fluxus group of experimental artists). The next major happenings books were Al Hansen's *Primer of Happenings and Time/Space Art* (1965), a sort of do-it-yourself popularization that had much to do with the modishness of happenings in the late 1960s, and Wolf Vostell and Jürgen Becker's *Happenings und Pop* Art (1966), the first international anthology and still the best overall source, though published only in German. Finally, Hanns Sohm and Harald Szeemann's massive *happening & Fluxus* (1970) is a chronology and bibliography, profusely illustrated, of the happenings and Fluxus artists.

Initially there was a good deal of resistance to defining *happening,* lest a definition prove restrictive, but here is a sampling of early attempts:

> *Allan Kaprow:* events which, put simply, happen ["'Happenings' in the New York Scene," *Art News* (May 1961:39)]; an art form similar to theater in that it takes place in a specific time and a specific location. Its structure and its content are a logical extension of the [performance] environment. [undated, circa 1965? In Vostell and Becker (1966:46)].

> *Claes Oldenburg:* the term invented by Allan Kaprow loosely used to refer to my ... work and [that of] others in a medium one way or another expanding the material of the artist to include events in time and people. [undated, circa 1962? in Sohm and Szeemann (1970) inside front cover].

> *Al Hansen:* a collage of situations and events occurring over a period of time in space [in Hansen (1966:24)].

> *Michael Kirby:* a purposefully composed form of theater in which diverse alogical elements, including nonmatrixed performing, are organized in a compartmented structure [in Kirby (1965:21)].

Dick Higgins: all the various performance forms in which the emphasis is placed not on who does a particular thing or why, but on, simply, what gets done [1966, in Sohm and Szeemann (1970) inside back cover].

Wolf Vostell: staged or improvised occurrence; phases of reality. Preparation of facts, theories, dreams untied to a specific kind of space; but at various places in the city [in Sohm (1970:46)].

Except for Kirby's definition, which is better worked out than the others, these attempts show the beginnings, when everyone agreed what a happening was, even if nobody knew how to verbalize it.

Other than a passing use of *happening* attributed to the writings of the Bauhaus artist Lazlo Moholy-Nagy, Kaprow's use of the word is the first in a special artistic sense. But its currency in art resulted in its widespread misapplication to a variety of staged situations or as a fashionable term for almost any event:

"Mealtime happenings are only part of the fun." [Italian Line cruise advertisement, 1965].

"Hoving Invites Public to 'Happening' in Park" [*New York Times* (26 May 1966:49)].

"HAPPENING / Basket ball at 7:00 PM on FRIDAY" [sign on a post-office door, 1967].

"The library hosts a broad range of community 'happenings' that range from jazz concerts to legislative reports." [Dorothy Humel, "Libraries—Las Vegas Style," *Library Journal* (1 June 1973:1780)].

"Dali recently presented a happening in Granolas with Kaisic Wong, creator of Oriental fantasy fashions, and Steve Arnold, underground movie director, both from San Francisco."

[*Women's Wear Daily*, (3 September 1974:16)].
"It's also nice *not to be* able to look up what's coming next (the virtue of no texts): everything on the tape comes as a surprise, and you listen hard so as not to miss a word. It's rather like a happening, with all the virtues and defects of that modern art form." [*New York Times Book Review* (6 April 1975:37)].

The term is not entirely meaningless, even today, but the art work it now covers is very different from what it once included. Surprise, though possible, was never particularly integral in the happening, but to the author of the last quotation it is. As *happening* came into general usage, it ceased to be useful as a technical term for artists. Many of us have regretted the loss. I tried to avoid the error of using a word that was too adaptable, such as *happening*, by my coinage *intermedia* (in Higgins, "Intermedia," *Something Else Newsletter*, February 1966, with a nod to Samuel Taylor Coleridge, who used the word in a lecture once in 1812 but who never systematically developed the concept).[36] *Intermedia* covers those art forms that are conceptual hybrids between two or more traditional media, such as concrete poetry (visual art and poetry), happenings (visual art, music, and theater), and sound poetry (music and literature). The term is sufficiently technical in effect that, though it has enjoyed some popular use, it is still applied only to the arts and, except for some careless confusion with "mixed media" (in which the elements remain distinct though simultaneous), is usually applied in my original sense. The curious evolution of *happening* shows that an artist who needs a new term ought to use a word that sounds technical, if possible one made from classical morphemes. It is now too late for *happening* as a precise term. What we need is a word that can be used to cover the following, which I offer as a definition (based on Kirby's) of the word as the happenings artists understood it:

A form of theatrical composition begun in the late 1950s, rejecting all narrative logic and all forms of stages in favor of maximum exploitation of the performance environment, lyrical performing elements within a matrixed structure, and an overall synthesis of music, literature, and the visual arts.

XII. The Importance of Caravaggio

About This Piece

The Importance of Caravaggio is intended to accompany an action by Alison Knowles. As one of the originators of Happenings and Fluxus, and one who particularly enjoys involving himself with the aesthetic underpinnings of those movements, I have based my lecture only partially on Caravaggio. The alternate focus tries to offer insight into our perception of the modern. Bringing the historic dimension periodically to the fore is crucial in emphasizing the overlaps between the concretism of the new arts and that of Caravaggio. Caravaggio's rejection of the Roman stress on *disegno* in favor of working direct from life and "nature," and his *arte senza arte* parallel the new arts' assumption of an art vs. life dichotomy, implicit in the concept of "anti-art." Additional parallels exist. Elements of Caravaggio's iconography bear an affinity to the imagery of many recent art works (for example, there is a strong affinity between *St. John in the Desert* and Geoffrey Hendricks's performance piece *La Capra*). Caravaggio's shift after 1600 towards the art of idea, embodied in religious painting, anticipates our art of idea, embodied in concept, minimal and schematic or structural art. I do not suggest that Caravaggio is the unique, first proto-modern of the recent avant-garde. By presenting parallels, I hope to bring Caravaggio's activity as a painter into an unexpected relation to the activities of those involved in the new arts.

We believe that we understand what is natural;
but the miracle is extremely natural, and the natural is extremely miraculous.

—Arnold Schoenberg, in "Gustav
Mahler"

Who says Caravaggio's too dramatic to be
real? One evening a friend of mine said something to that effect. The night was clear. Rain
was expected. Outside my window, farmers
were haying by tractor light, doing their best
to rush the hay off the field before the storm.
Seen in chiaroscuro, they looked as dramatic
as anything Caravaggio ever painted. I said
nothing. I pointed to the men at work.

The Youth with a Bowl of Fruit is possibly a self-
portrait. The young man is not elegant. He
would look utterly out of place in a work by
Titian or Raphael or Botticelli; even
Michelangelo would send him away, if only
to work out in a gym for a few months before
painting him. Not Caravaggio, who prefers
life in the raw, prefers to paint what he sees.
He rejects the Platonic idea in favor of the
Democritan concept. He atomizes—deals with
the broken and the particular, not the virginal
and the general. Caravaggio's treatment of
Christian myth runs counter to prevailing
attitudes. Myths as myths need no embellish-
ing, no prettifying. Caravaggio refuses to allow an assumed meaning to dominate his
response to myth. By displacing the allegorical focus, Caravaggio opens up that nexus of
power and delight central to myth's direct
appeal. He need no longer use details of ico-

nography to track a meaning lying outside the
formation of the visual imprint he wants to
create. Not every detail is required to add up
to inevitability.

David and Goliath —one of two versions. The
finer version, the taller, is at the Galleria
Borghese in Rome. The other, its picture plane
horizontally disposed, is at the Kunst-
historisches Museum in Vienna. In the latter
painting, David registers less enigmatically.
He has not calmed down after killing the
giant. He appears ready to toss the head he is
holding to some fishes somewhere. The giant's
head is less tired, less sensual. There is no
mystery here: it's a piece for a set.

The slides—sheets on a line, shoes in a group,
broken metal parts—they add up to a set.
They can be taught the facts of life—intruded
on physically, scorched or a transfer letter put
on them. The innocence of the photographer's
eyes—look but don't touch—is not required
of them.

St. Jerome—In his own age, St. Jerome was
celebrated for his caustic wit and scholarship.
The late Renaissance revered him as the
epitome of the ascetic. In stressing one dimension the age lost sight of others informing the
man and his teachings. Through Caravaggio's
myth-making process St. Jerome, with the
obligatory skull, becomes a poetic fiction, a
metaphor as much as a subject. Even here, all
is particularized. Note the coarseness of the
hands of Caravaggio's *St. Jerome*, the rough-
ness of the arm. There is no elegant, sensuous,

and painterly modeling. In spite of his halo,
this St. Jerome looks more like a garage me-
chanic than the patrician translator of the
Vulgate.

Giordano Bruno, Caravaggio's slightly older
contemporary, stresses divine frenzies—
"Furori." The concept comes from Plato's
Phaedrus, the great love and rhetoric dialogue.
Doesn't this philosophy typify Caravaggio's
activity as a painter? How much of the early
Baroque can be defined in terms of the decline
of Aristotelian classicism in the face of Platonist
fervor?

A connection can be made between things by
argument, by juxtaposition, or it can be made
physically with string. Who is to say which is
most profound?

St. Francis and the Angel—a better title for this
painting would be "the meaning of sleep."
The work is allegorical in our modern sense,
though not in a Neoplatonic one. Is St. Francis
sleeping or dead? How can he tell the difference?

Rope and muscle, cross and an old man, shoul-
der and push, light and dark, shiny and dull,
shovel and dirt and stone and inexplicable
cloth.

St. Catherine of Alexandria—Caravaggio shows
us an assemblage of emblematic objects—the
broken wheel, the palm which usually stands
for martyrdom, the sword at right angle to the
palm, St. Catherine projecting mystery, coy-

ness. Note her face, the lidless eyes, the long upper lip. We've seen it before: the young men in Caravaggio's earliest paintings; the *Medusa*, the *Young Man with Fruit*, the *Boy Bitten by a Lizard*. Did a man pose for this painting. What ironies are at work?

St. Peter in *The Crucifixion of St. Peter* has his eye on his arm, not on his crucifiers. He seems almost indifferent to the pain that he must be experiencing.

A hysterical response to pain is perhaps more typical of a suburban life style, for instance, than of a place where terrible pain is common, a concentration camp or a hospital. Here Caravaggio's realism goes beyond the normative conventions and assumptions of his age as well as of ours.

A man with a scythe—you can take him as a symbol of time or death, or you can take him as a gardener. Maybe the grass was simply too long for the ordinary mower and some scything was what was needed.

Places—universal or particular, unique or widespread. The Danish stock exchange, a garden in Japan, towers or rocks by the Baltic Sea. Except for a quick trip to Malta, Caravaggio never left Europe. What a shame he never got a close look at the mosques and madresas of Konya in Turkey, for instance. His locales are never as particularized as his people and objects.

Il Concerto Ideal (The Ideal Concert) is known for some reason or other to New Yorkers, in whose city the painting hangs, simply as *The Musicians*. The point is missed. It has many of Caravaggio's trademarks — un-aristocratic faces, so similar to each other as to suggest that the same model posed repeatedly, or that Caravaggio was obsessed by one particular face. In this as in other paintings, Caravaggio avoids making drawings, going straight to the canvas to work, making changes and corrections on it instead of preparing *disegni*. Scumbled brushwork — in the lutenist's sash, for example — gives the cloth a remarkably sheer look. The damaged leaves in the fruit are emblems of nature's imperfection. For Caravaggio, as for Shakespeare, nothing is perfect; art is a means of extending nature. Note also the irregular cropping; not just the signature, but the whole composition is eccentric, not preplanned.

Rare indeed are the moments when natural people look natural. We are always in motion, always expressing something. Tranquillity is an illusion, a fiction. Caravaggio saw this, and was alone among painters up to his times in this recognition.

Dutch beans or Danish beans, Dutch shoes or Danish shoes. Green peppers and fish. What is unique and what is general?

The Martyrdom of St. Matthew shows the saint, apparently one of Caravaggio's favorites, being slaughtered by a physically gorgeous young man. The saint looks like a very ordinary man, but the beautiful yet deadly young man seems aristocratic, another instance of Caravaggio's populism. There appears to be a relationship between this piece and *David and the Head of Goliath,* where, again, the handsome young man fulfills perhaps a death wish of an older one.

X-rays of the painting reveal a very beautiful and terrified young woman on the left, possibly Iphegenia of Ethiopia. Caravaggio painted over her a young man of fashion, wearing a plumed hat, indifferent to the goings on.

An angel threatens St. Matthew with the palm of martyrdom, clutching the palm tightly, not just to point to the saint, but as if he had just struck him with it. Again, an interplay of themes so common to Caravaggio: indifference and involvement, expression and a lack of expression.

Madonna, Child and Saint Anne—known as "The Madonna of the Serpent"—is over ten feet high. This huge painting is marvelously inconsistent as a stylistic whole. This visual effect vies with the consistency of rendering that Caravaggio gives to each of the figures in the painting. The virgin is rendered smoothly, St. Anne roughly. The child is rendered in part precisely, in part approximately. The painting fits the ambiguity of the text in the Vulgate, which can be read so that either the Virgin or the young Jesus is the one to kill the snake of "sin and heresy." It's your guess who will do it. Maybe that nice old lady St. Anne, if mother and child will but move their feet—which seem to be touching the snake, but not killing it.

In *The Death of the Virgin,* the Virgin's flesh is greenish, her body is bloated, and her feet are dirty, scarcely the dignified kind of representation most of Caravaggio's patrons would have thought was appropriate. The older men in the foreground are grief-stricken, but some of the younger ones farther back are chattering away, not looking, apparently indifferent.

Or are they? It's another Caravaggio ambiguity; to live is to doubt.

The story goes that the priests of the church where the painting was first hung had it removed; they said the Virgin looked too much like a courtesan. Bellori says it was because she looked too much like a common woman. In speaking of this painting most observers, it seems to me, see something of themselves, or at least each is obliged to make interpretations of the artist's deliberate ambiguities. For instance, the young man to the back whom I described as indifferent is described by Walter Friedlaender as engaged in quiet contemplation.

I see a statement of the universality of death, the Virgin becoming all women. What is she lying on? Is she levitated? Why must her body float?

Concretism, the concept that all ideas in any art (in poetry or painting or anything else) must be embodied in specific things and images, is basic to our reaction in the last twenty or so years against the abstraction that came before. Yet, such concretism is all there in Caravaggio, nearly 400 years ago, in his reaction against the abstract and intellectualized art that came just before him. He seems more relevant to us than many of his contemporaries because of this reaction.

In an art performance, why use this silk-screen squeegee and not that one, these stones and these keys but not that box of jars and cooked eggs, these little boxes that a Japanese friend of mine made but not those that were found in the street, some fabric for tearing and tying but not other fabric that was just recently bought, some tape but not some glue, and so on?

> *The Nativity* or *The Adoration of the Shepherds* is a perfect Caravaggio subject: the Lord, the humble birth, the shepherds, the implicit populism. Nobody, nothing in the painting, is "beautiful" except the situation. Those donkeys would never win a prize at the county fair. The shepherds' hands and feet are dirty. Yet, one of the shepherds is almost naked. Here, where one would least expect it, the issue of the beauty of the natural, at least of the natural body, is raised.

Caravaggio's method is opposed to *disegno*, working from design or from drawings. Caravaggio's method starts—touch, feel, look. Work directly with the material on the canvas. Criticize and doubt yourself, and make changes, overpaint and overcome, do not work *a priori* but *a posteriori*. This is the method of the folk singer rather than the composer of fugues and canons. Each work must create its own form, become its own paradigm.

> *Still Life* is an early, minor painting in which the tradition of Lombardy still lives. "The

Imperfections of Nature" would serve as a descriptive title. One of the big leaves in the upper left is sere and cracked. The apple and one of the pears have worm holes. Yet, the moisture on the leaves—the bloom on the grapes, too—these things are exquisitely portrayed. The perfect is wed to the imperfect.

She photographed me asleep in the field. I became her subject, and in describing, this became my own subject. This process would not be strange to Caravaggio.

St. John with a Ram. There are four St. John paintings, two of them very similar. The image is strong, for any man sensitive to his maleness—the hair of the head, and the hair of the ram's skin. A postcard of this painting, in black and white, provoked Geoffrey Hendricks into doing his nearly pagan performance piece, *La Capra,* in Italy, called *Sheep* when it was done in North America. He made that piece nearly 375 years after Caravaggio's work was completed, but a myth is always made anew, its images recast, given fresh inflections. The faith that inspired an earlier recasting and elaboration can be gone, but the emotional need that faith answered remains. This need will generate a new fiction. More than simple allusion and reference are needed to join a work to a tradition or lineage.

The old man, writing at his table. Light and shadow. Three books and a skull Something beyond the mortality of the old man is suggested. The mortality of the books?

The contexts change. Two cans of Goya-brand "frijoles negros" and "habichuelas blancas," intended for dinner, but instead put into a work of art. The death of a saint, intended to show the triumph over death, but instead put into a work of art and enjoyed. Draw your own conclusions: I find there's a case for iconoclasm.

Caravaggio's *St. John in the Desert* in Rome's Capitoline Museum is a good work to refute the Ruskin (and, later, Berenson) myth that Caravaggio was incapable of appreciating traditional beauty. Just as Richard Wagner felt he had to include a fugue in the overture to *Die Meistersinger* to demonstrate that he was a master of the kind of counterpoint that he had rejected, in this painting Caravaggio presents a dazzling variety of "pretty" textures in brilliant, slick brushwork that would put even a Jan Breughel to shame: it's the perfect Caravaggio for people who don't like Caravaggio.

I enjoy meditating on the meaning of the *Young Man With a Basket of Fruit* in the Villa Borghese. The man has the Caravaggio face, but it is radiant, erotic, healthy, and lyrical rather than dramatic. The fruit, by contrast, is unwholesome, its leaves wilted. The attitudes prevailing in Caravaggio's time, the time of the Counter-Reformation, coalesced in a thoroughgoing suspicion of the physical world. "The world, the flesh, and the devil" was the popular phrase. Caravaggio displaced this emphasis, reversing the acceptable order of things. Was Caravaggio saying that this flesh was more beautiful than that nature, that work of God?

Unrollables, and cups, and spoons, and forks. A fan. And earth. I will feel differently about each of these, depending on what goes on what or how it is placed.

The Deposition of Christ. Mary with her hands upraised looks more thankful than despairing. What real attitude towards death does this painting imply? The man bending, holding Christ's body, must be Nicodemus. What is Caravaggio, living in a virulently anti-Semitic milieu, saying about the Jews?

Narciso (Narcissus). Most writers up to Walter Friedlaender, accepted it as a Caravaggio. But how can this be? The myth is too deeply pagan, and the young man is, somehow, too tidy. A very handsome picture, but less likely a true Caravaggio than a piece by one of the "Caravaggisti," as his followers are known.

In *La Musica Ideal* (known in the English-speaking world as "The Musicians," not a translation but, then, the titles were not always given by Caravaggio), what is the young man at the left doing? Why isn't he playing an instrument? Does he provide the musicians with an audience?

David and the Head of Goliath. In the great version of this subject, the myth is of the young and presumably helpless conquering the older, the gigantic, the more powerful. David has the Caravaggio face, like some of the Saint Johns, the youths with fruit, or the musicians. Goliath has sensual but tired eyes, dead-looking, as if he were searching for his death. David looks clinical, impassive about what he has done. It was merely necessary. What does this say about death in general? What new myth emerges from the old?

On my Caravaggio slides, I considered masking out the backgrounds against which I photographed the pictures of the paintings. How utterly out of spirit, I realized. The frames, the pictures' environments, form a part of the work to a far greater extent than in the work of other Italian Renaissance painters. Caravaggio's concreteness is one of its main attributes and uniquenesses, similar in its way to those late 1950s collages by Allan Kaprow or Robert Rauschenberg in which mirrors are included, to reflect both the viewer and the environment in which the work is seen.

A dog's ear and wheat. The connection is arbitrary but nonetheless real. Now that we think about it, how similar are the photographs of them we have seen?

The Seven Acts of Mercy juxtaposes the six images from the Gospel of St. Matthew — "For I was hungered, and ye gave me meat; I was thirsty and ye gave me drink; I was a stranger, and ye took me in; naked and ye clothed me; I was sick, and ye visited me; I was in prison, and ye came unto me." To these six, traditionally the Middle Ages added a seventh act; "I was dead, and ye buried me." The first impression one gets of this enormous work — it is thirteen feet high—is of incredible chaos, to which the Madonna and child and a pair of seraphs floating overhead add their own grotesqueness. If ever there was a baroque work—and one meaning of the word "baroque" is "grotesque," as another meaning, used, for instance, of pearls, is "irregular"—if ever a work can be said to epitomize the Baroque, then this is it. Note how each of the figures is involved in one of the acts, yet some ambiguity remains as to which figure matches up with precisely which act of mercy. Another thing: those who are performing merciful acts seem to be doing them very cold-bloodedly. What does Caravaggio mean by this?

St. Francis and the Angel. Saint Francis with his head in the angel's lap. Isn't this an erotic relationship? When one man's head is in another man's lap, it seems to suggest something of that kind. The composition is the calmest of the whole of Caravaggio's surviving corpus. What might this imply about his attitude towards love?

Giordano Bruno, Caravaggio's contemporary, was burned by the Papal Inquisition in 1600 as a heretic. He developed a philosophy using two main catchwords: the infinite, which in Caravaggio becomes the vast; and movement—stasis is death, or at least closely akin to it. For memory and idea to find embodiments in the real world, only moving objects will suffice. These ideas, whether absorbed directly from reading Bruno's works or whether picked up through popularized versions of, for instance, the various Llullist tracts

on the art of memory (which have their own
novel stress on the dramatic and the centrality
of the theater), Caravaggio seems to have
taken to heart, drawing on them, at least in
spirit, in working out such complex paintings
as *The Seven Acts of Mercy*.

Materials, concrete materials to embody the
daily: staples and a staple gun, thread, poker
chips, a brush, scissors, wooden shoes, and a
model #180-7 1/2D wooden form.

We are not smug, and ours is not a trusting
time. Many of Caravaggio's contemporaries
seem to us too bland, with their typical neo-
Pythagorean look, with figures constructed
according to preconceived proportions instead
of according to the eye or heart. The Greeks
told of a man named Procrustes, who made
strangers lie in a bed he had made. If they
were too tall, he lopped their feet off, if too
short, he stretched them and killed them.
Paintings done according to preconceived proportions strike us, often, as being like a
Procrustean bed. But Caravaggio's drama is
less conceptual than empirical. Thus, it seems
more modern to us, as if he were asking,
sincerely, "What does it look like when a god
goes to heaven?" Not merely stating the belief
that he does.

The inventory of the things that are in a
Caravaggio painting suggests the style it is
painted in and the effect of the painting as
well—jail bars, the bare breast, the sword, the
naked man, the angels, the mother and child,
the gloves and the plumes, the wine skin

spilling, the gesturing hands, the swords, the
light and dark, and the yards and meters of
cloth—very heavy textured cloth. You could
never make a Verocchio or a Grandma Moses
out of that. But you could make a very
Caravaggiesque Happening from it: in a sense,
Geoffrey Hendricks has done just that. Con-
tents, then, determine content, in Caravaggio's
work as in much of the most concrete and
imagistic of the new, post-cognitive art forms.

> *The Madonna of the Rosary* was painted for the
> Dominicans and, naturally enough, includes
> some Dominicans. The whole iconography is
> extraordinary—the movement of the rosary
> from Virgin Mary to monk (St. Dominic him-
> self?) to the common people. The flow is unmis-
> takable. The arrangement of figures in the
> lower left is not so much a pyramid as an
> inverted funnel or a horn of plenty, pouring
> downwards. We see a man at the right. His
> eyelids do not lie over the eyeballs' surface.
> He is dressed as a monk and is gesturing
> towards the virgin. He resembles an older
> version of the young men I have several times
> noted as being similar in the early paintings.
> He also looks like a balder version of the
> portrait of Caravaggio in the frontispiece of
> Pietro Bellori's biography of him. Could this
> be a self-portrait? Incidentally, he also re-
> sembles the gesturing figure of Pontius Pilate
> in the as yet unauthenticated *Ecce Homo* at
> Genoa.

In a typical Caravaggio painting, the subjects
are set off by isolation against a very dark
background: the only alternative would have

been to have a mirror background, which was not among the technical possibilities of his day.

> *The Calling of Saint Matthew*. What ordinary people these are, from whom Matthew is chosen. This may explain the setting of the painting in what was then modern costume. It is another instance of Caravaggio's populism, almost unique in its time. Traditionally, St. Matthew is said to have been a tax collector, scarcely a beloved trade in his day or in ours. Yet Caravaggio shows a certain fondness for him, makes him one of his most-painted subjects.

"No ideas but in things!" says the twentieth century poet, defining his working principle. But when William Carlos Williams said this to describe his "new" discovery, he was actually echoing the "Fifth Ennead" of Plotinus, written sixteen centuries before. In between come Caravaggio and Giordano Bruno, among others, doing the same. Of course, there are differences, but there are also affinities, and these are usually glossed over. By seeing these affinities and calling attention to them we feel closer to the works involved, thus enriching our understanding of these games of art and life.

The ideas are always there, but they are embodied in things, always in things, never just superimposed over the subject. After 1600 the secular themes disappear from Caravaggio's work, and he paints only religious subjects. They are his microcosm in an age for which the microcosm and the macrocosm were

crucial concepts. Thus, the religious subjects
of his paintings always have secular, universal implications. 1600 was the year in which,
as I mentioned, the Papal Inquisition finally
burned Italy's great heretic, Giordano Bruno.
All Italy took note. No doubt, for all the defi-
ance in his life and work, Caravaggio took
that under consideration in making his deci-
sions.

> *Boy Bitten by a Lizard.* They say it's a boy, but
> how can we tell? Isn't Caravaggio giving us
> the myth of human sexuality here? The occult
> significance of lizards—the alchemical writ-
> ings abound with them—bears on this. This
> would be consistent with the sexual ambigu-
> ity of the person being bitten: the hermaphro-
> ditic figure is equally crucial, in alchemy, to
> the lizard.

Notation. This causes that to happen. All art is
the result of the performance of an aesthetic
act. Why not use an old performance to provoke a new one?

> More materials for an art performance: stamp
> pad and stamp, buttons, mirror, wood, and
> apples. Or bowl and withering leaves, and
> aging fruit.

The woman's foot and the child's are on the
snake's neck. Neither foot is pressing down
taut or strong enough to kill the snake. What
is the message?

> The apparent awkwardness of Caravaggio's
> compositions, their staginess and theatrical-

ity, can be perceived as an intrusion of reality—a reality of a kind religious experience
centers on—into the more sedate flow of traditional beauty and convention in art. Life
enters. That is to say, *natura naturans* enters,
giving us the Caravaggiesque *arte senza arte*,
art without the manner of art. It remains, after
all this time, disturbing. And current.

Section Three
Three Considerations of Fluxus

XIII. Fluxus: Theory and Reception

Fluxus is not:	— a moment in history, or
	— an art movement,
Fluxis is:	— a way of doing things,
	— a tradition, and
	— a way of life and death.[37]

i. To begin with . . .

To BEGIN WITH, this is not an introductory text on Fluxus. To explain what Fluxus is and was and where it came from is not my primary purpose at this time, having already done so in my long essay *Postface* (1962) and my short one, "A Child's History of Fluxus," among other pieces as well. Others have done so, too, of course, each in his or her own way. My concern here is, rather, to try to deal with some aspects and questions in Fluxus: what do we experience when we experience a Fluxus work? Why is it what it is? Is there anything unique about it, and so on?

In other words, this is an essay intended for the thoughtful person who already knows some Fluxus materials, who has perhaps thought about Fluxus in relation to Dada and Surrealism and the other iconoclastic art movements of our century, who may have attended a Fluxus performance, who may have reservations about Fluxus works in one way or another, but who, at any rate, already has some ideas on the subject. For him or for her I want to frame some questions and suggest some answers. With any luck, the whole inquiry should have an erotic, that is, a pleasure principle, one of its own.

One must, here, bear in mind that Fluxus was something that happened more or less by accident. In the late 1950s we Fluxus artists began to coalesce, sometimes thinking of ourselves as a group, unnamed, doing the work that later became known as Fluxus. We did not consciously present ourselves *to the public* as a group until 1962 when George Maciunas organized his festival at Wiesbaden, intended originally as publicity for the series of publications he wanted to issue that were to be called *Fluxus*. The festival caused great notoriety, was on German television, and was repeated in various cities beside Wiesbaden, which is well documented elsewhere and need not concern us here. The point I am getting at is that in connection with these festivals the newspapers and media began to refer to us as "die Fluxus Leute" ("the Fluxus people"), and so here we were, people from very different backgrounds. Knowles, Vostell, and Brecht were originally painters. Watts was primarily a sculptor. Patterson, myself, and Paik were composers. Williams and Mac Low were writers (I was that, too), and so on. Here we were, being told we were The Fluxus People. What *should* that mean? If we were to be identified publicly as a group, should we become one? What did we have in common?

The concept arose of consciously constituting ourselves as some kind of "collective." Maciunas was particularly pleased by that idea, since he was very much a leftist and, instinctively, a goodly portion of his approach to organizing us and our festivals had at least a metaphorical relationship with leftist ideology and forms. The collective clearly needed a spokesman, to be what a commissar was supposed to be in the USSR but seldom was. Maciunas was not yet an artist but a graphic designer,[38] and, as editor of the *Fluxus* magazine or annual or whatever it was to be, he seemed the best suited of us to be the commissar of Fluxus, which role he assumed and held until his dying day. In this there was a parallel to the role of André Breton in Surrealism, though Maciunas was less monolithic and more ceremonial (or he was supposed to be).

We never accepted Maciunas's right to read people out of the movement, as Breton did. Besides, it wasn't really a movement, but more of that later. Occasionally Maciunas tried to do this, but few others followed him on this point. We would continue to work with the artist who was banned by Maciunas until, eventually, Maciunas usually got over his own impulse to ban the person and accepted him or her back into the group. Surrealism without Breton is inconceivable, but, crucial though Maciunas's contributions were, Fluxus was less centralized on him. The degree of centralization is even today a matter of discussion.

As for us, looking back into history, we saw Futurism as important but as having no strong or direct relationship with us in any direct sense. Dada works we admired, but the negative side of it, its rejections and the social dynamic of its members, splitting and feuding, that we did not wish to emulate. Surrealism had, perhaps, minimal influence on us so far as form, style, and content were concerned, but aspects of its group dynamic seemed suitable for our use, subject only to the limitations on Maciunas's authority that lay in our nature as having already been a group with some aspects of our work in common *before* Maciunas ever arrived on the scene. More of this in a moment.

Fluxus was therefore:

a) a series of publications produced and designed by George Maciunas;

b) the name of our group of artists;

c) the kind of works associated with these publications, artists, and performances that we did (and do) together;

d) any other activities that were in the lineage or tradition that was built up, over a period of time, which is associated with the publications, artists, or performances (such as Fluxfeasts).

Whether or not Fluxus still exists and—if it does, then in what sense—depends on whether one is talking about history, works, forms, or some general spirit. Fluxus was not a movement in that it had no stated, consistent program or manifesto that the work *must* match, and it did not propose to move art or our awareness of art from point A to point B. The very name, "Fluxus," suggests change, being in a state of flux. The idea was that it would always reflect the most exciting avant-garde tendencies of a given time or moment (the Fluxattitude), and it would always be open for new people to "join." All they had to do was to produce works in some way similar to what other Fluxus artists were doing. Thus, the original core group expanded to include, in its second wave (after Wiesbaden), Ben Vautier, Eric Andersen, Tomas Schmit, and Willem de Ridder; in the third wave (by 1966) Geoffrey Hendricks and Ken Friedman; and, in the later waves (after 1969), Yoshimasa Wada, Jean Dupuy, Larry Miller, and others. It was thought of as something that would exist parallel to other developments, providing a rostrum for its members and a purist model for the most technically innovative and spiritually challenging work of its changing time(s). One received one's Fluxhood from Maciunas, but after that it was up to one to justify it.

An overview of how the Fluxus forms developed might be mapped out like this:

1) Once upon a time there was collage, a technique. Collage could be used in art, not just in visual art.
2) When collage began to project off the two-dimensional surface, it became the combine (Rauschenberg's term?).
3) When the combine began to envelop the spectator, it became the environment. I don't know who coined that term, but it is still a current one.
4) When the environment began to include live performance, it became the Happening (Allan Kaprow's term, usually capitalized in order to distinguish it from just *anything* that happens),

5) When Happenings were broken up into their minimal constituent parts, they became events. I first heard that term from Henry Cowell, a composer with whom both John Cage and, many years later, I myself studied. Any art work can be looked at as a collation of events, but for works that tend to fissure and split into atomized elements, this approach by event seems particularly appropriate.

6) When events were minimal, but had maximum implications, they became one of the key things Fluxus artists typically did (or do) in their performances.

That is, I think, the real lineage of Fluxus.

A digression into language seems in order here. In Fluxus one often speaks of Fluxfestivals, Fluxconcerts, Fluxpeople, Fluxartists, Fluxevents. . . . I myself am to blame for that one. Maciunas was very much interested in the odd byways of baroque art. I told him about the work of the German baroque poet, Quirinus Kühlmann (1644-88), a curious messianic figure who was eventually burnt at the stake in Moscow where he had gone in an effort to persuade the Tsar that he was a reincarnation of Christ. Kühlmann wrote various exciting books of poetry using "proteus" forms and other unconventional means, among which is the *Kühlpsalter*. This includes Kühlpsalms, evidently to be performed on Kühldays by Kühlpeople, and so on. Maciunas was delighted by this, and thenceforth made parallel constructions of his own that were based on it. There were "Fluxfests" or "Fluxfestivals," to be performed by "Fluxfriends" who were also "Fluxartists," wearing "Fluxclothes" and eating "Fluxfood," and so on. This dissociated such artists, festivals, and the like from regular ones. Its purpose was to get beyond accusations that this was "anti-music" as our aural works were sometimes accused of being, or even "non-music" (which would mean anything not music, from mushrooms to silverware). Our aural pieces were, simply, "Fluxmusic." Of course one was not an "artist" or even an "anti-artist" but a "Fluxartist," something presumably quite different.

I began this essay by observing that I was trying to write theory here, not to give a basic history or critical discussion. The difference, as I see it, is that criticism attempts to provide an understanding of individual works, to explain why and how they work, or why and how they fail to do so. Theory, on the other hand, attempts to provide the underlying assumptions and policies of those works and of the criticism of them, if such criticism is to be appropriate. If one were to undertake both criticism and theory, one would have to describe a great many works, and this essay would become hopelessly cumbersome and lengthy. Therefore, at the risk of frustrating the reader, I will concentrate on the theory and only bring up the individual works where it is necessary to provide examples. Thus, there is no need for such purposes to mention all the major Fluxartists. No slight is intended to those who are not discussed. Instead, the focus must be on works and artists who make good examples of the key points, who typify something or other, and let us hope that the reader has some familiarity with at least some of the works alluded to, or with some of the artists.

ii. Some Antecedents of Fluxus

On one hand, Fluxus appears to be an iconoclastic art movement, somewhat in the lineage of the other such movements in our century—Futurism, Dada, Surrealism, and so on. Indeed, the relationship with these is a real and valid one. Now we are ready to go into more detail concerning these in relation to Fluxus.

Futurism was the earliest such movement. It was founded by Marinetti in the first decade of the century, was proclaimed on the front page of the *Figaro Litteraire* and elsewhere, and it developed a group character which was sustained from its early years until World War II. This means it lasted at least thirty-plus years

Marinetti was its leader, though not in a totally dictatorial sense. Its members were supposed to follow along pretty much with what he said, but he usually forgave them when they didn't. He proclaimed *parole in libertà* ("words at liberty," a form of visual poetry); *teatro sintético* ("synthetic theater," that is, performance pieces that were synthesized out of extremely raw-seeming materials, similar to the *musique concrète* of the post-World War II era); simultaneity, a time-related form of Cubism; music of noises; and many such formal innovations or unconventional arts that are still fresh to consider. If, however, one hears the existing recordings of the music of Luigi Russolo, for example, one of the main futurist composers, one finds something far more conventional than what one might have expected from reading his famous *Arte de Rumori* ("Art of Noises") manifesto. One hears, to be sure, amazing noises being made over a loud-speaker—roars, scraping sounds, and such-like. But one hears these superimposed over rather crudely harmonized scales. If one goes into the content of Marinetti's writings, one finds him a very old-fashioned daddy type, rather hard on women, celebrating war as an expression of masculine virtue, and the like. Even the visual art, in the works of Balla and others, being the summit of Futurist fine art, is rather conventional with regard to its formal structures and implications. It is certainly rather conservative when compared to the innovative Cubism of France at the same time. In other words, Futurism is a goddess, nineteenth-century style, with one leg in the future and one in the conventional past and not too much in the present. Considering that the two legs are moving in opposite directions, it is no wonder that Futurism falls a little flat in the evolution of modern sensibility. Of course, it is of great technical and historical interest, as a starter and a precursor, but its works have only moderate intrinsic interest as works.

Dada, when one looks at it in isolation, seems more unique than it is. But most of the Dada artists and writers came out of Expressionism, and if one compares the Dada materials with those of their immediate antecedents, they are less unique than one might have imagined. Perhaps an anecdote is appropriate here. In the 1950s and 1960s, the journalistic image of Dada had become so extreme, so far from the reality of the work, that Dada was considered to be the limit of the extremely crazy in art—as wild as possible, as droll as possible, simply inexpressibly "far out," to cite the slang of the time. Thus, early Happenings and Fluxus (like the works of Rauschenberg and Johns) were often dismissed as "neo-Dada."[39] This was, of course, extremely annoying and embarrassing to those of us who knew what Dada was or had been. For example, I knew several of the old dadaists, had been raised on their work, and there was no doubt in my mind that what we Happenings and Fluxus people were doing had rather little to do with Dada.

Skipping ahead to 1966 for a moment, when I was publisher of Something Else Press, in various ways a Fluxus enterprise, I knew that, before the split between the French and German dadaists, Richard Huelsenbeck had published an anthology of Dada materials, the *Dada Almanach*. I therefore got Huelsenbeck's permission to reissue it in facsimile. The response to it was very revealing: I was told that this was "not real Dada!" The material seemed too conservative, far too close to the Expressionism of the pre-World War I years to gibe with the image that my 1960s friends and colleagues had built up in their mind as to what Dada was. Yet Huelsenbeck, at the time he did the *Dada Almanach*, was not a conservative at all. He had published a wildly leftist booklet, *Deutschland Muß Untergehen!* ("Germany Must Perish!"), and he saw no difference between political and cultural innovative and revolutionary thinking. His poems were as experimental as those of the other dadaists, Raoul Hausmann, for example. In other words, the journalistic myth had come to replace the substance to such an extent that the substance was overwhelmed. It is for this reason that the very term "neo-Dada" seems naive and inadequate today, since we now know a great deal more about Dada than was the case in the 1950s and early 1960s.

Surrealism is, of course, an outgrowth of Dada, historically. It was, quite self-consciously, a movement, unlike
Dada, which was more unruly, spontaneous perhaps, and
undirected. Surrealism was presided over by the relatively
benevolent Trotskyite *littérateur,* André Breton. Breton was
much given to care politics, to reading people out of his
movement or claiming them for it, proclaiming them and
disowning them according to their conformity or non-con-
formity with the theoretical positions he built up analogously
to Marxist theorizing in his various Surrealist manifestoes.
Ideology may have masked personal feeling in many cases,
as if to say. "If you hate me, you must be ideologically
incorrect." The commonplace about Surrealism is that it is of
two sorts, historical and popular.

Historical Surrealism usually refers to what was going on
in Breton's circle from the mid-1920s until the late 1930s in
Paris (or in Europe as a whole), usually involving the transformation of social, aesthetic, scientific, and philosophical
values by means of the liberation of the subconscious. This
led, of course, to a kind of art in which fantastic visions were
depicted extremely literally. A concern with the subconscious was typical of the time, and the story is told of that
great liberator of the subconscious, Sigmund Freud, that
someone asked him about surrealist art. His reply? Normally, he said, in art he looked to see the unconscious
meaning of a work, but in surrealistic art he looked to see if
there was a conscious one. Well, to return to my main
concerns, with the passage of time and of the entry of Surrealism into popular awareness, "surrealist" came to be more
of less synonymous with "fantastic" or "dreamy" in art.
Popular Surrealism, then, has little to do with historical
Surrealism, although careless critics tend to equate the two.

However, historical Surrealism has a far fuller history
than our usual image of it. Breton lived on into the 1960s, and
as long as he lived, "Surrealism" as a self-conscious, self-
defined movement continued, with new people joining and

old members being obliged to withdraw. During the years of World War II and immediately after, Breton and many of the surrealists lived in the United States, and their impact is not sufficiently understood either in Europe or America. They became the most interesting presence in the American art world. Magazines such as *VVV* and *View* were the most exciting art magazines of the time. The surrealists constituted the nucleus of the New York avant-garde. Some of us who later did Fluxus works were very conscious of this. I, for example, attended school with Breton's daughter Aubée ("Obie," to us) and, being curious what her father wrote, acquired a couple of his books. That was my *entrée* into Surrealism as a place to visit. Furthermore, from time to time there would be surrealist "manifestations," and some of these were similar to the "environments" out of which Happenings developed. These were, in any case, locked into our sensibility, as points of reference in considering our earlier art experiences, and for Americans at the time Surrealism was absolutely the prototypical art movement as such. We shall return to this, but I would like to consider a few points along the way.

1) Fluxus *seems* to be a series of separate and discrete formal experiments, with rather little to tie them together. In this way it seems to resemble Futurism. This is a point I will answer when presently addressing the actual ontology of Fluxus.

2) Fluxus *seems* to be like Dada, at least like the popular image of Dada, in being, well, crazy, iconoclastic, essentially a negative tendency rejecting all its precedents, and so on. In fact, there *is* some truth to this, but it is oblique. Fluxus was never as undirected as Dada, never as close to its historical precedents. Dada was, in fact, a point of discussion on those long nights at Ehlhalten-am-Taunus, during the first Fluxus Festival at Wiesbaden in 1962, when George Maciunas, myself, Alison Knowles, and, occasionally, others would talk into the wee hours of the morning, trying to determine what

would be the theoretical nature of this tendency to which we were giving birth, which we found ourselves participating in. Maciunas was intensely aware of the rivalry between the French and German dadaists; we wanted to keep our group together and avoid such splits as best we could. What could we do to prevent this fissioning? The answer was to avoid having too tight an ideological line. Maciunas proposed a manifesto during the 1962 festival at Wiesbaden that is usually printed as "The Fluxus Manifesto." But only a few of us were willing to sign it. Some did not want to confine tomorrow's possibilities by what they thought today. Others did not like its tone. I myself felt it was a poor job since it was so unclear, and I urged Maciunas to rewrite it. That manifesto as it stands is perhaps Maciunas's own manifesto, not a full-fledged and programmatic manifesto of Fluxus. Interspersed with cut-up images from a dictionary definition of "flux," the manifesto says that one must "Purge the world of . . . bourgeois sickness, 'intellectual', professional & commercialized culture . . . of Europanism" [sic] . . . PROMOTE A REVOLU-TIONARY FLOOD AND TIDE IN ART, . . . promote NON ART REALITY." It says little about how one is to do this; it is too general. It says nothing about *why* one should do this. It says nothing about who will carry it out, nor does Maciunas say what "non art reality" is or should be. At the time when Maciunas put together this manifesto, I hoped it would be rewritten in a more persuasive and less strident way with more concrete points. Today I believe it would have been a mistake to do anything of the kind, since the group would have split apart, just as the dadaists did, if our program seemed too confining.

3) Surrealism lasted more or less forty years as a viable tendency and, among other things, spun off a popular version, as I have said, lower-case surrealism. This seemed like a fine model for the Fluxus people. But how could we make Surrealism a model for Fluxus?

Before we leave this matter of antecedents and basic definition, it would be well to mention some individual artists who are sometime reckoned among the forefathers of Fluxus, and a few of those who are thought of as Fluxus but who are not.

When Ben Vautier speaks of Fluxus, he usually evokes the names of John Cage and Marcel Duchamp so repeatedly that one might well wonder if he had ever heard of any other artists at all (he has), nor is he the only person of whom this is true. In fact, an editor from a newspaper once became quite indignant at me for suggesting that Cage was not the actual founder of Fluxus (and Happenings as well).

The fact is, both Cage and Duchamp *are* much admired by the Fluxartists. Duchamp is admired largely for the inter-penetration in his work of art and life, the "art/life di-chotomy," as we used to call it in the early 1960s. In 1919, as is well known, Duchamp exhibited a men's urinal as an art work, a simple, white, and pristine object, classical in form, when one separates it from its traditional function. Since many Fluxus pieces, most notably the performance ones, are often characterized by their taking of a very ordinary event from daily life, and by then framing these as art by presenting them on a stage in a performance situation, there is a clear connection between such Fluxus pieces and Duchamp's uri-nal. For example, one often-performed Fluxus piece is Mieko (formerly "Chieko") Shiomi's "Music for Face," in which the performers come on stage and smile, gradually relaxing their faces until the smile disappears.[40] This is something that happens often in daily life, and it is somehow refreshing to think of an art performance that is both daily, un-insulated from one's diurnal, non-art existence, unlike most art works. Nevertheless, apart from a couple of musical experiments, Duchamp never did a performance work, nor did he have any great interest in them. At Allan Kaprow's seminal *18 Happenings in 6 Parts, the* first Happening presented in New York (in which I performed, and which has some oblique relationship with Fluxus), Duchamp was in the audience and I watched him; he seemed quite uninterested in what he was seeing, and I do not recall that he even stayed through the entire performance. It seems doubtful that he saw any particular connection between the performance he was watching and his own work. Nor, later, when he knew some of us and our work, did he see such a connection then, either. It seemed to be his effort to make life visually elegant, while we, on the other hand, chose to leave life alone, to observe it as a biological phenomenon, to watch it come and recede again, and to comment on it and enrich it in or with our works. We focused on different aspects of his work from those that had concerned him. When one sees a Duchamp work, one knows whether it is sculpture or painting or whatever; with a Fluxus work, there is a conceptual fusion; "intermedia" is the term I chose for such fusions, picking it up from Samuel Taylor Coleridge, who had used it in 1812.[41] Virtually all Fluxus works are intermedial by their very nature: visual poetry, poetic visions, action music and musical actions, Happenings and events that are bounded, conceptually, by music, literature, and visual art, and whose heart lies in the midground among these. Duchamp was an extreme purist; we were not, are not. He, therefore, makes an awkward ancestor for us, much as we may admire his integrity and his *geste*.

Cage was rather a different matter. Some of us (myself, Brecht, Maxfield, Hansen, and others) studied with Cage. But in his case, like Duchamp, he strove towards "nobility." This, for him, meant the impersonal or the transpersonal, often obtained by means of systems employing chance, in order to transcend his own taste. For us the greatest contribution he made was in his way of noticing a piece in external reality, rather than dragging it out of himself as most artists had done.[42] Mac Low, Brecht, Maxfield, and myself used chance systems, "aleatoric structures," but few of the other Fluxus artists did, at least with any frequency. As for Cage, he seemed to find Fluxus works simplistic, at least when he first saw them. They did (and do) often employ some extreme minimalism that was not one of his concerns. Too, Fluxus pieces can be quite personal, and this would place them beyond Cage's pale. For most of his life his own work was seldom intermedial. Though he wrote poems and composed music, one tended to know and be conscious of which was which. Of course, Cage's work changed throughout his life, and in later years he wrote a great deal of visual poetry. But at the time when Fluxus appeared this still lay in the future. Cage and Duchamp should,therefore, be thought of more as uncles of Fluxus rather than as direct progenitors or father figures. Fluxus, it seems, is a mongrel art, with no distinct parentage or pedigree. There is a relationship to Cage and to Duchamp, but it is mostly by affinity and the example of integrity, rather than that Fluxus developed out of their work in any specific way.

To summarize the discussion so far, the better one knows the Fluxworks, the less they resemble Futurism, Dadaism, Surrealism, Duchamp, or Cage.

iii. Is There a Fluxus Program (or Was There)?

Is there a Fluxus program?

I have already argued that Fluxus is not a movement, and this is, I feel, the case. Maciunas called it a "tendency," as we shall see. Nonetheless, if Fluxus is to be a useful category for considering work, it must have more of a meaning than simply as the name of Maciunas's proposed publications or the artists associated with it. That is to say, there must be certain points in common among the works in a body of works; they must hang together by more than mere *Zeitgeist*. This means that the works will have some aspects of a movement, though not all of them.

Usually a movement in the arts begins with a group of artists coming together with some common feeling that something needs doing, that, as I put it a while ago, the arts have to be moved from point A to point B. A kind of imagery has been neglected and needs to be introduced: Pop Art. Art has become too cold, and it must be warmed up with an appeal to the transrational: Romanticism. In other words, there is a program, whether or not that program is ever actually written out in a prescriptive manifesto, describing what is to be done and by whom and how, or whether or not the discovery is made by a critic that certain artists have something in common and constitute a group of some sort. Naturally, the world is full of pseudo-movements—works with something or other in common, which some ambitious critic then claims as a movement or tendency in the hopes of earning professional credit—"Brownie points," one might say—for having "discovered" the movement. But if these points are too artificial, if there is no natural grouping that enforces the feeling that these works belong together, it will soon be forgotten as a grouping.

But with a real movement, the life of the movement continues to take place until the program has been achieved; at that point the movement dies a natural death, and the artists, if they are still active, go on to do something else.

Fluxus had (or perhaps has) no concrete prescriptive program. Maciunas's "Fluxus Manifesto" is, as noted, very general and intellectual (for all its strident anti-intellectualism). Few Fluxworks were intended to destroy or even change the world of cultural artifacts that surrounded them, though they might affect how these were to be seen.

Nevertheless, there are some points in common among most Fluxworks:

1) internationalism,
2) experimentalism and iconoclasm,
3) intermedia,
4) minimalism or concentration,
5) an attempted resolution of the art/life dichotomy,
6) implicativeness,
7) play or gags,
8) ephemerality,

9) specificity,
10) presence in time, and
11) musicality.

These eleven points (really, they are *almost* criteria) can be taken up one by one.[43]

Fluxus arose more or less spontaneously in various countries. In Europe there were, in the beginning (others joined shortly afterwards) Wolf Vostell, Nam June Paik, Emmett Williams, and Ben Patterson, among others. In the United States there were, besides myself, Alison Knowles, George Brecht, Robert Watts, and the others I have already named, also La Monte Young, Philip Corner, Ay-o, and still others. In Japan there were Takehisa Kosugi, Mieko Shiomi, and more. Probably there were about two dozen of us in six countries, with little besides our intentions in common (for one thing, not all of us had studied with Cage). Thus, Fluxus was not, for example, the creature of the New York art scene, the West German art scene, the Parisian one, or anything else of that sort. It was, from its outset, *international*. At one point Maciunas tried, in structuring his proposed Fluxus collections, to re-nationalize them, but it simply did not work. One might also note here that Fluxus, aiming to be inclusive, consciously sought to include people from backgrounds as diverse as possible, notably women and blacks. In the latter it was less successful, including only Ben Patterson and the elusive Stanley "This Way" Bro[u]wn. But there were a number of women: Alison Knowles, Mieko Shiomi, Shigeko Kubota, Yoko Ono, Carla Liss, and (later) Alice Hutchins. In this respect, Fluxus was like Berlin and Zürich Dada but unlike Futurism, French Dada, or Surrealism.[44]

It was a coming together of *experimental* artists, that is, or artists who were not interested in doing what all the other artists were doing at the time; they mostly took an iconoclastic attitude towards the conventions of the art establishments of their various countries, and many have since paid the price of doing so, which is obscurity and poverty. No matter: they have their integrity intact. This experimentalism took the form, in all cases, however, of formal experimentalism rather than of content as such. There was the assumption that new content requires new forms, that new forms enable works to have new content and to lead to new experiences.

In many cases this experimentalism led the artists into *intermedia,* to visual poetry, some varieties of Happenings, sound poetry, and so on. At the time, we called these "hybrid artforms," but that term disappeared in favor of "intermedia."

In order to state such forms in a very *concentrated* way, a great measure of purification and distillation was necessary, so that the nature of the form would be clear. One could not have too many extraneous or diverse elements in a work. This led, inevitably, to a stress on brevity, since, by keeping a work short or small, there would be less time for extraneous elements to enter in and to interfere. This brevity constituted a specific sort of *mini-realism,* with as much concentration in a work as possible. As noted, La Monte Young wrote a musical piece that could last forever, using just two pitches. Wolf Vostell composed a Fluxus opera using just three words from the Bible for his libretto. George Brecht wrote many Fluxus events in his *Water Yam* series, using just a very few words, three in one event, twenty in another, two in a third, and so on.

Working so close to the minimum possible made the Fluxus artists intensely conscious of the possibility that what they did would not be art at all in any acceptable sense. Yet, there was also the sense that most art work was unsatisfying anyway, that life was far more interesting. Thus, a great deal of attention was given to the resolutions of the *art/life dichotomy,* which has already been mentioned.

A sense existed that working with these materials implied an avoidance of the personal expression so characteristic of the arts in the period just before Fluxus began, in the early and middle 1950s. But the personal, as a mode, was by no means rejected out of hand in Fluxus if it could be presented in a way that was not overly subjective, which would be limited in relevance. Thus, Alison Knowles performed with her infant daughter, for example.

There was also the danger that working with such minimal material would lead to facile meanderings, to Fluxartists grinding out endless mountains of minimalist pieces that had no real *raison d'être*. Thus, a very important criterion for avoiding this danger came to be the notion that a Fluxpiece, whether an object or a performance, should be as *implicative* as possible, that it should imply a maximum of intellectual, sensuous, or emotional content within its minimum of material.

In the period just before Fluxus began, the dominant style in visual art had been abstract expressionism and in music post-Webernite serialism. Both of these were apt to be extremely solemn and tendentious affairs indeed, and, in fact, seriousness tended to be equated with solemnity. Fluxus tended often to react against this by moving in the direction of humor and gags, introducing a much-needed *spirit of play* into the arts. This also fitted well with the iconoclastic side of Fluxus.

"Play" covers, of course, a good deal of territory. One plays for fun, but there is also the play of a cat with a mouse, of water in a fountain, the play of championship sports or bridge. All have their place in Fluxus, especially the humor. The private lives of the Fluxpeople were frustrating; most were poor, and spirits had to be kept up. Maciunas especially was oriented towards comedy and even farce. Further, it was startling and even shocking to many viewers that grown people would *play* their art. There was often, then, something defiant about the playful Fluxpieces, a lost quality now that Fluxus is better known and is even presented as mostly fun and games. This is, of course, a misprision and an unseemly one at that. The other sorts of game are also part of the picture, and the high seriousness of Fluxus cannot be understood without recognizing this.

There was also the sense that, if Fluxus were to incorporate some element of ongoing change, which is what "flux" implies, then the individual works should themselves change. Many of the Fluxus objects, therefore, were made of rather *ephemeral* materials, such as paper or light plastic, so that as time went by the work would either disappear or would physically alter itself. A masterpiece in this context was a work that made a strong statement rather than a work that would last throughout the ages in some treasure vault. Also, most of the Fluxartists were (and are) very poor, and so they could not afford to work with fine and costly materials. Many of Robert Filliou's works eventually disappeared into the air, for example, though other Fluxworks are, in fact, made of standard materials and will perhaps last (for example, works by Vostell or myself).

Maciunas's background, as I already mentioned, was in graphic and industrial design. The design approach is usually to design *specific* solutions to specific problems. Designers characteristically distrust universals and vague generalities. Generalizations are used in Fluxus works only when they are handled with all the precision of specific categories and necessities. They must not be vague. This was Maciunas' approach, and it remains typical for us now that he is gone.

Presence in time is an inadequate way of describing the quality that the longer Fluxperformance works have of incorporating time as a sort of equivalent of a large canvas with the events revealing themselves gradually. This presence in time becomes, in effect, the form of the piece in such works as La Monte Young's "Composition 1960 #7" (already noted) in which a B and an F-sharp are "to be held for a long time," hours or days or longer. The sound becomes not just an environment but a frame of reference for whatever is around it. Also, some patterns (or horizons of experience) simply cannot be absorbed in a minimalist statement. They require time to reveal themselves effectively. The pieces are, necessarily, harder to understand for an audience; the past experience of the members of the audience usually has led them to expect more entertainment values than they are likely to get. One hears it said, "I liked the little pieces, but the big ones went on too long." What one hopes is that the boredom, if any, will be temporary, while the receiver tries, hopefully, to fit his or her horizon to that of the piece. Boredom is, of course, not the aim of the piece, but it may be a necessary stage on the path to liking it. Therefore, with such pieces the characteristic length is apt to have to be sufficiently long to allow the receiver to get through the boring phase and into the spirit of the event afterwards. This is why Fluxus pieces are apt either to be very short (two minutes perhaps) or very long (twenty minutes or more).

Musicality here describes the quality of many Fluxperformance works of behaving like lyrical music rather than the theater or vaudeville. They are without climax or dramatic structure and are, in one way or another, sensuous or intellectual investigations of the nature of reality. In ancient times, in Boethius's *De Musica,* for instance, the term for this kind of piece is *musica speculativa.*[45] In a sense John Cage revived the concept in composing pieces that reflected the reality around them, and many Fluxpieces, such as my "Constellations" series, took off from this point. Audiences and participants alike seem to sense this and, for this reason, evenings of Fluxus performances seem better described as Fluxconcerts than as Fluxtheater.

Clearly not every work is likely to reflect all eleven of these characteristics or formal points, but the more of them a work reflects, the more typically and characteristically Fluxus it is. So, supposing one sees a work and wants to decide if it is Fluxus or not (whether or not it happens to be by a Fluxartist is not the issue here), all one need do is match it against the eleven formal points. The more it matches, the more Fluxus it is, logically enough. Perhaps there are other such formal points, but these eleven are sufficient.

Similarly, not every work by a Fluxartist is best described

as a Fluxwork; typically Fluxartists do other sorts of work as well, just as a collagist might also print, or a composer of piano music might try his hand at writing something for an orchestra. In this way, also, Fluxus differs from music. *All* the work of a surrealist was expected to be surrealistic. An abstract expressionist would be unlikely to produce a hard-edged geometrical abstraction. But a Vostell would do such a performance piece as "Kleenex" (1962), which he performed at many of the early festivals, while at the same time he was also making his "de-coll/age" paintings and happenings, having nothing to do with his Fluxus work except for their frequently intermedial nature. Maciunas used to like to call Fluxus not a movement but a *tendency;* the term is apt here, when one is relating a kind of work to its historical matrix.

Returning to intermedia, not all intermedial works are Fluxus, of course. For instance, the large-scale Happenings of Kaprow and Vostell are not Fluxworks in that their centers of gravity lie in areas outside those of Fluxus.[46] Nor are most sound or concrete poems. These usually have their intermedial nature in common with Fluxworks, but Fluxus was certainly not the beginning of intermedia. For instance, the concrete-poetry intermedium of the 1950s and 1960s was an immediate predecessor of Fluxus. The visual impulse in poetry is usually present, even if only subtly. After all, one customarily experiences it first with one's eyes. Nevertheless, visual poems (that is, poems so visually oriented that they are both visual *and* literary art) have been made at least since the second millennium before Christ, and they are found in most literary languages, European and non-European.[47] These pieces existed well before 1912 when Apollinaire made his *calligrammes* and so focused the eyes of the Western poetry world on the potentials of this intermedium. But, with concentration enough and with the other formal points I have mentioned, a visual poem could indeed be a Fluxwork.

Many intermedial performance works existed before

Fluxus. For example, in his anthology, *Technicians of the Sacred*, Jerome Rothenberg presented an enormous number of rituals and "performance poems" from the so-called primitive people which, when taken out of their usually sacred context, are so close to Fluxus pieces as to be nearly indistinguishable from them. Even had there been no immediate precedent of futurist performance pieces, no Dada or Surrealism, Fluxus might still have developed out of the materials of folklore. This point was not lost on Rothenberg, who included several examples of Fluxus performance pieces in his book.

Also, in the nineteenth century there was a tradition of parlor games that are sometimes very close to Fluxus. My Something Else Press, already mentioned as a publishing project that was in various ways a Fluxus enterprise, published a collection of such games by one William Brisbane Dick, *Dick's One Hundred Amusements*.[48] Fluxus might well have developed out of this popular-culture tradition as well. In fact, a few of the pieces from both the Rothenberg and Dick collections have been included in Fluxperformances with no noticeable incongruity.[49]

There are two other points worth mentioning in this part of the discussion. These are more in the way of Fluxtraditions.

Usually Fluxus performances have been done in costume. Either one wears all white, or one wears a tail suit, tuxedo, or formal evening dress. The former reflects the desire for visual homogeneity, which Maciunas, as a designer, tended to prize. The latter reflects his fondness for the deliberately archaic, formal, and obsolescent being presented in a new way. One sees a similar current in his use in his publications of extremely ornamental type faces, such as Romantique, for the headings, box covers, or titles.[50] These contrast with the very austere type he used in most of his setting of the body texts in Fluxus publications, IBM News Gothic, this last the version of the sans serif News Gothic on the IBM typesetter he used most of the time in the early days of Fluxus. There is no reason in particular why either of these traditions should be preserved; they are not integral to Fluxus. Perhaps this is one of the few areas in Fluxus in which there is room for sentimentality; both traditions have been carried on in Maciunas's absence.

Another tradition of Fluxus that is not a criterion as such is the emphasis on events that center around food. Many art works and groups of artists have dealt with food, but in Fluxus it becomes one of the main areas of involvement, perhaps because of its closeness to the art/life dichotomy. There were not only pieces themselves using apples, glasses of water on pianos, beans, salads, messes made of butter and eggs, eggs alone, loaves of bread, and jars of jam or honey, to name just a few that come immediately to mind, but also there were innumerable Fluxfeasts of various sorts, concerts or events that used the feast as matrix. No doubt these will continue as long as many of the original Fluxpeople are alive. One might speculate that the reason for this is the typical concern with food on the part of poor or hungry artists. But that seems secondary to the art/life element, and for me the fact that for works that are so much on the border of art and life, art and non-art, as Fluxpieces, the convention of a concert is not always suitable. For casual occasions with small audiences, feasts using food art are the equivalent of chamber-music concerts. Feasts have included such non-delicacies as totally flavorless gelatin "Jell-O," side by side with delicious loaves of bread in the form of genitals, chocolate bars cast in equally startling shapes, blue soups, and so on. Whether or not such foods are totally satisfying from an æsthetic point of view is not the question. The point is, rather, that there are non-determinative but nevertheless typical involvements in Fluxus side by side with the characteristic formal points.

iv. Evaluating Fluxpieces

But what of quality? How do we judge these works? Clearly, with Fluxus the normal theoretical positions will not apply. Fluxus works are simply not *intended* to do the same things as a Sophoclean tragedy, a Chopin mazurka, or a Jackson Pollock painting, and it is absolutely pointless to make the effort to fit Fluxus into a system to do this. Fluxus may have its thrills, but it is qualitatively different from most other art at least with respect to its teleology, its purposes, its ends.

First of all, what is it *not?*

1) It is not mimetic. It does not imitate nature in any narrative way, though it may be "natural" in the sense of "imitating nature in its *manner* of operation" (Coomaraswami's phrase)—its craziness, the kinds of patterns that it evokes, and that sort of thing. This is only to say that Fluxus could, in its own way, be realistic, very much so. There could be a genre of the Fluxus story, but it would have to be extremely generalized, stripped down to a bare minimum. A kiss—that might be a Fluxstory. But we don't usually think of that as mimesis.

2) Neither does it fit into the normative Romantic/Classic or Apollonian/Dionysian dichotomies. Perhaps it has something in common with the work of Novalis and the Schlegel brothers in German Romanticism, but it does attempt what either romantic or classical art attempts, a world transformed by the imagination or by feeling; it is not visionary; quite the opposite, in fact. In terms of its assumed effects, it does not attempt to move the listener or viewer or reader emotionally or in any other way. Neither does it attempt to express the artist emotionally or intellectually. Thus, one would not call it expressive in the normal meaning of the term. The Fluxartist does not even *begin* to reveal himself or herself through the work. Perhaps the viewer or listener is to reveal himself or herself by experiencing it, at least to himself or herself, but that is a different matter, and we shall return to it later. The important thing here is that the artist is as far away from the assumed eye or ear of the viewer or listener as is possible in an art work. Any expression is objectivized and de-personalized to the point of becoming transpersonal. One does not, as

in experiencing so many works of art, see through the work to the artist. There may be an individual style (most Fluxartists have those), but that, too, is a different matter, more akin to having one's own idiolect than to presenting a subjective vision of something.

3) Neither are Fluxworks, in the main, pragmatic. That is, they teach nothing except, perhaps, by example. They do not convey moral principles, nor do they present "correct" political or social views. They may be political, but this is apt to be in a symbolic way. For example, all the elements of a performance behave democratically; none dominates the others. But this is more apt to be the sort of thing that the artist thinks about than anything a viewer is concerned with.

4) Nor could they be called "objective" in the T. S. Eliot sense. They are not simply objects to contemplate; they are too minimal for that and, often, too active as well. They imply too much. Actually, some few Fluxworks do belong in this vein, but atypically.

5) Neither is the Freudian or symbolic analysis of a Fluxpiece apt to be very rewarding or extensive. One does not have enough materials to work on. Ninety-eight percent of Fluxus pieces have no symbolic content. Their psychological processes are too far and few between. Since the artist is not making a statement of any personal, psychological nature, an analysis of this sort would make very little sense.

6) A political analysis, Marxian or otherwise, might be interesting, but it would more likely satisfy the critic than the reader of the criticism, since Fluxus is only metaphorically political.

7) Since meaning is not the point and the conveyors of the meaning are so incidental that rather few patterns can be detected, the semiotics of a Fluxpiece are minimal enough to be problematic or even irrelevant. Of course, there *are* some such conveyors, but these require only the simplest of identifications. No patterns of communication would be likely.

8) The same holds true of structuralist analysis. The

linguistics of Fluxus would be a mentalistic exercise, not that Fluxus lacks its overall grammar, but the typical is only sixty per cent of the corpus, with the rest being exceptions of one kind or another. The whole analysis, rather than developing a meaningful critique or picture, would devolve into hair-splitting distinctions of *langue* and *parole*. Few patterns would be revealed. One might analyze a concert as a whole, but the concert *as a work* is a fairly arbitrary unit, and each concert tends to be quite different from each other concert (within certain limits), so that a structuralist analysis of recurring patterns would be rather pointless.

Yet, a person who attends a Fluxconcert, after the first shock, typically gets caught up in the spirit of it and begins to enjoy it, without consciously knowing why. Perhaps, there isn't even any shock. What is happening? To get to the answer to this will take a moment.

There is one critical approach that usually works, hermeneutics, the methodology of interpretation, both with regard to the artist and the recipient (the viewer, hearer, or reader). This approach, pioneered in recent times (it has an earlier history, too) by Heidegger, Betti, Gadamer, Jauss, and others in philosophy, can be used to theorize the workings of Fluxpieces fairly well. Usually the relationship between the recipient and the work is described in terms of a hermeneutic-circle idea of a work, leading to manifestation of work, leading to recipient, leading to recipient's own thought processes, leading to new idea of work, leading to further thought processes, leading to modified perception of work being manifested, leading back to altered perception of the idea of work. In other words, what the recipient sees is colored by his or her perception of it. This is an implied part of the piece, even though it may be quite different from what the artist thought of it or as the performer manifested it.

In practice, going through the whole hermeneutic circle is a terribly cumbersome process to consider. My own prefer-ence is to streamline it by borrowing the horizon metaphor from Gadamer. Let's take performance as the standard, for the moment. The performer performs the work. He or she establishes a horizon of experience; what is done, its implications, and whatever style the performer uses are all aspects of this horizon.

The viewer has his or her own horizon of experience. He or she watches the performance, and the horizons are matched up together. To some extent there is a fusion of these horizons (*Horizontsverschmelzung*). When the horizons fuse, wholly or in part, they are bent, warped, displaced, altered. The performance ends, and the horizons are no longer actively fused. The viewer examines his or her horizon. It is changed, for the worse or for the better. The best piece is the one that permanently affects the recipient's horizon, and the worst is the piece that the recipient, acting in good faith, cannot accept at all.

The key processes here are being conscious of the two horizons, completing the fusion process (by paying close attention to the performance), and then the discovery of the alterations in one's own horizon, as one notices that, for example, the performance has affected how one has been thinking about beans, butter, smiles, or eggs. Such criticism focuses a great deal, of course, on the viewer. In performance work it more or less ignores the original Fluxcomposer, who may or may not be the same as the performer.

But this is only true as far as the viewer is concerned because there is a similar fusion of horizons taking place between the composer and the performer. The composer makes the piece. The performer looks at the performance area and available materials, and only then decides just how to do the piece under the specific conditions of the performance. The performer next matches the horizon he or she has built up with the horizon of the original piece as he or she sees it. Even if the performer is performing his own work, there will still be something of such a fusion of horizons between X-as-composer and X-as-performer, because X adapts his or her own piece, takes the responsibility to make slight changes. If a piece is performed many years after it was written, perhaps X has changed it, and the interaction with the piece suggests different significances. The piece is viewed from many different angles, with different aspects revealed by each.

Now we can see why the viewer can enjoy the concert without knowing why, instinctively, he or she is matching horizons, comparing expectations, participating in the process; the more actively he or she does so, the more likely he or she will be able to enjoy the experience.

Nonetheless, for the viewer of Shiomi's "Music for Face," already mentioned, the composer is more or less an object of speculation. One wonders who might this "Mieko Shiomi" be. It is surely a Japanese name, but more one cannot tell. All one sees is the work being done. One does not really have any way of knowing if the performance is staying close to the Fluxcomposer's work or if the performer is taking liberties with it. What the recipient sees is the performance, no more, no less. But in the case of works as minimalist as Fluxus ones are apt to be, the more actively the performance is observed, the more likely one is to enjoy it, as noted above.

A question may well occur at this point, a natural question in viewing any unfamiliar art work: "Of what is this thing that I am seeing an example?" That is part of discovering one's meaning for a work. We love to classify. We involve ourselves in the naming of things, frame the work in its context, investigate its taxonomy. Of course, while I am talking about performance work, *any* Fluxwork—literary or fine art—would have analogical processes. But if one goes to a concert of familiar music, this question is minimized, because one knows, before one sets a foot in the door, that if Chopin is on the program, the concert is likely to include at least some Romantic music with a certain kind of sound to it. Thus, the taxonomy is not so important here. On the other hand, if one turns on a radio and finds oneself enjoying some unknown piece, part of the key to enjoying the piece is recognizing the question "Of what is this an example?" One tries to figure out what it is to match it with similar experiences in one's memory bank and so enjoy the work even more.

The fusion of horizons takes place in any hermeneutic art process. It is inherent in the discovery of the horizons. But in watching a Fluxperformance, examples are all the more important since they involve discovering the pattern of the performance, the what-is-being-done. Quite often this discovery, detecting the example aspect of the horizon, comes to the viewer with a striking impact; it is like "getting" the point of a joke. In fact, the similarity between even non-humorous Fluxpieces and jokes is striking.

Even when the piece is serious, one tends to react *as if* the piece were a joke, since a joke is the nearest thing on one's horizon to many Fluxpieces. For example, one is in an audience watching the stage. A balloon appears. A second balloon comes along. A third balloon comes along. One notices that the name of the piece is "Eight." Suddenly the pattern is clear. One laughs. Why? There is nothing inherently funny in the pattern, but it has enough in common with jokes so that each balloon, as it appears and confirms one's anticipation that there will in fact be eight balloons, feels like a stage along the way. Perhaps the metaphor of "joke" is implied by the piece. But what would happen if, in the piece, only seven balloons appeared? One would be annoyed, probably feel cheated. It would seem as if the Fluxcomposer were being overly clever. That would not be interesting. It would be like a tricky joke that dissolves into excesses of cleverness and amuses only the teller.

Some assemblages of Fluxpieces have been presented as other things besides concerts and feasts: rituals have a certain place in Fluxus, too. A ritual is, basically, a ceremonial act or series of such acts, symbolically recognizing a transition from one life stage or situation to another. Three notable Fluxrituals have been a Fluxmass, a Fluxdivorce, and the Fluxwedding of George Maciunas himself. In this last, Maciunas and his bride cross-dressed, as did the bridesmaids and best man (Alison Knowles). The wedding ceremony was based on a traditional Anglican one, but was altered with deliberate stumbling and falterings, the substitution of "Fluxus" for various of the critical words in prayers, and so on. Instead of anthems and special music, there were various special Fluxus pieces that were, in one way or another, suitable for a wedding. Afterwards there was an erotic feast, which included the special bread already mentioned above. According to classical theory one might expect such a reversal of the normative, with the solemn made light of and the religious made profane, to seem like a satire upon marriages in general. But no, the dominant feeling was one of joy. It was not a travesty but an incorporation of the horizon of Fluxus into that of marriage. The result was certainly serious: Maciunas and his bride Billie did, in fact, actually marry, though they also had a civil ceremony at another time. One felt that the participants were sharing the joy of the basic ritual with their Fluxfriends including one fifteen-year-old girl, a friend of one of my daughters, who came to the Fluxwedding without ever having seen a Fluxconcert or any other such event before. This young woman, whose horizons were thoroughly conventional, might have been expected to be shocked or offended or at least startled by the erotic feast. But as a whole the situation was so far from the normative that normative standards did not apply; she did not reject the fusion of horizons but entered into the situation and enjoyed herself as thoroughly as one might at any other kind of wedding.

Ultimately, of course, the purpose of achieving such a fusion of horizons is to allow the possibility of their alteration. I have not gone into Fluxobjects, Fluxboxes, and Fluxbooks, but the situation is the same as with the performances; one sees the work, considers its implied horizons, matches them with one's own, and these last, if the piece works well, are altered and enriched.[51]

In one of the "pages" (works) in George Brecht's series

"The Book of the Tumbler on Fire," one sees the words "notice green" in cork letters on a large wooden tablet. The tablet and words are painted red. There is a displacement: should the piece be green? One matches what one is seeing with what one might expect to see.[52] Should the piece have been green? The word says something different from what one would expect from the color. One thinks about labels, green and life, craft and its absence, simplicity and complexity. Perhaps one turns one's head away from the piece and looks at a white wall. After staring at red, one will see its complement, green. Perhaps one imagines a whole rainbow of "green" on tablets ranging from red through violet and brown, perhaps even including black and white. Any of such pieces would work reasonably well, though arguably the red-green juxtaposition is the most vivid. Still, had the piece been painted black or white, other meanings would appear from the color/non-color dichotomy. The horizons would work, and the implications, while different, would follow somewhat along the same pattern: see, identify what it is, compare it with what it might be, consider, digest, anticipate the next possibility, observe the transformation of one's own horizons, and enjoy the process. Each of such pieces is *an example* of the possibilities. When one sees such a piece, one imagines its alternatives. The alternatives are implied in the piece. The work is, in this sense, exemplative: it does not exist, as most art does, in its most definitive and perfect form possible. It exists in a form that suggests alternatives. This is true of many recent works, not just Fluxworks. They encourage the creativity of the viewer, listener, or reader, that is, of the receiver.

Such implications are a key criterion for evaluating the quality of a Fluxwork. If it has them, if one is conscious of them on the intuitive and imaginative level (rather than forcing them through an act of will), the work is good. That is, it is achieving its potential. The extent to which it lacks implications, conversely, is the extent to which it is not good, the extent that it fails. One can, for metaphysical reasons, reject such value judgments on the conscious level, of course, but one experiences them nonetheless and performs an act of criticism and, hopefully, of self-enrichment when one allows one's horizons to be changed.

The best Fluxworks imply a whole set of other possible Fluxworks; they are exemplary. In terms of performance style (or style of execution as Fluxart, Fluxboxes, and Fluxbooks), the best performances are, therefore, those that are most direct, so that one can perceive at least some of the alternative possibilities to the form in which a given work appears. This avoids what would be a problem in these works of becoming involved with noticing craftsmanship and the definitiveness of the statement they may contain. The best performance style for Fluxpieces is, thus, that which allows the piece to be experienced with a minimum of consciousness of the performer intervening between piece and receiver.

The same is also true of some kinds of non-Fluxus performances, of comedy, for instance. A comedian who intrudes on his joke by laughing, by expressing himself in a subjective way, by commenting "This is a great joke," by reducing the joke's effect by calling attention to himself, is likely to wind up as the only person laughing at his joke. In such cases the horizons of "joke" and "audience anticipation" fail to fuse. Buster Keaton, whom Maciunas claims in the lineage of Fluxus on his chart histories, always presents the humor in his films in an altogether deadpan way, while a twelfth-rate jokester in a hotel bar does much of the laughing and expressing himself—and bores the audience. So it is with Fluxus. The proper style for Fluxus is the most low-key and efficient one. One does not mystify the audience (that is not the point), but one lets it have exactly enough information to discover the horizon, and then one lets the piece do the rest. It is *never* necessary to joke about the Fluxpiece or to comment about it in an evaluative way—"Next we will have a great piece from 1963 by Ben Vautier . . . " That would constitute an intrusion, and, far from making the piece more likable, would detract from it.

What a pity it is that the public, including the professional public of organizers as well as performers, likes to lay emphasis upon the Fluxus artist him- or herself, and to encourage the production of what one might call "signature performances," those that derive their authority from their association with the originator of the work. Yet, I know I am not the best performer of my work, and most of us in any case can only present one perspective. We need more. It is always exciting to see what a new performer can contribute to an old piece. Of course, there is a certain numismatic thrill, not unlike collecting coins, in saying, "Oh, I saw Tschaikowsky on his last tour of America in 1898," or it might be Paderewski ca. 1938 or Nureyev or Julian Beck just a few years ago. Dear me, just what was it that he *did?*

Thereby hangs the problem: the personality and presence of the performer in such a signature performance tend to dominate the performance, to blind the spectator to what is being seen or heard or done, to break, putting it technically, the hermeneutic circle with an extraneous element that establishes new and perhaps irrelevant ones. Too, such performances are not good for the signer, since they convince him or her that *only* he or she can do the work. This would establish a silver umbilical cord to the work that may be nurturing but is not healthy after a certain point.

What is to be done? Of course, one must not avoid signature performances entirely or, for the Fluxartist, avoid doing them; it may be the only occasion when one will see some work one wants to see, or one can do whatever one wants to and not some (by now) familiar old work. But one must take the signature performance with a grain of salt, must note it as only one of the possibilities. That way the works will live as they should, and so will we, as artists, spectators, and thinkers. Pieces grow and change, just as people do, according to their changed contexts.

There is a slight difference between European Fluxus and American Fluxus. The Europeans have tended to perform their Fluxus works in the context of festivals, while the

Americans have tended to let the life situations predominate more often. Almost all the Fluxperformances in Europe have been in such concert situations, except for a few in the street: in America both of these have happened, but the feasts and the Fluxrituals have virtually all happened in America. The reason for this is not a difference in attitude, but rather, the European Fluxartists are more scattered so it takes a well-financed festival to bring them together. On the other hand, in spite of the worse financial situation in America, there are more Fluxartists or Fluxpeople there, and they form one or several communities. For instance, in New York City alone there are perhaps thirty Fluxpeople in residence, so to bring them together is not hard.

Also, the European Fluxworks, more typically than the American ones, come out of an expressive tradition. Since, to build up an emotional impact, one usually needs to work on a scale that is beyond the minimal, the collation sort of work is more typically European, while the minimalist one is more typically American or Japanese. Besides, even if an American wanted to work on the larger scale, funding and obtaining rehearsal time would be problematic, so that the economics militate against doing such pieces in America in contrast to Europe.

To return to the question of judging the work, then, it is my opinion that the most appropriate method, one that viewers or experiencers of Fluxworks often do intuitively, is to match their own horizons with those implied by the work. If their own horizons are thereby made more vivid or are expanded, emotionally or intellectually or however else, then the work is doing its job. If not, the work has failed.

v. Horizons of Reception and Expectation

What about other aspects of reception—artists, public, and institutions?[53] The reception of Fluxus—its popularity, influence and, in general, its acceptance—varies considerably, according to who is seeing the work. The least problem-

atic area is that of the general public. If even a relatively
unsophisticated person attends a Fluxperformance or an
exhibition of Fluxus works, such a person is apt to have an
interesting and pleasurable experience. Even at the very
beginning of Fluxus this was true. At Wiesbaden in 1962 the
Hausmeister (janitor) of the museum was so delighted by the
performances that he brought his family and friends to the
concerts as well. Not a formally cultured man, he nevertheless was sufficiently enthusiastic about the concert to exert
himself and bring those with whom he wanted to share it.
Furthermore, some of the more successful Fluxus performances have been done in the street or on boardwalks and in
other public spaces. One performance by Benjamin Patterson
comes to mind. It took place in New York's Times Square, on
the edge of a red-light district. He stood on street corners,
waiting till the lights turned green, and then simply followed
the light to the next corner. Several young women (they
appeared to be prostitutes) watched him do this for a while,
and then they joined in. This situation was not as exceptional
as one might imagine. Thus, it cannot be argued that, simply
because it is formally unconventional, Fluxus is lacking in
potential popularity. Because of the comparative simplicity
of most Fluxus pieces, this is less true of Fluxus than of other
avant-garde tendencies.

For most avant-garde art, one needs to know quite a
considerable amount of art history and even of technical
procedure in order to get one's bearings enough to be able to
fuse one's horizons and experience pleasure. The difficulty of
doing this is apt to become more pronounced, in fact, with the
progressive intellectualism of the audience, since it has more
expectations of what will or should happen. An audience
with the baggage of ideas to which it feels some commitment
has more to overcome than an audience without them, and it
must overcome the false horizons in order to be able to fuse
them and experience pleasure. An audience with a strong
commitment to one or another alternative set of ideas—

intellectual or derived from precedent and fashion—has to learn that these ideas are not under attack in Fluxus situations, that they are simply irrelevant to the work at hand, and this takes time.

As I have said, Fluxus performances and situations are popular with the public once the public is confronted by them. Many, many times "professionals" in charge of the programs of institutions have grossly underestimated the appeal of Fluxpieces; they devote an evening to Fluxperformances when they might have devoted several, and then they are surprised at the frustration among those who have to be turned away. They program an exhibition, print 500 catalogues, then find that the exhibition breaks attendance records and that they must print another thousand or so catalogues. The public, therefore, is not the problem.[54]

As for artists, few who do performance works can attend a Fluxus performance without, subsequently, including Fluxus-type elements in their own next performance. Naturally, these are usually not acknowledged, but a sensitive viewer can detect them. For example, in the 1960s, the famous Living Theater picked up fragments of Fluxworks, especially from Jackson Mac Low and myself (we had both worked with the Living Theater at various points), and included them in their program, "Shorter Pieces."

An interesting instance of the absorption of Fluxus into a larger context happened during the 1970s, when "performance art" or "art performances" became common. Typically, performance art was different from Fluxus, in that it included much more narrative and subjectively personal content, usually focusing on generating a public persona for the artist. Works by Laurie Anderson are a good example of this, stressing the bright young ingenue in the high-tech world of New York City (not always justifiable, but usually fairly convincing in performance). The persona may be quite different from the private personality of the artist. However, the minimalist structure within which the performance takes place, the untraditional narrative matrix, the absence of most theatrical techniques, suggest a debt to Fluxus (and perhaps to Happenings). The performances of "performance artists" match many of the Fluxus formal points given above, and, but for their knowledge of Fluxus, it is unlikely that their work would assume the form it did. Since the artists who did this work were, for the most part, younger than the Fluxus people, they naturally did not wish to present themselves as traveling in the wake of Fluxus or Happenings. They describe themselves as qualitatively new and different, although there are at least three overlaps, artists who have done major Fluxwork but who are accepted as performance artists as well. These are Alison Knowles (one of the original Fluxpeople), Geoffrey Hendricks, and Jean Dupuy. This legacy area can and should be explored more fully at some point.

Fluxus has had a complex relationship with museums and galleries. Maciunas himself pretty much despised them as playthings of the rich and purveyors of corrupt views, presenting dead art as the only possibility. Many Fluxartists, however, have seen them as the best means of breaking beyond the charmed circle of *cognoscenti* into a larger, more real world, and whatever it would take, short of a complete misprision, to make this break seemed (and seems) desirable. In recent years there have been at least a dozen major museum exhibitions of Fluxus works, sometimes accompanied by performance evenings. These have expanded the public enormously, but at the same time they have led to the propagation of simplistic views, an over-stress on the fun-and-games side of Fluxus, best explained as a horizon of expectation: 1) Fluxus's main participant was Maciunas; 2) Maciunas's most unique contribution was his playful designs for the covers of the Fluxboxes, his games; 3) therefore such games are the heart of Fluxus.

The would-be curator or collector constructs a horizon of expectations built on that notion and is then confronted by works by most of the other Fluxus artists or works made since Maciunas's death in 1978 by almost any of the Fluxartists. These present a horizon of some other sort. Rather than abandoning his or her horizon, the curator or collector concludes that this other work is not really Fluxus.[55] This can be a real problem, since it leads to misprisions and a false image of what Fluxus includes. But how does one expand the horizon of how Fluxus is perceived? Does one call work done since 1978 "post-Fluxus?" Is it meaningful to speak of an artist today (1994) as a Fluxartist? Can one do so without downgrading Maciunas's importance to the group as a whole? For all his occasional deviousness, Maciunas remained loyal to his group; he would probably say to downgrade him and survive. But most of us are reluctant to survive by attacking him. Anyway, that is a problem more for the artist than for the larger public. Time will surely resolve the problem one way or another. It always does. Many Fluxartists have produced their best work since 1978. This simple fact is sure to be discovered sooner or later, whether the collector or curator wants to call it "Fluxus" or by some other name. When the horizon of expectations viewers have, whether looking at the objects or the performances made by the Fluxartists, no longer matches what we are told "Fluxus" covers, then a new name will appear. It is not something the Fluxartists can control, because theirs is the horizon of poesis, which is quite different. Their focus is on the nature of what they intend, and this is only partly what the viewer sees and experiences.

To reiterate what I have said, before closing off, Fluxus differs from most art in being more conceptual or formal, less craft-oriented. It is of course a group of people and a historic tendency, but one of its main contributions is to show that one can make works with the eleven typifying characteristics I already mentioned (internationalism, experimentalism and iconoclasm, intermedia, minimalism, an attempted resolution of the art/life dichotomy, implicativeness, the spirit of play, ephemerality, specificity, presence in time, and musicality).

The best ingress into the work, since it does not usually offer the same experience or have to match our normative expectation for art, is via hermeneutics, via the horizon concept. Historically, Fluxus had an influence on art performance but also on artists' books (bookworks), which I have not discussed. Its real impact, however, will probably be when new artists can take up the Fluxus format without being self-conscious about it, to make into their own whatever they themselves need from the area.

XIV. Two Sides of a Coin:
Fluxus and Something Else Press

i.

IN THE LATE 1950s, when Happenings and events began to be performed in New York and elsewhere, while there was some consensus that the works that visual artists performed in spaces of their own devising (usually constructed in art galleries or sponsored by these) constituted "Happenings," there was no name for the works made by people who were not primarily visual artists. These were spoken of, simply, as "events" because that was a convenient term for them used by myself and my fellow students in John Cage's class in "Experimental Composition," taught at the New School for Social Research.[56] At first, the artists who were doing the latter had no agreed-on name for what they were doing, but the performances of this kind of works at Yoko Ono's loft on Chambers Street in New York (1960-61) and at George Maciunas's AG Gallery on Madison Avenue (1961), also in New York, made it obvious that a name was needed. Maciunas gave up his art gallery in 1961 and undertook the design and production of La Monte Young and Jackson Mac Low's *An Anthology*.[57] When his work was done, he found that he still had a large amount of intriguing material he wanted to publish, so he proposed a magazine and publication series, to be called "Fluxus." Maciunas went to Europe at the beginning of 1962 and, to promote *Fluxus*, organized a series of performances, called "Festum Fluxorum" ("Feast of Fluxusses"), the first of which was to take place at the art museum in Wiesbaden, Germany. Alison Knowles, Emmett Williams, and I were among the participants in those "Fluxus Concerts," which would later be described as "Fluxconcerts." These concerts caused a great scandal. The press began to call the work "Fluxus," and, as already mentioned, the participants they named *die Fluxus Leute*, that is, "the Fluxus people."

After performances we stayed at Maciunas's house outside Wiesbaden, at Ehlhalten am Taunus, staying up most of the night, trying to figure out the implications of what we were doing, discussing Turkish music and Heideggerian hermeneutics,[58] which I saw as an appropriate theoretical underpinning to our work. Along the way we planned the tactics of our next steps, mapped out new pieces, dined on such delicacies as pink or green mashed potatoes (we put food coloring into the dish), and imbibed Unterberg, a bitter liqueur. If we were "the Fluxus people," what was this Fluxus we had unleashed, and what was it for?[59]

At Ehlhalten we had lots of time to talk about the history of what we were doing. Maciunas was well aware of Greek visual poetry that paralleled our colleagues' concrete poetry, though he mistakenly ascribed it to the Byzantines.[60] As already mentioned some pages ago, I told Maciunas about Quirinus Kühlmann (1644-88), a German visionary poet who made visual poems called "Kühlpsalms" that were printed in his *Kühlpsalter* and recited on "Kühldays." Eventually Kühlmann was burnt as a heretic by the Tsar of Russia in Moscow, whither he had gone to see if the Tsar would like to found a new church with him. Maciunas was delighted by the story. From Kühlmann we picked up the habit of using terms like "Fluxconcerts," "Fluxartists," "Fluxfriends," "Fluxreasons," and "Fluxanythings." These terms were useful to us since we were not happy with the connotations of "art" with its liminality and perhaps overly elitist associations. We preferred to think of the art-life dichotomy lying at the basis of Fluxus, of "Fluxart" as being somehow closer to life than other art forms.

ii.

Before Maciunas returned to America in 1963 to present Fluxus formally in the USA, he had asked me to prepare for publication the large manuscript of what became *Jefferson's*

Birthday, a cross-section of my work from 1962 to 1963. Since I had been trained as a printer, was working at Zaccar Offset,[61] and was used to copy-editing, design, and all the technical side of printing and publishing, it was a natural thing for me to be involved in the production of my book. However, when my book did not materialize in what seemed to me a reasonable amount of time, and when Maciunas could not promise when he could get to it, I founded Something Else Press,[62] incorporated on February 2, 1964, as "Something Else Press, Inc." *Jefferson's Birthday /Postface* was bound in August, 1964. *Postface* was an account of the background and beginning of Fluxus, and the two books were bound together so that theory would not be divorced from practice. I called myself the "President" (and, for a time, sported a necktie in "presidential blue," while the first editor of Something Else Press was Barbara Moore.[63] When she left in 1966, Emmett Williams moved from Europe to New York and became the next editor. The Board of Directors varied slightly, but it usually consisted of myself, Alison Knowles, and Emmett Williams. While the Press never had more than five employees at one time—as many people as one could stuff into a taxi cab—we did have some interesting people aboard over the years who went on to distinguished careers elsewhere. At the shipping and order desk alone we had dancers Meredith Monk and Judy Padow, composer-violinist Malcolm Goldstein, artist Susan Hartung, poets Denis Dunn and Lawrence Freifeld, writer Mary Flanagan, and others, not to mention the artists and writers who worked for the press in other capacities, Fluxartists Al Hansen, Ken Friedman, and Ann Noël Stevenson.

Between 1966 and 1973, when I finally left "the Press," we produced 95 books. After my departure, two others were produced: Manfred Eaton's *Bio-Feedback Music* and a facsimile edition of Gertrude Stein's *A Book Concluding with as a Wife Has a Cow,* which was printed but not distributed. My successor at the press was Jan Herman, a good editor who wanted to run the operation, but it turned out he had no gift for fund-raising or for diplomacy. While he would wrap packages and do chores, he would not do what the president of an organization should do: write grant proposals, visit with possible patrons, handle major sales, and so on. By the autumn of 1974, the debts of Something Else Press had accumulated to about $240,000, and, though its assets were worth much more than that, I was in no position to return to the Press and work this out. As co-owner (with Emmett) of the Press, I filed for bankruptcy for it.[64]

The problems we faced at Something Else Press were typical of those of any small, independent publisher. Even though the prices of the books were high for the times, we lost so much money through distribution that our best-selling titles[65] were a threat to our very existence. Furthermore, although I was interested in publishing, I was above all an artist. My art work had been suffering because of my extensive responsibilities at Something Else Press. I could not simply go away and work somewhere: who would pay my co-workers? My secretary, Nelleke Rosenthal, saw these things clearly, as did I, but it was she whose advice it was to discontinue the Press, to self-publish for a while, and to start a new small press when another opportunity arose. I followed the first part of her advice in 1972 and started a program of publishing very small, model editions of my works using the name "Unpublished Editions." In 1976 Alison Knowles joined me in the project, and in 1978 so did John Cage, Philip Corner, Geoffrey Hendricks, Jackson Mac Low, and, soon thereafter, Pauline Oliveros and Jerome Rothenberg.[66] In 1978 we also changed the name of this new small press to "Printed Editions," as witness to our new identity (as our catalogue put it). Structurally, the new press was an unincorporated syndicate. The books were produced by each artist-member and sold through the network that had been built up for Something Else Press. All promotions were done on a cooperative basis (mainly a catalogue), and the moneys received were credited to the artist-author and paid out. There was only a minimal overhead to deal with. The system worked well until the end of 1986, at which time so many other publishers wanted to produce our main titles that we had no major books for Printed Editions. So we agreed to disband. Mission accomplished. That was the end of my formal involvement in book publishing.

As for Maciunas, his own first publications appeared in 1962 and 1963. *Fluxus*, intended as a magazine, never appeared except as an annual, while the reproduction proofs that we had carefully corrected at Ehlhalten were never printed and were eventually destroyed in a flood in Maciunas's car. But it was also the imprint on the yearbooks, books, and "Fluxboxes" that did appear, starting in 1963. Maciunas set up shop in Canal Street among the surplus stores, and there he bought plastic boxes, collected the makings of kits, and pasted Fluxlabels onto the covers. At the time of his death, in 1978, Maciunas was still producing Fluxus publications of one sort or another,[67] mostly Fluxboxes. A few were even produced to his specifications posthumously by Barbara Moore's Reflux Editions.

iii.

This is the matrix, then, of the Fluxus publications and of the Something Else Press. The stories that surround the various books and the people who worked on them—authors, artists, editors, and so on—are worth telling, too, but that must await another time. Every book has two stories, the story it tells and the story that surrounds it. I like to think that the stories surrounding the Something Else books are more a part of them than those of most other publications and have begun the "anecdotalization," if there be such a word, of the Press in a videotape lecture,[68] but that is a major project. What we can note now is the relation between Fluxus and Something Else Press, how they fit into their context at the time, and the relation between their legacies and traces today.

Maciunas' way of publishing stressed the original design, the unusual materials, and the hand-made. Objects in boxes and printed sheets held together by nuts and bolts — that was his orientation. But making these is, of course, hand work. The advantage of object books is that it costs little to prepare in advance to make a work; there are minimal editorial costs, no binders' dies and sample cases to worry about, and the like. However, the unit cost (the cost of making each copy) is relatively high. Their disadvantages are that the results cannot be sold universally and that the production of large numbers of them takes too much time. For example, Maciunas set us up with piles of papers to crumple and then unfold for Mieko (formerly "Chieko") Shiomi's page in the *Fluxus Yearbox* (1963). It took three people an evening to produce the papers for her one page. There were to be forty or so pages. How on earth could we produce all those? This is why so few copies of the *Fluxus Yearbox* were produced. In fact, Maciunas sometimes only produced each copy of the publication to order, waiting a few weeks until the orders had built up and then assembling whatever was needed.

Maciunas's politics were crypto-Communist; while never a party member, he loved to affect a conspiratorial manner, and his adoration of the USSR was not precisely rational. However, he had very little of the popular touch. Most of our circle, Fluxartists and Fluxfriends, were liberal in our politics, or leftist, but we had a strong populist streak that made us concerned about whether the Fluxboxes and publications were too elitist. Our productions were "collectibles," and perhaps we were simply producing as much "for the collector" as traditional artists. With this on my mind, around 1964 I began to have a vision of our publications being sold in supermarkets. How could this be brought about?

Nobody seems to know how Maciunas first learned graphic design. But throughout the 1960s he made his living doing design, paste-ups, and mechanicals, what was known in the trade as "finished art," often for the Jack Marchard

Studio.[69] But Marchard's main business was brochures, labels, logotypes, posters, and pamphlets. The normative style of the time was the "Helvetica look;" set everything in Helvetica typeface, give it lots of room, and let it go. Maciunas favored a tight, energetic look, which he achieved by using sans serif types, especially News Gothic, which he then juxtaposed with old-fashioned and florid display faces, such as the old wood type faces in the Romantique family. The layouts themselves were those appropriate to Marchard's business. Usually they were based on grids, into which or over which the types were laid out so as to suggest a cellular form. For the Fluxus publications, for which Maciunas was not limited by the needs of Marchard's clients, Maciunas frequently placed his types upside down or at least on their sides; this, too, had the effect of emphasizing the grid, as well as having a humorous effect.

By contrast, though I, too, rejected the "Helvetica look," after a brief time making bank checks (which taught me type face recognition, if nothing else), I worked mostly for offset printers and, eventually, book publishers and manufacturers. I, therefore, became familiar with the available materials and suppliers, with cost-accounting practices, and so on. As for design, my design style became whatever was appropriate to book formats. Grids were, for the most part, useless for such large-scale work. So I laid out my pages rectilinearly but lined up the elements along the diagonals of the pages, setting my type to form triangles and trapezoids wherever possible, and, also, where feasible, I set poems and short chapters flush bottom on the type pages (usually they are set in the middle). I used larger and bolder running heads at the tops of pages than is customary in order to tie the page together and because I liked the legibility it gave to a sometimes rather scattered or unorthodox page. Since I did not wish to develop favoritism among type faces, I used whatever faces a particular supplier had, often making my selections by means of chance operations, using dice.[70] In this way,

I became familiar with many seldom-used or old-fashioned fonts that later gave the Something Else Press books their look of old-but-new. I liked Maciunas's designs, but he never commented on mine, so I assume he didn't reciprocate. But what Maciunas really did *not* like was the withdrawal of my energy from the production of Fluxus publications.

Yet, the move had been all but inevitable all along. I wanted to offer Fluxus to everybody, to have Fluxus and Fluxus-type work (similar works by other artists who were outside our circle) available in airport book shops and grocery stores. Maciunas focused on the work being cheap but gave little attention to making them accessible to ordinary people, to promotion and distribution beyond the order forms that were printed in his *CC V TRE* newspapers, which, of course, had to circulate among the right people to function at all, people who already had some idea what they were looking at. Concern about this made my withdrawal from the production of the publications more or less just a matter of time.

I had protested strongly to Maciunas over his threat to withdraw his legal sponsorship of Ayo and other foreign Fluxartists (whose status required letters of support) if they participated in Allan Kaprow's production of Karlheinz Stockhausen's *Originale,* which was being produced as part of Charlotte Moorman's Festival of the Avant-Garde for 1966. Both Moorman and Stockhausen were anathema to Maciunas, the former as an exponent of European cultural chauvinism (was American cultural chauvinism any better? I asked) and the latter as an unprincipled opportunist. This was in line with the Marcyism of the *Workers' World* politics of Henry Flynt, a marginal Fluxperson who took an interesting but, I felt, unproductive anti-art position that saw art as bourgeois, a view even Lenin had once denounced as "typically Trotskyite." In fact, this is why, by way of contrast, Emmett Williams and I, the next year, invited the W. E. B. DuBois Clubs, a Communist youth group, to contribute a manifesto to the *Manifestoes* pamphlet published by the Something Else Press in our inexpensive Great Bear Pamphlets series in 1967. All the other manifestoes in that booklet were either by Fluxus artists or were somehow in the same spirit as these. I was adamantly opposed to our potential marginalization for the sake of ideological purity; we were already marginalized enough in the cultural world without adding to the problem. Most of the Fluxartists were, in any case, quite apolitical in spite of the typical political militancy of the times.

Maciunas chose to view my protest and involvement in the production of *Originale* as a withdrawal from Fluxus. He denounced me in the chart histories he constantly revised as histories of and statements about Fluxus. He said in two of the versions of the chart that I had withdrawn from the group to found a rival organization. However, I kept describing myself as a Fluxperson, and my Fluxfriends kept including me in their projects. So I was not really excluded from Fluxus. Then in the summer of 1966, Maciunas and I sat down in the city park that was outside the Something Else Press office and which served me as a private conference room, and we talked over our objectives. Maciunas and I might not have agreed about the relation of our activities to society as a whole, but we did agree on the objectives of our publishing activities. While the Fluxus publications should serve as paradigmatic models or prototypes of various sorts, the best role for Something Else Press was as an outreach series, useful for getting our ideas beyond the charmed circle of *cognoscenti* to which, reluctantly, we belonged, one which could present to the larger public all kinds of alternative and intermedial work. Maciunas would do his boxes, while I would be the one to do books. The Press tried always to be "something else" than what commercially oriented trade publications were doing or, since there was The Something Else Gallery in the front room of Alison's and my home, what commercial galleries were showing. This was a position Maciunas heart-

ily approved, and thus the schism ended. I was again included by Maciunas in Fluxus, and so it continued until his
death, which occurred in 1978. There also developed another
kind of reciprocity. For example, when Ken Friedman appeared on the scene in 1967, I felt he belonged in Fluxus as
much as in Something Else Press, and so I brought him to
Maciunas, with whom he worked from then on as well
serving as the Director of Something Else Press in 1970-71
while it was located in California for a year.

Fluxus was, then, to be thought of as having four aspects:
a series of publications, a group of artists, the forms associated with the publications and their performances, and the
theoretical positions inherent in these. This made it not so
much a movement, with a clearly defined group of artists
setting out to achieve a particular program, as a "tendency,"
organized on a collective basis, something more pluralistic
and less exclusive than the other iconoclastic movements of
our century that it resembled in one way or another—Dada,
Futurism, Surrealism, and Russian Constructivism. Fluxus
was also pluralistic and in any case more suited to the cultural
climate of the 1960s and 1970s, usually (and inadequately)
defined as "postmodern."

By contrast, Something Else Press was to be a parallel
expression, covering much the same ground but with historical and other related materials added, through which we
could develop the context of Fluxus and intermedial art
forms by bringing the work to the largest possible public in
an undiluted form. But whatever we did, it would have to
follow with our name, to be "something else" from what the
commercial publishers were doing. Already in the 1950s the
Fluxartist Robert Filliou had issued his *Manifesto d'Autrisme,*
declaring the need always to be doing something other than
the normative routine. This was very close to the Something
Else Manifesto, which I had written in 1963 when I decided
to start Something Else Press and before any of the books had,
as yet, appeared.[71] But if the purpose of the Press always

would be to publish the valuable work that differs from the fashionable or the conventions of the times, then to fulfill its role, however, the Press would have to include other kinds of intermedia than simply Fluxus. Otherwise, we would not be creating an appropriate context for our reception. The editorial board—Emmett Williams (and, earlier, Barbara Moore), Alison Knowles, myself, and, at the end, Jan Herman—focused on other possibilities, printing such intermedial areas as concrete poetry (which Emmett Williams had pioneered),[72] new forms of fiction or proto-novel,[73] and works of past avant-gardes we felt were important and either misunderstood or under-appreciated.[74] This was in keeping with Maciunas's and my view that cultural innovation is cumulative, that each innovation adds to the store of possibilities and does not simply replace some earlier mode forever as, by contrast, is often true in science. The assumption that replacement applies to culture and art as much as science, that the introduction of a new form does not simply add to the available possibilities but makes the older ones obsolete, is what I call the "neoteric fallacy" ("neoteric" is a rare word but it is not my coinage; it denotes a taste for or interest in the new). Opposed to this fallacy would be Maciunas's and my view that brothers and sisters in artistic innovation have always been active, that the avant-garde is eternal, but that many of the most worthwhile innovations have been lost over the centuries or have been repressed. This would be true of secular drama in the Middle Ages, of unusual styles of music in the late fourteenth and early fifteenth centuries, or in some non-Western classical music traditions (notably Central Asian, Turkish, and Mongol styles), as well as of such forms of intermedia as visual poetry and graphic musical notation. Maciunas announced several issues of his *Fluxus* magazine that would be devoted to this kind of material. However, they never appeared, and, in fact, he barely had a chance to scratch the surface, gathering together the actual materials. I was more fortunate, because when I left Something Else Press I had the leisure to gather materials of this sort together, resulting in my book *Pattern Poetry: Guide to an Unknown Literature* (1987).[75] I also worked out the start of a hermeneutic theory for intermedia art in general and Fluxus in particular,[76] thus completing some of the objectives that had been set out during our late-night discussions at Ehlhalten in 1962, namely, clarifying the historical context and roots of Fluxus and beginning the task of establishing its theoretical matrix, without which it is hard to evaluate individual works or to develop a critical vocabulary for Fluxus or, indeed, for many other art currents of recent years—conceptual art, art performance, or, arguably, of Language poetry.[77]

iv.

So Fluxus and the Something Else Press had related objectives, but they were different, too; the Press largely grew out of Fluxus and Unpublished/Printed Editions out of the Press. The Press could not have performed its outreach if it had used the kind of experimental formats that were appropriate to Maciunas's Fluxus publications, nor could he have provided the experimental prototypes if he had confined himself to books. Of course, there are exceptions to this, as well as overlaps. Maciunas did, in fact, do several traditional-format books early on in Fluxus, as already mentioned, and Something Else Press issued several books in boxes or on cards or portfolio books.[78] But these are just that, exceptions. Most of the Something Else books were only experimental as regards the printed page, not in format, trim size, or binding. We also published twenty pamphlets on handsome colored papers, the Great Bear Pamphlets. These cost up to $2 and were thus rather inexpensive, even for the time. They were in fact our vehicle for achieving my dream of having our works available in at least one grocery store, the Berkeley Coop in Berkeley, California, where they were available for some time on a display case beside the vegetable counter.[79] We also became the object of a satirical wisecrack in an article in *Harper's Magazine,* which mocked the "poetry readings at the Something Else Gallery." The only reading we ever had there was a non-stop marathon reading of James Joyce's *Finnegans Wake.* Maybe Joyce was too modern for them. Anyway, the appearance of such a mention in an establishment magazine, or the reviews of the Williams *Anthology of Concrete Poetry* in *Vogue* and *Newsweek,* indicated that we were getting to places the new arts seldom penetrate, and this too was appropriate to our program.

Not only did Fluxus and Something Else Press include many of the same participants, but our objectives were closely parallel. They were twin sides of the same coin. Although it included fewer people, Printed Editions had similar objectives to those of Something Else Press, objectives more suited to the role of Printed Editions as a smaller small press, a term that covers too many independent publishers, but our needs and purposes were appropriate to a cooperative, and our entire program was devoted to aspects of our *members'* work and its contexts rather than to the larger problem of promoting broader art forms — as did the program of Fluxus performances and Fluxboxes and as did Something Else Press with its purview and programs in Fluxus and concrete poetry, new fictions, avant-garde theory, and so on. The relationship between Fluxus and Something Else Press was, therefore, a symbiotic one, while Printed Edition was a focusing in on a portion of Something Else Press. All three form an overall story.

XV. A Fluxessay for a Few of my Fluxfriends

Project for Dick Higgins
Devise a hermeneutic of the spread of Buddhism in America to be taken as a performance piece.

Project for Takehisa Kosugi
Develop a realization for the above using electronic crickets and cans that make sounds.

Project for Eric Andersen
Define the ambiguities and tautologies in the above project and realize these with flashing lights.

Project for Alison Knowles
Base an ethics on the horizons of the above, to be expressed in terms of shoes, beans, and fishes of the Philippine Seas.

Project for Philip Corner
Teach the above as if they did not exist.

Project for Geoffrey Hendricks
Project all horizons of the above into ontology and perhaps epistemology using mythical imagery.

Project for Ben Vautier
Shorten the above; demonstrate its roots in Cage and Duchamp to all of the possible kinds of art students.

Project for Jackson Mac Low
Scramble all written materials resulting from the above and construct twenty-one new kinds of old-fashioned poems from them.

Project for Joe Chick and Glue Mama
Make food versions of all the above.

Project for Hala Pietkewicz
Eat the above.

Project for Takako Saito
Catch and box the sounds of all the above.

Project for Emmett Williams
Make portraits of all the artists doing their projects, leaving out any you regard as non-existent (except for two).

Project for Robert Watts
Make one object epitomizing the psychological processes of all the above.

Project for Larry Miller
Point in all directions implied by the above.

Project for Kuniharu Akiyama
Conduct Fluxorchestral versions of all the above.

Project for Toshi Ichiyanagi
Make piano arrangements of all the above, but keep them a secret.

Project for Addi Køpcke
Explain all the above in the form of celestial jokes.

Project for Richard Maxfield
Make music for the angels out of the explanations.

Project for John Lennon
Make a song about all these projects intended to place exactly eighth on the celestial hit parade.

Project for George Maciunas
Organize a tour through all the heavens with these projects on a cosmic mine-sweeper.

Project for Yoshi Wada
Trumpet all these projects back to earth with an earth trumpet made of plumbing parts.

Project for Joseph Beuys
Creatively misinterpret all the above projects to produce an interesting identity.

Project for the Zaj Group
Parallel all the above, keeping a minimum distance of 31,3 cm away.

Project for the Hi Red Center
Question all the above, distributing the results in tabular form.

Project for Al Hansen
Anticipate everyone's solutions of their projects in popular terms, but only tell the results to very young people.

Project for Erebo
Disappear carrying aspects of the above.

Project for Serge Oldenburg
Follow Erebo from all possible directions.

Project for Bengt af Klintberg
Prepare a book paralleling the projects in terms of traditional jokes from all Nordic cities.

Project for Lugo Gosewitz
Develop a glass cabbala using the letters of a Hebrew translation of texts that result from the above projects.

Project for Sten Hanson
Base a set of athletic procedures on the realizations of all these

projects and intensify their sounds with appropriate vocal effects.

Project for Shigeko Kubota
Realize exactly seven of these investigations as video sculptures, detailing their precedents in Dada, Futurism, and late surrealist manifestations.

Project for Nam June Paik
Cause all these and related projects to short-circuit in a positive manner on preselected dates.

Project for Joe Jones
Automate all the projects and plug them in.

Project for Ay-o
Color all the projects as rainbows and match them with a set of corresponding textures.

Project for Robert Filliou
Express all the projects as algebraic equations, including the hermeneutic of experiencing them.

Project for Benjamin Patterson
Consider all the projects in silence for fifteen years, then reappear with games that sum them up.

Project for Vostell
Make a marriage ceremony from all the projects and from this derive a series of visual notations with words in Spanish.

Project for Milan Knizák
Lead all these ideas among the quiet people.

Project for George Brecht
Summarize all concrete aspects of all the above in a set of five words for possible performance.

Project for Mieko Shiomi
Indicate the weights and directions of all the above on a three-dimensional atlas of the earth.

Project for La Monte Young
Locate a single tone in the above and sign it with capital letters.

Project for Tomas Schmit
Insist on being invited to produce a footnote for each of the projects, so that you can decline to accept the invitation.

Project for Ken Friedman
Prepare 6,000 alternatives to each of the projects and reveal their prices in a commercial newsletter.

Project for Henry Flynt
Picket all the realizations.

Project for René Block and Gino di Maggio
Record all the sounds of all the above.

Project for Jean Dupuy
Analyze the perception of each realization in terms of Leonardo da Vinci's optics.

Project for Yoko Ono
Apologize to the sky.

Project for Jan Van der Marck
Propose a final resting place for all the objects, realizations and processes.

Project for Sarenco
Enlarge all the projects to mammoth scale.

Project for Daniel Spoerri

Classify and exhibit any artifacts resulting from the above projects according to their sentimental factors balanced against their potential applications.

Project for Knud Pedersen

Identify the Danish aspect of each of the projects; isolate and translate only these aspects for television broadcast and for debate in the Danish parliament.

Project for Jean Brown and Hanns Sohm

Document all the above, and file the result both alphabetically and by date.

Project for Jon Hendricks

Catalogue all artifacts and graphic spin-offs that relate to the above.

Project for Barbara Moore

Take any leftovers and make something wonderful from them.

Project for Mats B

Understand and edit all the above into a book.

Project for Peter Frank

Review the above book and derive all possible lectures from it.

Endnotes

Modernism Since Postmodernism

[1]*Journals of Ralph Waldo Emerson. 1820-1872*, ed. Edward Waldo Emerson and Waldo Emerson Forbes. 10 Vols. (Boston: Houghton Mifflin, 1909-148:79). Quoted in Ihab Hassan, *The Postmodern Turn: Essays in Postmodern Theory and Culture* (Columbus: Ohio State University Press, 1987:182).

[2]Hassan 1987:198). "Fatidic" is a synonym for "prophetic."

[3]Accounts of the history of "Postmodernism" appear in Hassan, (1987: 85-86) and Calinescu (1987:267-69). Jencks (1987) offers a good study of the term in architecture.

[4]Calinescu (1987:267-69).

[5]The earliest use of the term "semiotic" that we know is in the chart facing the title page of Ernesto Friderico's *Galenicæ et Hermeticæ Anatome Philosophica* . . . (Hamburg: Michael Hering, 1626:frontispiece), a work on medicine. On the chart it denotes signs indicating the nature of diseases and diagnosing them. This term, too, then, like "postmodern," has been with us longer than is generally realized.

[6]Hassan (1987:135).

[7]Hassan (1987:168-173).

[8]In *The Dismemberment of Orpheus: Toward a Postmodern Literature* (2nd ed. Ann Arbor: University of Michigan Press, 1982) and *Paracriticisms: Seven Speculations of the Times* (Urbana, IL: University of Illinois Press, 1975).

[9]This is a point which Paul Mann makes repeatedly in his *The Theory-Death of the Avant-Garde* (Bloomington: Indiana University Press, 1991). Also, Calinescu (1987:273) points out that some

German critics, notably Jürgen Habermas, do not accept an autonomous conception of Postmodernism, as in Habermas's article "Die Moderne: Ein Unvollendetes Projekt" ("The Moderns: An Uncompleted Project") published in the United States in *New German Critique* 22 (Winter 1981) as "Modernity versus Postmodernity," surely a misrepresentation of Habermas's position.

[10]I deal with this later in this book. Not dealt with are the various forms of "Postmodernism" in the theater and performance, which often revolve around the question "How did Western theater originate—in game or in ritual?" The question posits the theoretical response of the critic. On the side of ritual are the excellent writings of Richard Schechner and the anthropologist Victor Turner. The game theory has no outstanding champion but seems to have more adherents. Some day I would like to write about this area.

[11]In Mann (1991:141). Mann's polemic, self-described in the very first sentence as "This overheated and distasteful little book" (1991:7) is invaluable for its critiques of Rosalind Krauss (1991:72) and others of her ilk.

[12]The term was a popular one among the German Romantics, first used by Herder in 1769. A good historical account of it is in Friedrich Kluge, *Etymologisches Wörterbuch der Deutschen Sprache* (Berlin: de Gruyter, 1975:878). It was imported into English by Matthew Arnold in such places as the "The Function of Criticism at the Present Time" (1865?) and *Literature and Dogma* (1883).

[13]I first used the term in my essay "Mediocracy," printed later in this book.

[14]See Hans Robert Jauss ("Sketch of a Theory and History of Aesthetic Experience" in Jauss, *Aesthetic Experience* (1982:3-151) and "Literary History as a Challenge to Literary Theory" in Jauss, *Toward an Aesthetic Reception* (1982:3-45). A more general definition of the hermeneutic method in criticism, i.e., a non-Jaussian one, is in Calinescu (1987:273). Richard Palmer's

Hermeneutics (1969) is the fullest and most lucid account we know of the method. See also footnote 21.

[15]The most sophisticated attempt to establish a real set of criteria that oppose Modernism and Postmodernism lies in Hassan's list, given later in my text and in Hassan (1987:91-92), already discussed. Besides the problems mentioned later, even within his conception there are problems. For example, he lists at the start "Romanticism/Symbolism" as Modern and "Pataphysics/Dada" as Postmodern. If so, Postmodernism is virtually as old as Modernism, thus calling into question its distinction from it. But was not a large current in what we might agree constituted a Modernism its revival of classical principles, as in Stravinsky's so-called "Neoclassicism," the poetry of T. S. Eliot, and so on? Isn't the corpus of work from Dada as distinct from its legend actually quite characteristically modernist? Isn't one reason why Pataphysics has its appeal its reveling in that which transcends normative, specific meanings, which is characteristic of abstraction and non-objectivism in fine art, for instance? Are not these last characteristic of modernist art more than of post-modernist in most taxonomies? Thus, his list becomes an argument for my own argument that Postmodernism is at best a phase of Modernism and is inherently too flawed a concept to be usable except possibly in architecture, where it has a very specific function, given later.

[16]Otto Gmelin, *Philosophie des Fernsehens* I (Pfullingen, BRD: self-published, 1967).

[17]One would like to know how other peoples have responded to their change of millennia, too.

[18]My own ambivalent feelings about this are expressed in "Fluxus Against Fluxus" later in this book.

[19]A good account of Andy Warhol's reception and prominence is in Mann (1991:137-138). To be personal for a moment, I knew Warhol for many years and, while terribly shy, he was an intellectual, well-informed and capable of carrying on a discussion of art when he chose to. The myth of Warhol as a *naïf* who

could say nothing besides "er . . . uh . . . " is just that, a myth. It is unfair to Warhol to cast him as the undertaker of Modernism with his Campbell soup cans signifying the "death of art," as some have claimed, or even the death of Modernism. They are simply elements of an environment and vision, to which many of his works belong. The most memorable aspect of Warhol's work, it seems to me, is the curious indifference it implies to its subject matter—Jackie Kennedy, automobile accidents, the death chair, Marilyn Monroe, and so on. On the positive level, it is a vision that tries to point towards a freedom from editorializing comment. For this, his emphasis on the surface level of art communication is indispensable, even if one does not (as I don't) share his vision.

[20]To detail this lies outside my discussion in this essay, but the Marxists have at least made a beginning of tracing the limitations of the assumption of the eternal in art or beauty. My point about the *Zeitgeist* has to do with this as well. If new spirits arise in each decade that must be expressed, then correspondingly older spirits will seem more distant and remote and will become more difficult to appreciate.

[21]This is the term which Hans-Jörg Gadamer calls *Horizonts-verschmelzung*. I have covered much of the ground I am discussing here in my book *Horizons: The Poetics and Theory of the Intermedia* (Carbondale: Southern Illinois University Press, 1983). The most succinct account of hermeneutics in literature (it could easily be applied to other arts as well) is Richard Palmer's entry on hermeneutics in Alex Preminger and T. V. Brogan, *The New Princeton Encyclopedia of Poetry and Poetics* (Princeton: Princeton University Press, 1993:516-21). Palmer's fuller account is his *Hermeneutics* (Evanston, IL: Northwestern University Press, 1969), already mentioned.

[22]The *Oxford English Dictionary* cites a first English usage of "neoteric" in the works of Thomas Nashe from 1596. However, as "neotericus" Cicero imported it into Latin from Greek. An account of this appears in Curtius (1953; an expansion of Curtius's account in Calinescu, 1987:14-18), relating the term to the idea of modernity. The *Oxford English Dictionary* cites a first usage of the noun "hermeneutics" from 1737 in the works of the

theologian Daniel Waterland, though in neo-Latin and and German it is older. In fact, the adjectival form, "hermeneutic" does not appear until 1807.

[23]See the essay "Innovation" in my *A Dialectic of Centuries* (1978:83-87).

[24]Dika Newlin's *Schoenberg Remembered: Diaries and Recollections, 1938-1976* (New York: Pendragon Press, 1980) is an account of Schoenberg's actual classroom procedures, as distinct from his theories. Newlin studied with him privately and in his classes in Los Angeles and understood his work profoundly, as her several other books on Schoenberg attest.

Five Myths of Postmodernism

[25]I discussed this in "Modernism Since Postmodernism," above. Cf. Calinescu (1987:14-18).

[26]Other early appearances of this term also are documented in "Modernism Since Postmodernism," above.

[27]Calinescu (1987:98) calls attention to the use of this term by Etienne Pasquier (1529-1615), a "French humanist lawyer and historian," possibly as early as 1562, but it appears to be a unique usage. Pasquier's text reads: "A glorious war was then being waged against ignorance, a war in which, I would say, Scève, Bèze and Pelletier constituted the avant-garde; or, if you prefer, they were the fore-runners of the other poets. . . ." However, we know of thirteen editions of Pasquier's *Recherches de la France*, the work in which the term appears, from 1562 to 1665, so it may well have been known to Saint-Simon and his circle. Saint-Simon's book, his last, was a collaboration, and the text in which "avant garde" appears may actually be by his colleague Olinde Rodrigues.

[28]Although they are named for their magazine, *L=a=n=g=u=a=g=e*, "Language" poets seems a more efficient name for the group.

[29]Obviously this was written before the changes in the Communist block, but the assumptions still hold among Western WFMs.

[30]Cited in Frederic Will (1965:74). This quotation is said to come from Cousin's *Du Vrai, Du Beau et Du Bon* (1818 and 1836).

[31]Cf. fn. 5.

[32]The idea that criticism is superior to art is not an especially new one. It is found in the early writings published as the *Cahiers de la Jeunesse* of the 1840s by the French philosopher and Orientalist Ernest Renan (1823-92), per Calinescu (1987:163-164).

Mediocracy

[33]I did not mention literature here because, after founding and running Something Else Press from 1964 to 1973, it might seem too partisan for me to point out how, in recent time, the small presses have had to pick up much of the load of quality publishing that was previously done by larger firms. However, the biggest inhibition on larger sales was from our public not understanding that small-press books cost more because production runs are shorter, so unit costs are higher. Besides, many (not all) small-press books are intended for re-reading by the same person, not for throwing away, so that both physically and editorially, we had to put more into a book. Even so, a good book remains a pleasure on second reading, while most "trade books" do not, but are like cotton candy, fading away as one eats into them. In the long run, the well-chosen small-press book is a better buy. One should never buy a book that one doesn't mean to read twice; that is the secret of real economy here.

Music from Outside

[34]My *Pattern Poetry* documents many examples of it over the past two millennia. See elsewhere in this book.

John Cage: Perception and Reception

[35]This piece was written in 1986-87, before Cage's death, which occurred in 1992.
The Origin of "Happening"

[36]Coleridge's only use of the term "intermedium," so far as I can discover, is in "Lecture Three 'On Spenser,'" in Coleridge, Samuel Taylor. *Coleridge's Miscellaneous Criticism*, ed. T. M. Raysor (1937:33). It reads: "Narrative allegory is distinguished from mythology as reality from symbol; it is, in short, the proper intermedium between person and personification. Where it is too strongly individualized, it ceases to be allegory . . . "

Fluxus: Theory and Reception

[37]This is the text of a rubber stamp I made up around 1966 and used to stamp the endings of my letters.

[38]Maciunas was educated in architecture and industrial design, but he seems always to have had an interest in art which intensified over the years. His major works date from the later years of his life. For a fuller biography of Maciunas, see Jon Hendricks's *Fluxus Codex* (1988).

[39]The first public Fluxconcert in Europe, which took place a few months before the Wiesbaden festival in 1962, was not called "Fluxus" but it included only materials later classified as Fluxus, it was organized by Fluxartist Ben Patterson and Maciunas. It was called "Neo-Dada in der Musik" after a lecture Maciunas had given soon after his arrival in Europe, thus suggesting that Maciounas did not yet think of Fluxus as a body of work apart from his proposed publications. An account of the term "Neo-Dada" is in Susan Hapgood's *Neo-Dada Redefining Art (1958-62)* (1994:11-12, 58 fn. 1).

[40]Another Fluxus tradition is making pieces which answer other pieces. For instance, I have a piece in my "Metadramas" cycle of the 1980s in which one "looks for the vanishing smile." This refers to Shiomi's much earlier piece, but one need not know this to enjoy it.

[41]This subject is discussed in greater detail elsewhere in this book and two others of my books, *Horizons* (1983) and *Dialectic of Centuries* (1979).

[42]He perceived his pieces rather than conceived them, as I have put it elsewhere in this book.

[43]In 1990, Ken Friedman expanded on my original nine criteria which were in the early versions of this essay, adding the last two which are specifically relevant to performance pieces. His articles were published as "The Twelve Criteria of Fluxus" in Friedman's catalogue essay *Fluxus and Company* for Emily Harvey Gallery and in Lund Art Press (vol. 1 no. 4). I am indebted to him on this point and others.

[44]For all that Surrealism included a huge number of participants, the only women who come to mind in it are Leonora Carrington and Meret Oppenheim.

[45]A "speculum" is a mirror. Two other ancient classifications are *musica mundana* ("music of the worlds"), which we call by the medieval term "music of the spheres," and *musica humana* (human music), which describes the normative "playable" music, whether art music or popular music.

[46]Maciunas, unlike the rest of us, had a stormy relationship with Kaprow, many of whose works of the late sixties seem appropriate to Fluxus and distant from his earlier Happenings. As for Vostell, with whom Maciunas's relationship was also stormy, some of his Happenings, such works as the *T.O.T.* (1973), seem like collections of small and concise Fluxus events.

[47]My *Pattern Poetry: Guide to an Unknown Literature* (1987) documents some 1,800 visual poems from before 1900 C.E. in Greek, Latin, Hebrew, Hungarian, Italian, French, German, Scandinavian, Dutch and Flemish, British and English-language, Spanish, Portuguese, Catalan, Polish, Russian, Ukrainian, Croatian, Chinese, Japanese, Sanskrit and the Prakrits, Gujarati, Hindi, Marathi, Tamil, Burmese, Persian, Turkish, Arabic, and

Ancient Egyptian literatures. No doubt there are more. Nor are these works necessarily by obscure poets, as is sometimes charged, but that is another story.

[48]Please note that it is the author's last name that is referred to in the book's title, not my surname.

[49]The Swedish Fluxus artist Bengt af Klintberg is a professional folklorist. Many of his works have a direct relationship to folklore.

[50]In the next essay Maciunas's design style is discussed more fully.

[51]This approach will work with many other works outside of Fluxus, of course, works which one's gut feeling tells one are "good" but which one finds hard to explain. It is through horizons that, for instance, I found myself enjoying such a Joseph Kosuth construct as his Wittgenstein show in Vienna; though not particularly a friend of Fluxus, Kosuth seems somehow very relevant to it.

[52]This is the Jaussian *Erwartungshorizont* ("horizon of expectations"), to which we will return later.

[53]The most thorough account of the reception of Fluxus by the public and of different interpretations of what it is is Hannah Higgins's "Fluxelephant: A Reception History of Fluxus" (Ph.D. Dissertation, University of Chicago, Chicago, IL, 1994).

[54]In 1979, a Fluxconcert was presented by The Kitchen in New York. Originally scheduled for three evenings, the staff reduced it to one. Several hundred people were crowded in over house capacity, and over a thousand people were turned away. In Paris in 1989, for a Fluxus evening at l'Ecole des Beaux Arts, more than three thousand viewers were unable to fit into the hall. Special Fluxus issues of magazines have all done well, some going out of print within a few days of publication.

[55]Many Fluxartists, including myself, have experienced this problem in their professional lives as well. The scenario goes like this: artist takes his or her work to good gallery. Gallery owner says artist is a Fluxus artist and they are not a Fluxus gallery: "Try so-and-so" (which has shown Fluxus). Artist goes to so-and-so. Work is shown. Collector comes along with his or her horizon of expectations build up into a fun-and-games focus. Collector says, of the new works, "This is not Fluxus." Thus, be it ever so fine a work, the work goes unsold. Artist is thus placed into a survival bind: should I conceal my Fluxus past (of which he is she is proud)? What should I do to downplay it?" Naturally, no new gallery wants to show the Fluxus artists, be they ever so famous, because they know almost all would-be Fluxus collectors have the old horizon of expectations. They also know there are very few surviving works from the early days of Fluxus which are not, by now, in museums or in collections which are likely to go there, certainly not enough to base a business on.

Two Sides of a Coin: Fluxus and the Something Else Press

[56]The term "event," used in this way, is of uncertain origin; the composer Henry Cowell, with whom both Cage and myself studied, used it, but Cowell may have picked it up from Cage as well.

[57]La Monte Young and Jackson Mac Low, eds., *an anthology* (New York: Jackson Mac Low, 1962). The book was reprinted by the Heiner Friedrich Gallery in New York in 1970.

[58]While Maciunas viewed Heidegger as a life-long fascist whose work was a justification for fascism, I didn't. If I wanted to persuade Maciunas of Heideggerian ideas, I had to phrase them so he would not recognize them.

[59]It was already several years too late to write a proper manifesto setting out our program, as most movements have. Maciunas drafted one, but only a few people signed; we were too far along in our work and too diverse for that. He never had the authority within our group that, say, André Breton did among the surrealists. Maciunas might try to read people in or

out of Fluxus, but as a group we operated more by consensus, regarding Maciunas as a member of the group who had great gifts for publicity and energy for correspondence, but ultimately as just one among equals. Though tempted to be dictatorial at times (who isn't?), Maciunas was glad to accept that Fluxus was a collective and, usually, to function within that context.

[60]As noted elsewhere in this book, actually the seven principal Greek visual poems are much older, and the few Byzantine pieces are derivative of earlier works. On all this I subsequently expanded in *Pattern Poetry*.

[61]Zaccar Offset became the main printer for Maciunas and Fluxus. The 1977 feast in honor of Maciunas took place on the premises of Zaccar Offset, though by then they had moved to a different space from the one described in my *Postface* (1964).

[62]The general story of Something Else Press has been described elsewhere, most fully by Peter Frank in his monograph *Something Else Press* ("DocumenText." New Paltz: McPherson and Company, 1983). I will therefore not repeat the anecdote of how "the Press" was named, how it ran its course, and, in 1974, died and was replaced by "Unpublished Editions," a cooperative whose name was changed in 1978 to "Printed Editions" and which lasted until 1986. Instead we will focus on how Something Else Press related to Fluxus.

[63]Since those days Ms. Moore has written memorably about Fluxus.

[64]Jan opposed the bankruptcy, as did Emmett, though he had no idea where new capital might be found. In the aftermath of the bankruptcy the two of them attacked me roundly,,accusing me, in an interview published in *West Coast Poetry Review* (Winter 1976-7), of, such things as, when "things got rough," taking a pleasure jaunt to Frankfurt, Germany, with my secretary, Nelleke Rosenthal, and implicitly wasting the Press's resources. Well, I did have a part-time secretary, Nelleke, who was Dutch and who had a brother in Frankfurt. In September 1973, although I had left the Press in July, I decided to attend the

Frankfurt Book Fair, and Nelleke came along to visit her brother and to help staff our booth at the Fair. We worked hard and sold more books in one week there than Jan Herman had sold during the entire year. While Emmett came to understand this, Jan Herman never did figure out just what had gone wrong.

[65]We produced a total of 18,000 copies of Emmett Williams's *An Anthology of Concrete Poetry* (1968) and 17,000 copies of Claes Oldenburg's *Store Days* (1969), respectable numbers by any accounting.

[66]All but Oliveros had been Something Else Press authors, and an Oliveros book had been proposed.

[67]Good documentation of these is in Jon Hendricks's *Fluxus Codex*.

[68]*The Something Else Press and Since* (Vancouver, BC: Western Front, 1981).

[69]Marchard's studio had the advantage of being a place where nobody smoked, important to Maciunas since he had terrible asthma.

[70]To do this, I would make a list of up to thirty-six faces, assign a number to each, then use dice to select a number between one and thirty-six, and then start from whatever face I had selected. This resulted in some of the Something Else books being set in unusual faces or faces which are normally only used for display.

[71]Both manifestoes are included in the *Manifestos* pamphlet, already mentioned. I have been unable to find out where Filliou's manifesto first appeared, and was unaware of its existence when I wrote my own manifesto; mine was first printed inside the dust jacket of the first Something Else Press book, *Jefferson's Birthday/Postface* (1964), also already mentioned.

[72]Such works include Emmett Williams, *An Anthology of Concrete Poetry* (1968), Eugene Gomringer, *The Book of Constellations*

(1970), and the various books of Williams's own poetry that we produced.

[73]Daniel Spoerri's A*n Anecdoted Topography of Chance* (1966), my *A Book About Love & War & Death* (1972), Kostelanetz, ed., *Breakthrough Fictioneers* (1972), and Toby Mac Lennan's *1 Walked Out of 2 and Forgot it* (1973) are of this sort.

[74]For example, such works would include Richard Huelsenbeck's *Dada Almanach* (1966) or Gertrude Stein's *The Making of Americans* (1969) and the four other Stein works we reissued. These last began the current popularity of Stein today, since, at the time we were doing our reissues, Stein was sometimes discussed but, since her works were so hard to obtain, she was very seldom read.

[75]This book, already mentioned, documents some 1,800 visual poems from before 1900 C.E. from all over the world (not just from the West) and also presents a gathering of related phenomena, such as old graphic musical notations.

[76]These theories originally appeared, for the most part, in the *Something Else Newsletter*, starting in February 1966 with "Intermedia," which revived that term from S. T. Coleridge. The early texts went through various revisions, as they began to compose parts of a whole, until they reached their final versions in two books, *A Dialectic of Centuries: Notes towards a Theory of the New Arts* (1st ed., West Glover, VT: Printed Editions, 1978 and [revised] 2nd ed., West Glover, VT: Printed Editions, 1979) and *Horizons: The Poetics and Theory of the Intermedia* (Carbondale, IL: Southern Illinois University Press, 1983).

[77]Most of what passes for criticism in those areas offers potential vocabulary but little insight, since the relationship among the words is not clear and no contextualization is offered for the work in terms of its diachronic or current relationships. This point I expand on in an article, "Five Myths of Postmodernism" in *Art Papers* 13:1 (1989).

[78]Robert Filliou's *Ample Food for Stupid Thought* (1965) came in two editions, a traditional book one and a postcard set in a box. Wolf Vostell's *De-coll/age Happenings* (1966) came in a box which included a set of black and white reproductions of his Happenings notations, a book with their texts, an Alka Seltzer® packet glued to a piece of aluminum foil, and a trimmed matzo cracker. Allan Kaprow's *Calling* (1968?) was arranged as a visual poem on vinyl sheets with plywood covers. My *foew&ombwhnw* (1969) was bound as a prayer book. There were also others. Somehow these publications can also be viewed as early artists' books.

[79]I used to have a photograph of the rack of Great Bear Pamphlets beside the green peppers.

List of References

Amman, Robert J. "The Musical Theory and Philosophy of Robert Fludd." *Journal of the Warburg and Courtauld Institutes* [London University] 30 (1967) 198-227.

Andrews, Edward Deming. *The Gift to be Simple: Songs, Dances and Rituals of the American Shakers.* 1940; New York: Dover Publishing, 1967.

Anonymous. *Das ABC cum notis vanorum, herausgegeben von einem dessen Nahmen in ABC steht.* Leipzig and Dresden: Johann Christoph Miethen, 1703.

A.L.F. Askins, "Manuel de Faria e Sousa's Fuente de aganipe: the unpublished seventh part," in Geary (1983,245-77).

Barthes, Roland. *S/Z,* tr. Richard Miller. New York: Hill and Wang, 1974.

Bayam. Andreas. *Panegyricus sine Verbis de S. Philippi Nerii Laudibus .* . . . Urbi Veteriex typographia Rainuldi Ruuli, 1629.

_____. *Cardiographia* . . . Roma: apud Jacobum Laurum, 1624.

Berne, Stanley and Zekowski, Arlene. *A First Book of the Neo-Narrative.* Stonington, CT: Metier Editions, 1954.

Black Mask Group. See Hahne, Ron.

Block, René. *Für Augen und Ohren: von der Spieluhr zum akustischen Environment (For Eyes and Ears: from Mechanical Clocks to Acoustical Environments).* Berlin: Akademie der Künste, 1980 [catalogue of exhibition at Akademie der Künste and elsewhere].

_____. *1962 Wiesbaden Fluxus 1982. Eine kleine Geschichte von Fluxus (A Small History of Fluxus).* Berlin: Berliner Künstlerprogramm des DAAD and Wiesbaden-Erbenheim: Harlekin Art, 1982 [catalog of exhibition at Nassauischer Kunstverein, Wiesbaden, and elsewhere].

Block, Ursula and Michael Glasmeier. *Broken Music: Artists' Recordworks.* Berlin: Daadgalerie, 1989 [catalogue of exhibition at the Daadgalerie and elsewhere].

Boethius. *De Institutionis Arithmetica Libri Duo. De Institutione Musica Libri Quinque*, ed. Gottfried Friedlein. 1867; Frankfurt am Main: Minerva, 1966.

Bouissac, Paul. *Circus and Culture: A Semiotic Approach.* Bloomington: Indiana University Press, 1976.

Brecht, George and Robert Filliou. *Games at the Cedilla, or The Cedilla takes Off.* New York: Something Else Press, 1967.

_____. See Martin, Henry.

Bürger, Peter. *Theory of the Avant Garde,* tr. Michael Shaw. Minneapolis: University of Minnesota Press, 1984.

Cage, John. *Empty Words. Writings '73-'78.* Middletown, CT: Wesleyan University Press, 1981.

_____. *M. Writings '67-'72.* Middletown, CT: Wesleyan University Press, 1979.

_____. *Notation.* New York: Something Else Press, 1969 (with Alison Knowles).

_____. *Pour les oiseaux: entretiens avec Daniel Charles.* "Les batisseurs du XXe siècle." Paris: Pierre Belfond, 1976. English translation: *For the birds.* Dover, New Hampshire: Marion Boyars, 1981.

_____. *Roaratorio.* Königstein: Athenäum, 1982 [comes with cassette].

_____. *Silence. Lectures and Writings.* 1961; Middletown, CT: Wesleyan University, 1973.

_____. See Richard Kostelanetz.

Calinescu, Matei. *Five Faces of Modernity: Modernism, Avant-Garde, Decadence, Kitsch, Postmodernism.* 2nd ed. Durham, NC: Duke University Press, 1987.

Canel, A. *Recherches sur les Jeux d'Esprit, les Singularités et les Bizarreries Litteraires principalement en France.* Erreux: de l'imprimeries d'Auguste Herissey, 1867.

Caramuel de Lobkowitz, Juan. *Ioannis Caramuelis Primus Calamus ob Oculos Ponens Metametricam, quae Cariis Currentium, Recorrentium, Abscendentium, Descerndentium nec non Circumvolantium Versuum Ductibus* . . . Roma: Fabius Falconius, 1663.

Cardew, Cornelius, ed. *Scratch Music*. London: Latimer New Dimensions, 1972.

Cerone, Pedro (=Pietro). *El Melopeo y Maestro*. 2 v. "Biblioteca Musica Bononiensis," 2 and 25. 1613; Bologna: Arnoldo Forni, 1969.

Chabrol, C. *Oriselle, ou les Extrèmes Mouvements d'Amour, tragicomédie* (Paris: Mathieu Colombei, 1633).

Charles, Daniel. *Gloses sur John Cage*. "Serie «esthetique»" Paris: Collection 10-18, 1978.

Chopin, Henri. *Poesie Sonore Internationale*. Paris: Jean-Michel Place, 1979 [comes with two cassettes; revised edition in preparation].

Coleridge, Samuel Taylor. *Coleridge's Miscellaneous Criticism*, ed. T. M. Raysor. 1936; Folcroft, PA: Folcroft Press, 1969.

Corner, Philip. *Ear Journeys: Water*. New York: Printed Editions, 1977.

_____. *I Can Walk Through the World as Music*. Cavriago: Edition Pari & Dispari, 1981.

_____. *I Can Walk Through the World as Music (first walk)*. New York: Printed Editions 1980.

_____. *Popular Entertainments*. 1968; New York: Printed Editions, 1980.

_____, Alison Knowles, Benjamin Patterson, and Tomas Schmit. *The Four Suits*. New York: Something Else Press, 1966.

Crane, Nichael and Stoffler, Mary, eds. *Correspondence Art. Source Book for the Network of International Postal Art Activity*. San Francisco: Contemporary Arts Press, 1984.

Curtius, Ernst Robert. *European Literature and the Latin Middle Ages,* tr. Willard R. Trask. Princeton: Princeton University Press, 1953.

Duchamp, Marcel. *Marchand du Sel: Écrits de Marcel Duchamp*. Paris: Terrain Vague, 1959.

Emerson, Ralph Waldo. *Journals of Ralph Waldo Emerson*, ed. Edward Waldo Emerson and Waldo Emerson Forbes. 10 v. Boston: Houghton Mifflin, 1908-124.

Erlhoff, Michael. *Kurt Schwitters Almanach*. Hanover: Zweitschrift, 1987.

Filliou, Robert. See George Brecht.

Fludd, Robert. See Robert Amman.

Fluxus: Aspekte eines Phänomens. Wuppertal: Kunst und Museumsverein, 1982 [exhibition catalogue].

Friedlander, Walter. *Caravaggio Studies*. Princeton: Princeton University Press, 1955.

Friedman, Ken. "The Twelve Criteria of Fluxus." See *Ubi Fluxus Ubi Motus*, below.

Geary, John S. *Florilegium Hispanicum: Medieval and Golden Age Studies Presented to Dorothy Clotelle Clark*. Madison, WI: Medieval Seminary of Hispanic Studies, 1983.

Gmelin, Otto. *Philosophie des Fernsehens I*. Pfüllingen, Germany: Self-published, 1967.

Gomringer, Eugen. *The Book of Constellations*, ed. and tr. Jerome Rothenberg. New York: Something Else Press, 1970.

Góngora y Argote, Luis de. *Obras Poéticas* Paris: L. Michaud, 1921.

Gryphius, Andreas. *Lustspiele,* ed. H. Palm. Stuttgart: Literarisches Verein, 1878.

Hahne, Ron, Ben Morea, and the Black Mask Group. *Black Mask and Up Against the Wall Motherfucker*. London: Unpopular Books and Sabotage Editions, 1993.

Hapgood, Susan B. *Neo-Dada Redefining Art 1958-62*. New York: American Federation of the Arts, 1994 [exhibition catalogue].

Harsdorffer, Georg Philipp, Sigmund Von Birken, and Johann Klaj[us]. *Fortsetzung der Pegnitz-Schaferey*. Nurnberg: Wolffgang Endter, 1645.

_____. *Pegnesisches Schafergedichtt*. "Deutsche Neudrucke, Reihe Barock," 8. 644; Tubingen: K. Carher, 1966.

Hassan, Ihab. *The Dismemberment of Orpheus: Toward a Postmodern Literature*. 2d ed. Ann Arbor: University of Michigan Press, 1982.

_____. *Paracriticisms: Seven Speculations of the Times*. Urbana, IL: University of Illinois Press, 1975.

_____. *The Postmodern Turn. Essays in Postmodern Theory and Culture*. Columbus: Ohio State University Press, 1987.

Hendricks, Jon. *Fluxus Codex*. New York: Abrams, 1988.

Hermannus de Santa Barbara. *Carmelo-Passus in xenium oblatus... d. Ioanni Gualterio Slusio* . . . Leodii: apud Arnoidum Bronckardt, 1687.

Higgins, Dick. *A Book About Love & War & Death*. Barton, VT: Something Else Press, 1972.

_____. *A Dialectic of Centuries: Notes towards a Theory of the New Arts*. 2nd ed. New York: Printed Edition, 1980.

_____. "Dick Higgins." in Zadrozny, Mark.

_____. *Horizons: The Poetics and Theory of the Intermedia*. Carbondale, IL: Southern Illinois University Press, 1983.

_____. "Intermedia." *Something Else Newsletter* 1 #1 (February 1966) 1-4. Reprinted in Higgins (1983:18-28).

_____. *Jefferson's Birthday/Postface*. New York: Something Else Press, 1964.

_____. *Pattern Poetry: Guide to an Unknown Literature*. Albany, NY: State University of New York Press, 1987.

_____. "Points Towards a Taxonomy of Sound Poetry," in Kostelanetz (1981) pp. 49-59; also *Precisely* 10-12 (1981).

_____. *Towards the 1970's*. Somerville, MA: Abyss, 1970.

Higgins, Hannah. "Fluxelephant: A Reception History of Fluxus." Unpublished Ph.D. Dissertation. Chicago: University of Chicago, 1994.

Huelsenbeck, Richard. *Dada Almanach*. 1921; New York: Something Else Press, 1966.

Iacobus Nicholai de Dacia [Jakob Nielsen]. *Liber de Distinccoine Metrorum,* ed. Aage Kabell. "Monografier utgina av K. Humanistiska Vetenskaps-Samfundeti Uppsala," 2. Uppsala: Almquist & Wiksell, 1967.

Jauss, Hans Robert. *Aesthetic Experience and Literary Hermeneutics*, tr. Michael Shaw. Intr. Wlad Godzich. Minneapolis: University of Minnesota Press, 1982.

_____. *Toward Aesthetic Reception*, tr. Timothy Bahti. Intr. Paul de Man. Minneapolis: University of Minnesota Press, 1982.

Jencks, Charles. *Post-Modernism: the New Classicism in Art and Literature*. New York: Rizzoli, 1987.

Jha, Kalanath. *Figurative Poetry in Sanskrit Literature.* Delhi: Motilal Banarsidass, 1975.

Jolas, Eugene. "From 'Jabberwocky' to 'Lettrism,'" *Transition* 48, 1 (1948), 104-20.

Kagel, Mauricio. *Die Umkehrung Amerikas (The Inversion of America)*. Köln: Westdeutscher Rundfunk, 1977.

_____. *Theatrum Instrumentorum*. Köln: Kölner Kunstverein, 1975 (catalogue).

Katz, Ruth. "On 'Nonsense' Syllable as Oral Group Notation," *Musical Quarterly*, 60 (April 1974), 187-94.

Kepler, Johannes. See D. P. Walker.

Kirby, Michael. *Happenings*. New York: Dutton, 1965.

Kircher, Athanasius. See D. P. Walker.

Klotz, Heinrich, ed. *Postmodern Visions. Drawings, Paintings and Models by Contemporary Architects*. New York: Abbeville, 1985.

Knizák, Milan. *Unvollständige Dokumentation. Some Documentation. 1961-1979*. Berlin: DAAD, 1980.

Knowles, Alison. *A Bean Concordance*. Barrytown, NY: Printed Editions, 1983.

_____. See John Cage, Philip Corner, and Michael Erlhoff.

Kostelanetz, Richard, ed. *Aural Literature Criticism*. New York: Assembling Press, 1981), pp. 49-59; rpt. *Precisely* 10-12 (1981).

_____, ed. *Breakthrough Fictioneers*. Barton, VT: Something Else Press, 1972.

_____, ed. *Conversing with Cage*. New York: Limelight Editions, 1988.

_____. *John Cage*. "Documentary monographs in modern art." New York: Praeger Publishers, 1970.

_____. "Person of Letters in the Contemporary World. A Memoir in Ten Parts." in Zadrozny, Mark.

Krauss, Rosalind E. *The Originality of the Avant-Garde and Other Myths*. Cambridge: MIT Press, 1987.

Liede, Alfred. *Dichtung als Spiel*. 2 v. Berlin: Walter de Gruyter, 1963.

Lienhard, Siegfried. "Enigmatisk vers och carmina figurata i sanskritdiktning," *Kung. Vitterhets Historie och Antikvitets Akademiens Årsbok* (1983), 79-88.

Lovejoy, Arthur O. *Essays in the History of Ideas*. Baltimore: Johns Hopkins University Press, 1948 [pp. 228-53].

Mac Lennan, Toby. *1 Walked Out of 2 and Forgot It*. Barton, VT: Something Else Press, 1973.

Mac Low, Jackson. *Asymmetries 1-260*. New York: Printed Editions, 1980.

_____. *French Sonnets*. Tucson, AZ: Black Mesa Press, 1984.

_____. *Representative Works: 1938-1985*. New York: Roof, 1985.

_____. *Stanzas for Iris Lezak*. Barton, VT: Something Else Press, 1972.

_____. *Twenty-Two Light Poems*. Los Angeles, CA: Black Sparrow, 1968.

_____. *The Twin Plays*. "Great Bear Pamphlets." New York: Something Else Press, 1966.

_____. See La Monte Young.

Mahlow, Dieter. *—Auf ein Wort! Aspekte Visueller Poesie und Visueller Musik (—For One Word! Aspects of Visual Poetry and Visual Music)*. Mainz: Gutenberg Museum, 1987 (catalogue of exhibition at the Gutenberg Museum and three others).

Mann, Paul. *The Theory-Death of the Avant-Garde*. Bloomington: Indiana University Press, 1991.

Martin, Henry. *An Introduction to George Brecht's Book of the Tumbler on Fire*. Milano: Multhipla, 1978.

Maupassant, Guy de. *Oeuvres Complètes* . . . Paris: Louis Canard, 1908).

Newlin, Dika. *Schoenberg Remembered: Diaries and Recollections, 1938-1976.* New York: Pendragon Press,
1980.

Nielsen, Jakob. See Iacobus Nicolae de Dacia.

Nyman, Michael. *Experimental Music. Cage and Beyond.* London:
Studio Vista, 1974.

Oliveros, Pauline. *Software for People: Collected Writings 1963-80.*
Barrytown, NY: Printed Editions, 1984.

_____. See Heidi von Gunden.

Palmer, Richard. "Hermeneutics." In Preminger (1993:516-21).

_____. *Hermeneutics.* Evanston, IL: Northwestern University
Press, 1969.

Passerini, Pietro Francesco. *Schedarium Liberale . . .* Piacenta:
Iohanni Bazachii, 1659.

Patterson, Benjamin. See Philip Corner.

Poggioli, Renato.. *The Theory of the Avant Garde.* Cambridge, MA:
Harvard University Press, 1968.

Porter, Lambert C. *La Fatrasie et le Fatras.* Genève:
Librairie E. Droz, 1960.

Pozzi, Giovanni. *La Parola Dipinta.* Milano: Adephi, 1981.

Preminger, Alex, and T. V. Brogan, eds. *The New
Princeton Encyclopedia of Poetry and Poetics.* Princeton:
Princeton University Press, 1993.

Robson, Ernest and Jet Wimp. *An Anthology of Contemporary
Mathematical Poetry.* Parker Ford, PA: Primary Press, 1979.

Russolo, Luigi. *The Art of Noise,* tr. Robert Filliou. "Great Bear
Pamphlets." New York: Something Else Press, 1968.

Saint-Simon, Claude-Henri de, Léon Halévy, and Claude Redon.
Opinions Littéraires, Philosophiques et Industrielles. Paris:
Bossanye Père, 1825.

Satie, Erik. *The Writings of Erik Satie,* tr. and ed. Nigel Wilkins.
London: Eulenburg Books, 1980.

Schafer, R. Murray. *The Tuning of the World: Toward a Theory of
Soundscape Design.* Philadelphia: University of Pennsylvania
Press, 1980.

Schmit, Tomas. See Philip Corner.

Schöning, Klaus, ed. *Hörspielmacher: Autorenporträts und Essays.* Königstein: Athenäum, 1983.

_____, ed. *Neues Hörspiel: Texte Partituren.* Frankfurt: Suhrkamp, 1969.

_____, ed. *Neues Hörspiel O-Ton: Der Konsument als Produzent.* Frankfurt: Suhrkamp, 1974.

_____, ed. *Spuren des Neuen Hörspiels.* Frankfurt: Suhrkamp, 1982.

Soundings. Purchase, NY: Neuberger Museum, 1981 (catalogue of exhibition curated by Suzanne Delahanty).

Southey, Robert. *The Poetical works of Robert Southey.* Boston: Houghton Mifflin, 1884.

Spoerri, Daniel. *An Anecdoted Topography of Chance,* tr. Emmett Williams. New York: Something Else Press, 1966.

Stein, Gertrude. *The Making of Americans.* 1925; New York: Something Else Press, 1966.

Tuwim, Julian. *Pegaz Deba.* Warsaw: Czylenik, 1950.

Ubi Fluxus Ubi Motus (exhibition catalogue, curator Gino di Maggio). Milano: Mudima, 1989.

Visible Language 26 #1-2 (Winter/Spring, 1992). Special issue: Estera Milman, ed. *Fluxus: A Conceptual Country.*

Vom Klang der Bilder: Die Musik in der Kunst des 20. Jahrhunderts (On the Sound of Pictures: Music in the Art of the Twentieth Century). München: Prestel, 1985 (catalogue of exhibition at Staatsgalerie Stuttgart, curated by Karin von Maur).

Von Gunden, Heidi. *The Music of Pauline Oliveros.* Metuchen, NJ: Scarecrow Press, 1983.

Walker, D. P. *Spiritual and Demonic Magic: From Ficino to Campanella.* 1958; Notre Dame: University of Notre Dame Press, 1975.

_____. *Studies in Musical Science in the Late Renaissance.* Leiden: E. J. Brill, 1978.

Warmington, E.H. ed. *Remains of Old Latin.* Cambridge: Harvard University Press, 1967.

Will, Frederic. *Flumen Historicum:: Victor Cousin's Aesthetic and Its Sources*. Chapel Hill, NC: University of
North Carolina Press, 1964, [pp. 74, 93 n. 89].

Williams, Emmett, ed. *An Anthology of Concrete Poetry*.
New York: Something Else Press, 1968.

Wilson, Colin. *The Outsider*. Boston: Houghton Mifflin, 1956.

Wilson, Martha. "Artists Books." New York: Abbeville Press,
1990.

Young, La Monte (with Jackson Mac Low). *An Anthology*. 1961;
New York: Galerie Heiner Friedrich, 1977.

Zadrozny, Mark, ed. *Contemporary Authors*. *Biographical Series*, 8.
Detroit, MI: Gale Research, 1988.

Discography

Recomended recorded versions of works mentioned in
the text:

Baude Cordier. *Tout par Compas*. Ensemble Ricercare de Zurich.
Harmonia Mundi LP HMU 592.

Beuys, Joseph. *Sonne statt Reagan*. EMI-Electrola, 1982. LP 7143.

_____, and Henning Christiansen. *Schottische Symphonie (Scottish
Symphony)* and *Requiem of Art*.. Edition Schellmann 2-rec.
LP.50-159-62.

_____, and Nam June Paik. *In Memoriam George Maciunas (Piano
Duet, 1978)*. Beuys and Paik. Edition Block, 1982 (LP).

Brus, Günther. See Rühm, Gerhard.

John Cage. *Amores* (1943). Many recordings, including
the one by the Kroumata Percussion Ensemble
(Swedish) BIS LP-272. Also Quatuor Helios. Wergo
0-286-203-2 (CD). This last has also the *First Construction (In Metal)*, see below.

_____. *Atlas Eclipticalis* (1961). With other works, Barton
Workshop. Etcetera KTC 3002 (CD).

_____. *First Construction (in Metal)* (1939)- Les Percus-
sions de Strasbourg, on Philips 6526 017; Kroumata
Percussion Ensemble. (Swedish) BIS LP-232. For
Paul Price's vintage recording, see below.

_____. *Fontana Mix* (1958). We know of no recording of this work alone, but it is in the background on various releases, perhaps most notably of *Aria with Fontana Mix*, Cathy Berberian, soprano, on Time Records LP S/8003.

_____. *HPSCHD* (composed with Lejaren Hiller, Jr., 1967-9)- On Nonesuch H-71224 (LP).

_____. *Imaginary Landscapes, nos. 1-3* (1939-42)- *Imaginary landscape no. 1* is performed by John and Xenia Cage, among others, on a classic album of Cage, *The 25-year retrospective concert of the music of John Cage* (May 15, 1938), which also includes *Sonatas and interludes* (1946-8) performed by Maro Ajemian and *First construction (in metal)* (1939) performed the Paul Price Percussion Ensemble. Other major works are also on the album. Produced by George Avakian on three Avakian Records (LP, no numbers), with a brochure designed by Robert Rauschenberg, available through New Music Distribution.

_____. *Music of Changes* (1951). Herbert Hencke, pianist, on Wergo 600099-50 (CD). David Tudor, pianist, on New World 214 (LP).

_____. *Roaratorio* (a 1982 realization, with John Fullemann, of _____ , _____ *circus on* _____ , (1979). Mode 18-9 (CD).

_____. *Six Melodies for Violin and Keyboard* (1950). Various good recordings, the most convincing being by Vera Beths, violinist, and Reinbert de Leeuw, piano, on Phillips 9500 920 (LP). The record also includes the *Amores* (see above).

_____. *Sonatas and Interludes* (1946-48). Many recordings available. Perhaps the subtlest is by Yuji Takahashi. Denon 33C37-7673 (CD).

_____. *String Quartet in Four Parts* (1950), Several fine recordings; including that by the La Salle Quartet, on DGR 2530735.

_____. *Variations I-VII* (1958-66). Various recordings for a variety of groups of instruments (these are often open). Compare the realizations of *Variations III* (1963) by Gerd Zacher on the organ, on Deutsche

Gramophon DGG 139442 with that by the San Francisco New Music Ensemble, on Wergo 60057.

Christiansen, Henning. *Abschiedssymphonie (Farewell Symphony).* Christiansen with Joseph Beuys.Edition Block LP EB 118.

_____. See Joseph Beuys.

Corner, Philip. *The Barcelona Cathedral* and *Gamelan.* "Vibrazioni del Sonorio," 8. Illasi: Edizioni Lotta Poetica and Napoli: Studio Morra, 1987? LP 0724.

Dubuffet, Jean. *Musical Experiences.* Finnadair, 1973 LP SR 9002.

Duchamp, Marcel. *The Entire Musical Work of Marcel Duchamp.* Petr Kotík and SEM Ensemble. Multhipla, 1976. LP n.1.

Franklin, Benjamin. *Quartetto for Three Violins and Cello.* Played by members of the Royal, Philharmonic Orchestra. Society for the Preservation of the American Musical Heritage, LP MIA-117 [with Sidney Lanier].

Górecki, Henryk Mikolaj. *Three Pieces in The Old Style* (1963). Kraków Philharmonic, conductor Rolands Bader. Koch 3-1041-2 (CD).

Grainger, Percy (with Barry Conyngham). *Free Music I and II.* Move Records, 1978. LP MS 3027.

Haydn, Joseph. *Canons.* Gyr Girls' Choir, Miklós Szabó conductor. Hungaroton CD HCD 12890.

Hays, Sorrel (then "Doris Hays"). *Hush.* On *Sleepers* (lullabies by eight composers]. Finnadair LP 7-902661.

Hoffmann, E. T. A. *Symphony in E-flat,* excerpts from *Undine* and *Die Lustige Musikanten (The Merry Musicians)* and *Quintet for Harp and String Quartet.* Berlin Radio Symphony Orchestra, Lothar Zagroek, conductor, and others. 1965; Musica Mundi, 1982. CD 11627.

Johnson, Tom. *Lullaby.* See Sorrel Hays.

Kepler, Johannes. *The Harmony of the World.* Willie Ruff and John Rodgers. Kepler (New Haven) LP 1571.

Knowles, Alison. *Mantra for Jessie.* See Sorrel Hays.

Kostelanetz, Richard. *Invocations.* Folkways LP FRS 37902.

Lanier, Sidney. *Wind Song* and *Danse des Moucherons.* Sebastian

Caratelli, flute and Raymond Viola, piano. See Franklin, Benjamin.

Lockwood, Annea. *Malolo*. See Doris Hays.

Lombardi, Daniele, ed. *Musica Futurista*. Cramps/Multhipla 2-LP. 5204 002 [includes Russolo, Marinetti, Casella and others].

Lora-Totino, Arrigo, ed. *Futura: Poesia Sonora*. Cramps/Multhipla, 1978. 7-LP 5206-301/7.

Marinetti, Filippo Tommaso. *Il Futurismo*. Milano?: "Historical Archives." EMI Italiana-La Voce del Padrone LP 3C 065-17982.

_____. See also Lombardi, Daniele.

Nietzsche, Friedrich. *Piano Music*. Jorge Zuleta, pianist. Edition Theater am Turm LP PHL 8001.

_____. *Songs*. Angela Dellert, Judy Roberts, Peter Hahn, singers, Jorge Zuleta, pianist. Edition Theater am Turm LP PHL 8003.

Nitsch, Hermann. See Rühm, Gerhard.

Oliveros, Pauline. *Horse Sings from Cloud* and *Rattlesnake Mountain*. Lovely Music LP VR 1901.

_____. *Vor der Flut*. Eigelstein 2-rec. LP LC 6767 and EFA 17-6025/26.

_____. *The Wanderer*. Lovely Music LP VR 1902.

_____. *The Well and the Gentle*. Hat Hut Records [Therwil, Switzerland] 2 LP Hat ART 2020.

_____. *Lullaby for Daisy Pauline*. See Sorrel Hays.

Paik, Nam June. See Beuys, Joseph.

Roth, Dieter. *Tote Rennen + Lieder* (Dead Heats + Songs). "Selten Gehörte Musik" series. Edition Hansjörg Mayer, LP F666.082.

_____. See also Rühm, Gerhard.

Rousseau, Jean-Jacques. *Le Devin du Village (The Village Soothsayer)*. Bernard Cottret, Ana-Marie Miranda and Serge Wilfart, soloists, chorus and chamber orchestra, conductor.

Roger Cotte. Musical Heritage Society LP MHS 1985.

Rühm, Gerhard, Hermann Nitsch, Dieter Roth, Günther Brus and Oswald Wiener. *Münchner Konzert Mai 1974. (Munich Concert May 1974).* "Selten Gehörte Musik" series. Edition Hansjörg Mayer. LP.

_____, Dieter Roth and Oswald Wiener. *November Symphonie (November Symphonie). 2. Berliner Dichterworkshop.(Second Berlin Poetry Workshop).* "Selten Gehörte Musik' series. Edition Hansjörg Mayer, 2-LP.

_____, Hermann Nitsch, Günther Brus and Dieter Roth *String Quartet.* . "Selten Gehörte Musik' series. Edition Hansjörg Mayer 3-LP 55-81-71.

_____, Dieter Roth and Oswald Wiener. *3. Berliner Dichterworkshop.(Third Berlin Poetry Workshop).* Edition Hansjörg Mayer LP F 65.040.

Russolo, Luigi. See Lombardi, Daniele.

Santos, Carles. *Voicetracks.* Santos, voice. P. A. Taylor LP CS-007.

_____. *Perturbacion Insperada.* Santos, voice and piano. Linterna Música LP A 586-013.

Schoenberg, Arnold. *String Quartet No. 3, Op. 37* (1927). LaSalle Quartet. Deutscher Grammophon DGR 419 994-2 (CD).

Stravinsky, Igor. *Pulcinella* (1919-20). Saint Paul Chamber Orchestra, conductor Christopher Hogwood. London CD 425 614-2.

Vostell, Wolf. *Dé-coll/age Music.* Wolf Vostell. Multhipla, LP M20137.

_____ *Garten der Lüste / Giardino delle Delicie (Fluxus Opera).* Esperanza Abad, Nancy Bellow, Marie-Louise Gilles, Else Nabu, H. Hamm-Albrecht, chorus, Vostell, director. Multhipla/Wewerka Edition, 1984. 2-LP M-20138.

Wada, Yoshi. *Lament for the Rise and Fall of the Elephantine Crocodile.* Wada. India Navigation LP IN 3025.

_____. *Off the Wall I and II.* Free Music Production (Berlin) LP SAJ-49.

Wiener, Oswald. See Roth, Dieter and Rühm, Gerhard.

Index of Persons Named in Text